Rachel,
a star. May the
pon you never be
n Jesus name
30/12/15

Praying the Word of

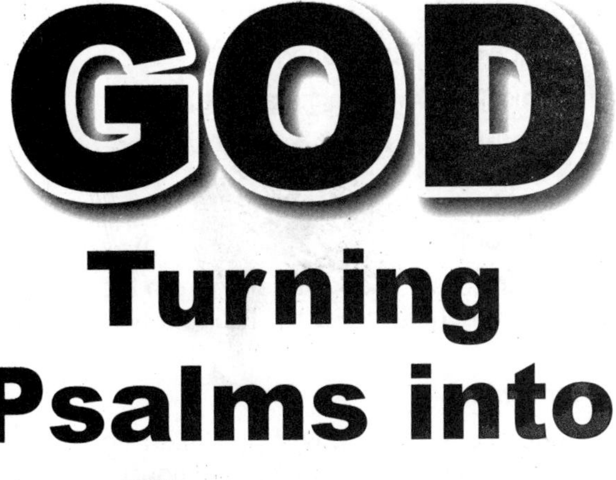

Turning Psalms into Prayer

Praying the word of God

ISBN: 978-0-9930393-0-0
Layout & Printing:
Boldstep Communications Ltd
+234 803 329 4531, +234 803 323 5835

Please note that I have used the British spelling of certain words rather than the American spelling.

Please note that I have capitalized certain pronouns in scripture that refer to the Father, Son and Holy Spirit and this may be different from some Bible publishers' styles.

Different Bible translations have translated the titles of God, LORD and Lord differently. For consistency I have used the title "Lord" where God is being referred to as Master and "LORD" where He is being referred to as the Sovereign God (YHWH pronounced Yahweh). No matter the title by which we refer to God, we must always show Him reverence.

Please note that satan is not capitalized anywhere in this book. I am happy to violate grammatical rules in doing so.

Dedication

This book is dedicated to my Lord Jesus Christ who paid the supreme price by dying for my sins.

This book is also dedicated to the women in my life, my beloved mother Josephine Aduke for what you gave up to ensure I had a good start in life, my wonderful wife Yewande who has stood by me through thick and thin and my darling daughter Temidire for her never failing encouragement. You carry the torch.

I also dedicate this book to Rev Olufemi Odubonojo and all my pastors who have pastored and taught me, and have encouraged me to fulfil my purpose in life.

This book is dedicated to all who encouraged me to write this book, including my late friend and colleague, Pastor Olawale Mohammed.

Finally I dedicate this book to all who are willing tools in the hands of God, standing up and interceding on behalf of the saints all over the world.

Acknowledgements

I would like to express great appreciation to Prof Yemi Osinbajo for writing the foreword to this book. I would also like to appreciate Revd Bunmi Fagbemi, Revd Tade Agbesanwa, Pastor Dunni Odetoyinbo and Ms Busola Thompson for the testimonials which they have given this book.

I give special thanks to Minister Goke Fawole for reading and correcting parts of the manuscript. Words cannot express my gratitude to my friend and brother, Muyiwa Jibowu for the painstaking efforts in reading through this book and the numerous suggestions which have greatly enriched this book.

I thank Deacon Rotimi Olanrewaju and my friend Soji Fagade for all that they did to get this book published and my website up and running. I also thank Wole Olugbode for the work done in formatting the book. God bless you all.

Content

Foreword

The Psalms have always held a deep fascination for believers and even those of other faiths. Many have been inspired to set its deep invocations, praises and petitions into lyrics for hymns and short choruses of praise and worship of the Almighty God. Others have created some of the best known choral chants from its inspired words.

Ola Tubi's PRAYING THE WORD OF GOD: TURNING PSALMS TO PRAYER however stands alone.

This effort is a painstaking, line by line transformation of the Psalms to prayer points. The concept is not only ground-breaking, it mines the depths of the word of God as contained in the Psalms.

The range of emotions and circumstances covered by the Psalms have always made them a deep and fertile source of prayers , but it is the careful, logical arrangement of all 150 Psalms into five books and further classification to subject heads from which prayer topics are drawn that is one of the finest points of this inspired work. From cries to God in times of distress, to high praises, thanksgiving and affirmations of his faithfulness, there are prayers for every season and circumstance.

If the Lord wills, this could well become one of the true prayer classics of our generation.

Prof. Yemi Osinbajo SAN
Professor of Law and a Pastor in the Redeemed Christian Church of God, Lagos, Nigeria.

Introduction

People want to pray to God because there are issues and concerns that need resolution. There are also times when there is a desire to express joy and gratitude to God too. Unfortunately it is a challenge to do so because they do not know how to. This book shows us that God's word is what we need to use in praying to Him. God calls on men in Isaiah 1:18 - Come let us reason together. As many people find it difficult to pray, this book has been written to show us how we can read the Bible and turn it into our prayer book.

The prayers in this book are simple day to day words as prayers are a conversation between children and their heavenly father. Reading the Bible and praying the word will help us develop an intimate relationship with God. God will no longer be "the man upstairs" as many call Him when we make a conscious effort to talk to Him as often as we talk to our loved ones around us.

It is also important to study the word of God because it is one of the pieces of armour that the Christian possesses in our battle with the devil who is our enemy. Chapter 6: 17 of the book of Ephesians tells us the sword of the Spirit is the word of God. It should be noted that the sword is the only offensive weapon among all those listed. Therefore the study of the word of God will equip us to do battle with our enemy.

The Bible is divided into the Old and New Testaments. There are 66 different Books and the Book of Psalms is part of the Old Testament.

I thank God that He has inspired me to write the first of a series of prayer books. I have started with the Book of Psalms because it is a book of prayer and praise to the Almighty God. All Psalms have a focus on God and His Son Jesus Christ. There are 150 Psalms written by several men. For organisational purposes it has been divided into five Books (Ps 1-41; 42-72; 73-89; 90-106, 107-150). Each Book ends with a concluding doxology.

My classification of Psalms into different types involves a lot of overlapping in a bid to make this book very user friendly for every child of God. Words used repeatedly in each Psalm and the title of the Psalm have driven many of my classifications.

In drawing out the prayers, I used the King James Version of the Bible, and then searched for the Bible versions that were closest to the King James Version to place alongside the prayers.

This book is a result of my decision to start studying the word and praying effectively. You are welcome to start the journey too.
God bless you.

Olatubosun Tubi

Classification

Blessings of righteousness and of being merciful
Psalms 1, 41, 49, 52, 101, 112, 128
Brotherly love and unity
Psalm 133
Consequences of ingratitude
Psalms 78, 81
Corruption and foolishness of man
Psalms 14, 36, 53
Covenant
Psalms 89, 132
Danger
Psalm 143
Direction
Psalms 25, 32, 37, 43
Early morning
Psalms 5, 30
Entering God's presence
Psalms 15, 24, 84, 122
Envy of others/Encouragement in God
Psalm 73
Evening
Psalms 3, 4
Favour
Psalms 5, 30, 87, 141
Fear of the Lord
Psalms 34, 128
Genuine worship
Psalm 50
Gift of children
Psalms 127,128

Psalms 9, 33, 34, 47, 48, 65, 66, 67, 68, 81, 89, 92, 95, 96, 98, 99, 100, 103, 104, 105, 107, 108, 113, 117, 136, 138, 145, 146, 147, 148, 149, 150

Prayer for earthly rulers

Psalms 72, 82

Prayer for servants of God

Psalm 134

Promotion

Psalm 75

Protection

Psalms 3, 16, 23, 27, 28, 71, 91, 121, 141, 144

Revival

Psalms 80, 85, 119, 138

Repentance and forgiveness of sin

Psalms 6, 25, 30, 32, 34, 38, 39, 51, 106, 130

Thanksgiving

Psalms 100, 124, 126

Thanksgiving for answered prayers

Psalms 18, 21, 30, 40, 116, 118

Thirsting for God (Remember me)

Psalms 13, 42, 44, 63, 69, 74

Times of unbelief

Psalm 77

Trusting/Dependence/Confidence in God

Psalms 11, 23, 27, 31, 37, 46, 62, 91, 125, 127, 139

Victory

Psalms 2, 52

BOOK 1

Psalm 1 NASB

This Psalm contrasts the character of the righteous man and the wicked man. The righteous is blessed and the wicked is destroyed. It also shows how God looks at both types of men.

BIBLE		PRAYER	
1.	How blessed is the man who does not walk in the counsel of the wicked, nor stand in the path of sinners, nor sit in the seat of scoffers!	**1.**	By Your grace I will not be ungodly and I will live in the fear of God. Steer my heart away from the counsel of the wicked. Help me run away from rebelling against God by sinning. With Your help I will not stand in the path of sinners. With Your help I will not be found in the company of those who mock You and all You stand for.
2.	But his delight is in the law of the LORD, and in His law he meditates day and night.	**2.**	Give me a heart that delights in the law of the LORD. Help my heart to stay on Your word at all times. As I delight in Your word, let my relationship with you grow closer and closer every day.
3.	He will be like a tree firmly planted by streams of water, which yields its fruit in its season and its	**3.**	I declare I will be fruitful continually, I will never go dry. Whatever I do and wherever I go I will

leaf does not wither; and in whatever he does, he prospers.	prosper in the name of Jesus. I choose the way of the blessed man rather than the way of wickedness.
4. The wicked are not so, But they are like chaff which the wind drives away.	**4.** Lord, cause the wind to blow away every agent of wickedness from my affairs, my household and my community in Jesus name.
5. Therefore the wicked will not stand in the judg-jment, nor sinners in the assembly of the right-eous.	**5-6.** On the day of judgement I pray I will not be part of the group of the unright-eous in Jesus name. Thank You Father for perfecting all that con-cerns me in Jesus name.
6. For the Lord knows the way of the righteous, But the way of the wicked will perish.	

Psalm 2 NIV

This Psalm shows the attitude of the nations – peoples, kings and rulers to God and His anointed i.e. Jesus Christ and every child of God. The Psalm lets us know God's reaction to them.

BIBLE	PRAYER
1. Why do the nations con-spire and the peoples plot in vain?	**1.** Lord as You sit in the heavens; terrify every gathering against my household and my community with Your fury.
2. The kings of the earth rise up and the rulers	**2.** Whenever the enemies rage and imagine or set

	band together against the LORD and against His anointed, saying,		and counsel one another may it continue to come to nothing in Jesus name.
3.	"Let us break their chains and throw off their shackles."	**3.**	Father let them feel Your wrath and let every rebellion against You including rebellion in my heart be put down now, in Jesus name.
4.	The One enthroned in heaven laughs; the Lord scoffs at them.	**4-5.**	Lord laugh at all the efforts of those who gather against my household and my community because they will all come to nothing for You are my Lord and Master.
5.	He rebukes them in His anger and terrifies them in His wrath, saying,		
6.	"I have installed My king on Zion, My holy mountain."	**6-7.**	I thank You for providing a King for Your people whose reign is forever more. You have said I should ask and You will surely give.
7.	I will proclaim the Lord's decree: He said to me, "You are my son; today I have become Your father.		
8.	Ask Me, and I will make the nations your inheritance, the ends of the earth your possession.	**8.**	Lord give me all the peoples, rulers and kings for my inheritance today in Jesus name. Lord I ask for the ends of the earth as my possession today in Jesus name.
9.	You will break them with a rod of iron; you will dash them to pieces like pottery."	**9.**	I break every gathering against me with Your divine rod of iron They are all shattered into pieces in Jesus name.

	Lord let Your wrath fall on all who gather against You and Your kingdom.
10. Therefore, you kings, be wise; be warned, you rulers of the earth.	**10.** Do not be angry with me, I do not want to miss the way.
11. Serve the Lord with fear and celebrate His rule with trembling.	**11.** I heart; help me serve You with reverential awe and rejoicing in Jesus name.
12. Kiss His son, or He will be angry and your way will lead to your destruct-ion, for His wrath can flare up in a moment. Blessed are all who take refuge in Him.	**12.** Thank You for giving refuge to all who trust in You. I bless Your name and I appreciate You.

Psalm 3 NASB

This Psalm is a cry to God to save us from our adversaries. It shows our dependence on God for protection and confidence that HE answers our prayers. This is an early morning prayer.

BIBLE	PRAYER
1. O Lord, how my adver-saries have increased! Many are rising up against me.	**1.** Lord I come to You this day.
2. Many are saying of my soul, "There is no deliverance for him in God." Selah.	**2.** Many are rising against me; they say there is none that will save me.
3. But You, O Lord, are a shield about me, my	**3.** I know You are my shield; do shield me from

glory, and the One who lifts my head.

every trouble. Lift my head from every trouble and restore my glory in Jesus name.

4. I was crying to the Lord with my voice, And He answered me from His holy mountain. Selah.

4. I cry to You today, You are the one that answers prayers; answer me from the heavens.

5. I lay down and slept; I awoke, for the Lord sustains me.

5. I sleep and I wake up daily because You are my sustenance. When I sleep I trust You will grant me rest.

6. I will not be afraid of ten thousands of people who have set themseve-es against me round about.

6. No matter the numbers of those against me, arise my Lord and my God, save me from my enemies.

7. Arise, O Lord; save me, O my God! For You have smitten all my enemies on the cheek; You have shattered the teeth of the wicked.

7. Silence my enemies, shut them up and shatter them.

8. Salvation belongs to the Lord; Your blessing be upon Your people! Selah.

8. My salvation is in Your hands. Thank You for saving me. Thank You for every blessing on me and all that is mine in Jesus name.

Psalm 4 NIV

This is a cry to God for help. The righteous man wonders when the seeming reproach in his life will turn to honour. He asks that God put gladness in his heart and he will have peace

For the director of music. With stringed instruments.
A Psalm of David.

BIBLE		PRAYER	
1.	Answer me when I call to You, my righteous God. Give me relief from my distress; have mercy on me and hear my prayer.	**1.**	Lord I call on You, hear my cry, answer my prayers and show me mercy. You who made me righteous, You have given me comfort in times of discomfort.
2.	How long will you people turn my glory into shame? How long will you love delusions and seek false gods?	**2-3.**	Men want to pull me down. I thank You as You have set me apart unto Yourself; when I call on You, hear me as You have promised.
3.	Know that the Lord has set apart His faithful servant for Himself; the Lord hears when I call to Him.		
4.	Tremble and do not sin; when you are on your beds, search your hearts and be silent.	**4.**	When I go to bed, fill my heart with Your word.
5.	Offer the sacrifices of the righteous and trust in the Lord.	**5.**	Let my sacrifices be acceptable to You. The wicked are saying where is my God? Help me not to doubt You; I do not want to fall into sin.

6. Many, Lord, are asking."Who will bring us prosperity?" Let the light of Your face shine on us.

7. Fill my heart with joy when their grain and new wine abound.

8. In peace I will lie down and sleep, for You alone, Lord, ake me dwell in safety.

6. I ask for Your light to overpower darkness in my life in Jesus name. My countenance must change.

7. Let me be confident of the security You have provided for me.

8. Jehovah Shalom I receive Your peace into my life in Jesus name, thank You Father in Jesus name.

Psalm 5 ESV

This Psalm shows God's attitude to those who are wicked and commit iniquity. This contrasts with God's blessing of the righteous man. This is an early morning Psalm

To the choirmaster: for the flutes. A Psalm of David.

BIBLE

1. Give ear to my words, O Lord; consider my groaning.

2. Give attention to the sound of my cry, my King and my God, for to You do I pray.

3. O Lord, in the morning You hear my voice; in the morning I prepare a sacrifice for You and

PRAYER

1. My God and my King, listen to me, I have no one to turn to but You.

2. Help me develop a relationship where I will always call on You every morning. My prayer is a cry of desperation to connect with You. Look upon the meditations of my heart.

3. Help me learn to wait to hear Your response to me too, for my expectation is that You will

	watch		answer me.
4.	For You are not a God who delights in wickedness; evil may not dwell with You.	4.	I appreciate You my Father for You do not take pleasure in evil.
5.	The boastful shall not stand before Your eyes; You hate all evildoers.	5-6.	Give me a heart that will always run away from wickedness, lying and deceit.
6.	You destroy those who speak lies; the Lord abhors the bloodthirsty and deceitful man.		
7.	But I, through the abundance of Your steadfast love, will enter Your house. I will bow down toward Your holy temple in the fear of You.	7.	Show me Your loving kindness which enables me to enter into Your presence. I bow and worship You.
8.	Lead me, O Lord, in Your righteousness because of my enemies; make Your way straight before me.	8.	I ask You to lead me into a life of righteousness.
9.	For there is no truth in their mouth; their inmost self is destruction; their throat is an open grave; they flatter with their tongue.	9.	Enemies have slandered maligned my character and their nature is wickedness.
10.	Make them bear their guilt, O God; let them fall by their own counsels; because of the abundance of their transgressions cast them out, for they have rebelled against You.	10.	Let all the wicked around me, fall into the traps they have laid carefully for me.
11.	But let all who take refu-	11.	I have got to learn to trust

ge in You rejoice; let them ever sing for joy, and spread Your protection over them, that those who love Your name may exult in You.

You and as I do, let rejoicing fill my mouth. Your protection and security causes me to shout for joy.

12. For You bless the righteous, O Lord; You cover him with favour as with a shield.

12. Let Your favour be a shield around me and all that is mine in Jesus name.

Psalm 6 NIV

The Psalm is a Psalm of repentance. The Psalmist appeals to the loving kindness of God and also shows us that we have a God that answers prayers.

For the director of music. With stringed instruments. According to sheminith. A Psalm of David.

BIBLE

1. Lord, do not rebuke me in Your anger or discipline me in Your wrath.
2. Have mercy on me, Lord, for I am faint; heal me, Lord, for my bones are in agony.
3. My soul is in deep anguish. How long, Lord, how long?
4. Turn, Lord, and deliver me; save me because of Your unfailing love.
5. Among the dead no one proclaims Your name. Who praises You from the grave?

PRAYER

1. Lord have mercy on me. Do not be angry with me.
2. Let Your grace abound towards me for I am suffering O Lord.
3. Jehovah Rapha, heal my body, heal my soul. I long for You.
4. I want to live so I will continue to give thanks to You.
5. The dead cannot give You thanks. Deliver me my Lord and my King.

6. I am worn out from my groaning. All night long I flood my bed with weeping and drench my couch with tears **7.** My eyes grow weak with sorrow; they fail because of all my foes.	**6-7.** I cry to You all night, my adversaries surround me.
8. Away from me, all you who do evil, for the Lord has heard my weeping.	**8.** I command every worker of iniquity to get out of my life now in Jesus name.
9. The Lord has heard my cry for mercy; the Lord accepts my prayer.	**9.** Instantly I know You have seen my tears and heard my prayers for You are a good God.
10. All my enemies will be overwhelmed with shame and anguish; they will turn back and suddenly be put to shame.	**10.** All my enemies will be ashamed and they will turn away from me dropping off like fleas in Jesus name. Those that refuse to turn away from sin shall remain ashamed forever in Jesus name.

Psalm 7 NASB

This Psalm shows that the righteousness of God will bring vindication to the righteous man and judgement on the wicked.

A Shiggaion of David, which he sang to the Lord concerning Cush, a Benjamite.

BIBLE	PRAYER
1. O Lord my God, in You I have taken refuge; Save me from all those who	**1.** Lord I trust that You are a just God. Father I take refuge in You.

	pursue me, and deliver me,		
2.	Or he will tear my soul like a lion, dragging me away, while there is none to deliver.	**2.**	Do not let my enemies succeed in their plans.
3.	O Lord my God, if I have done this, if there is injustice in my hands,	**3.**	Deliver me from my enemies. I have no other help but You.
4.	If I have rewarded evil to my friend, or have plundered him who without cause was my adversary,	**4.**	I have not done evil to anybody but the progra-mme of the enemy is to steal, kill and destroy.
5.	Let the enemy pursue my soul and overtake it; And let him trample my life down to the ground And lay my glory in the dust. Selah.	**5.**	Lord would deserve all the enemy is doing to me if I have lifted up my hand against them in sin. Help me live with integrity.
6.	Arise, O Lord, in Your anger; Lift up Yourself against the rage of my adversaries, And arouse Yourself for me; You have appointed judge-ment.	**6-7**	I come to You in humility, arise Father in anger and cause the hosts of heaven to fight for me.
7.	Let the assembly of the peoples encompass You, and over them return on high.		
8.	The Lord judges the peoples; vindicate me, O Lord, according to my righteousness and my integrity that is in me.	**8.**	Judge them and let them see Your rage. Let the enemies know that You are on my side.
9.	O let the evil of the wick-ed come to an end, but	**9.**	Today I decree that the wickedness of the

	establish the righteous; for the righteous God tries the hearts and minds.		wicked must come to an end.
10.	My shield is with God, who saves the upright in heart.	**10.**	You are my defence. Save me for my righteo-usness is in You.
11.	God is a righteous judge, And a God who has indignation every day.	**11.**	Touch the heart of the wicked, let them turn to You. You are a righteous God; You are my shield and my support.
12.	If a man does not repent, He will sharpen His sword; He has bent His bow and made it ready.	**12.**	Those who refuse to turn away from righteousne-ss will feel Your fire.
13.	He has also prepared for Himself deadly weapons ;He makes His arrows fiery shafts.	**13-16.**	Let every worker of mischief, every agent of the devil fall into every trap, every hole and every barrier or obstacle that has been laid against my household and my community.
14.	Behold, he travails with wickedness, and he conceives mischief and brings forth falsehood.		
15.	He has dug a pit and hollowed it out, and has fallen into the hole which he made.		
16.	His mischief will return upon his own head, and his violence will descend upon his own pate.		
17.	I will give thanks to the Lord according to His righteousness and will sing praise to the name of the LORD Most High.	**17.**	I will continue to give You thanks, Your praises will never cease on my lips. Thank You Jehovah El Elyon, the Most High God.

Psalm 8 NIV

The Psalm allows us appreciate the majesty of God.

We also see man in relation to God

For the director of music. According to gittith. A Psalm of David.

BIBLE		PRAYER	
1.	LORD, our Lord, how majestic is Your name in all the earth! You have set Your glory in the heavens.	**1.**	O LORD my Lord Your name is excellent. LORD God Your majesty is displayed in the heavens for us to see. Your glory fills the heavens.
2.	Through the praise of children and infants You have established a stronghold against Your enemies, to silence the foe and the avenger.	**2.**	You show Your strength through the protection and care You give to children. Help us teach our children to appreciate and testify of Your strength. I pray this act of Yours will continue to silence the enemy in Jesus name.
3.	When I consider Your heavens, the work of Your fingers, the moon and the stars, which You have set in place,	**3.**	All You created continue to amaze me, I see the heavens, the moon and the stars, You ordained them and nothing can ever change the works of Your hands. I worship You, awesome God.
4.	What is mankind that You are mindful of them, human beings that You care for them?	**4.**	Thank You for where I am in relation to You and in relation to all You have created. Thank You for loving me so much that

	You gave up Your Son Jesus Christ to die for me.
5. You have made them a little lower than the angels and crowned them with glory and honour.	**5.** As man Jesus was a little lower than the angels, but You have crowned Him with glory and majesty.
6. You made them rulers over the works of Your hands; You put everything under their feet:	**6.** LORD You have given Him dominion over the works of Your hand.
7. All flocks and herds, and the animals of the wild, **8.** The birds in the sky, and the fish in the sea, all that swim the paths of the seas.	**7-8.** All You created are under His feet. Let this glory extend to all Your children.
9. LORD, our Lord, how majestic is Your name in all the earth!	**9.** I thank You for favouring me. Blessed be Your holy name.

Psalm 9 NKJV

The Psalm shows different reasons why we should give praise to God.

To the Chief Musician. To the tune of "Death of the Son." A Psalm of David.

BIBLE	PRAYER
1. I will praise You, O Lord, with my whole heart; I will tell of all Your marvellous works.	**1.** Lord I praise You with my whole heart. I remember what You have done for me in the past. I praise You for what You are doing now and what You are in the process of

doing for the future.

	Scripture		Prayer
2.	I will be glad and rejoice in You; I will sing praise to Your name, O Most High.	2.	I am joyous that I have a God like You, the Almighty, the All-Knowing, and the Most High God. JEHOVAH EL ELAYON
3.	When my enemies turn back, They shall fall and perish at Your presence.	3.	Let me live in Your presence for it is enough for every one of my enemies to turn away from me and perish be- fore You in Jesus name
4.	For You have maintained my right and my cause; You sat on the throne judging in righteousness.	4.	You are a righteous judge.
5.	You have rebuked the nations, You have destroyed the wicked; You have blotted out their name forever and ever.	5.	I ask that You rebuke and destroy the works of my enemies' hands in Jesus name.
6.	O enemy, destructions are finished forever! And You have destroyed cities; Even their memory has perished.	6.	Every agent of the enemy will end up in ruins in Jesus name.
7.	But the Lord shall endure forever; He has prepared His throne for judgment.	7.	Let them be uprooted together with their roots in Jesus name.
8.	He shall judge the world in righteousness, and He shall administer judgment for the peoples in uprightness.	8.	You execute judgement fairly.
9.	The Lord also will be a refuge for the oppress-	9.	You are my stronghold at all times, and I know I am

	ed, a refuge in times of trouble.		safe in You.
10.	And those who know Your name will put their trust in You; For You, Lord, have not forsaken those who seek You.	**10.**	I know You Father and all my trust is in You, and I know You do not turn away from those who seek after You.
11.	Sing praises to the Lord, who dwells in Zion! Declare His deeds among the people.	**11.**	I praise You LORD as I declare the works of Your hands; the heavens declare Your glory. The seasons show that You are indeed Almighty. Help me encourage the people around me to praise Your name.
12.	When He avenges blood, He remembers them; He does not forget the cry of the humble.	**12.**	Remember me in my time of trouble; my enemies are desperate for my blood.
13.	Have mercy on me, O Lord! Consider my trouble from those who hate me, You who lift me up from the gates of death,	**13.**	Those who hate me continue to send affliction my way. Let my cry come unto You. Be gracious unto me. Lift me up from death and until I die I will testify of You.
14.	That I may tell of all Your praise in the gates of the daughter of Zion. I will rejoice in Your salvation.	**14.**	Let me rejoice in my salvation.
15.	The nations have sunk down in the pit which they made; In the net which they hid, their own foot is caught.	**15.**	Let all who have made a pit for me fall into the pit in Jesus name.
16.	The Lord is known by the	**16.**	Lord You are known to

judgment He executes; The wicked is snared in the work of his own hands.
Meditation. Selah

17. The wicked shall be turned into hell, and all the nations that forget God

18. For the needy shall not always be forgotten; The expectation of the poor shall not perish forever.

19. Arise, O Lord, Do not let man prevail; Let the nations be judged in Your sight.

20. Put them in fear, O Lord, that the nations may know themselves to be but men. Selah

be a just God. Let the wicked not escape the work of their hands.

17. Let them be turned into hell, especially those wh who forget You are Almi-Almighty.

18. By Your grace my expectation shall not perish in Jesus name.

19-20. Arise O God, show Your power, let Your fear overwhelm them, let them realise they are ordinary men and they must bow down to You.

Psalm 10 NKJV

This Psalm shows how the wicked think and it is also a call for Justice. We also see that God hears our prayers.

BIBLE

1. Why do You stand afar off, O Lord? Why do You hide in times of trouble?

2. The wicked in his pride persecutes the poor; Let them be caught in the plots which they have

PRAYER

1. Do not hide Yourself from me O God. In my time of trouble, hear me as I call.

2. As the wicked pursue me, let them fall into the devices they have asse-assembled for me.

devised.

3. For the wicked boasts of his heart's desire; He blesses the greedy and renounces the Lord.

4. The wicked in his proud countenance does not seek God; God is in none of his thoughts.

5. His ways are always prospering; Your judgments are far above, out of his sight; As for all his enemies, he sneers at them.

6. He has said in his heart, "I shall not be moved; I shall never be in adversity."

7. His mouth is full of cursing and deceit and oppression; Under his tongue is trouble and iniquity.

8. He sits in the lurking places of the villages; In the secret places he murders the innocent; His eyes are secretly fixed on the helpless.

9. He lies in wait secretly, as a lion in his den; He lies in wait to catch the poor; He catches the poor when he draws him into his net

10. So he crouches, he lies low, that the helpless

3. The wicked are boasting and the greedy are cursing and reject You; they say there is no God.

4. In their pride they feel they do not need You.

5. As obvious as Your judgements are, the wicked do not see them.

6-7. They speak falsehood, they are cunning and deceitful, they are full of themselves, and they continue to do mischief.

8. The wicked kill the innocent and unassuming; they are on the lookout for the unfortunate.

9. They think You do not see them and they will not pay for their deeds.

10. Grant me strength to withstand every action of

may fall by his strength.

11. He has said in his heart, "God has forgotten; He hides His face; He will never see."

12. Arise, O Lord! O God, lift up Your hand! Do not forget the humble.

13. Why do the wicked renounce God? He has said in his heart, "You will not require an account."

14. But You have seen, for You observe trouble and grief, to repay it by Your hand. The helpless commits himself to You; You are the helper of the fatherless.

15. Break the arm of the wicked and the evil man; Seek out his wickedness until You find none.

16. The Lord is King forever and ever; The nations have perished out of His land.

17. Lord, You have heard the desire of the humble; You will prepare their heart; You will cause Your ear to hear,

18. To do justice to the

the wicked.

11. Arise Lord show up and lift up Your hand, remember the oppressed.

12. The wicked think there is nothing You can do about their wickedness because they have gone on for too long.

13. Lord let there be an end to our indifference to evil in our midst and in our community in Jesus name.

14. The poor and the oppressed commit themselves to You. You are the helper of the helpless.

15. Jehovah Saboath, break the arm of the wicked; ensure they are totally wiped out.

16. You are the same yesterday, today and forever. As You have done in the past remove all heathen from the land.

17. I ask that You strengthen my heart. Help me hold on to You.

18. Vindicate me such that

fatherless and the oppressed, that the man of the earth may oppress no more.

the wicked will be unable to cause me any more terror in Jesus name. Thank You Father for listening to me and answering my prayers.

Psalm 11 NASB

The Psalm is about trusting God. It also shows God's reaction to the righteous and the wicked.

For the choir director. A Psalm of David.

BIBLE	PRAYER
1. In the Lord I take refuge; How can you say to my soul, "Flee as a bird to your mountain;	**1.** I put my trust in You O Lord. I thank You Lord for being my refuge. I have no other God but You.
2. For, behold, the wicked bend the bow, they make ready their arrow upon the string to shoot in darkness at the upright in heart.	**2.** As the wicked plan to shoot me down, be my shield and protect me. I pray Lord that You will keep me from failing.
3. If the foundations are destroyed, what can the righteous do?"	**3.** My foundation is in Christ the Solid Rock; therefore it will not be destroyed in Jesus name.
4. The Lord is in His holy temple; the Lord's throne is in heaven; His eyes behold, His eyelids test the sons of men.	**4.** Lord You are seated on Your throne in heaven. I come boldly to Your throne of grace and mercy. You see every act of man from Your throne in the heavens.

5. The Lord tests the righteous and the wicked, and the one who loves violence His soul hates.

5. As You test the righteous and the wicked, help me to be upright in Jesus name. You hate all those who love violence and You will punish them all.

6. Upon the wicked He will rain snares; fire and brimstone and burning wind will be the portion of their cup.

6. I ask that You rain snares on them all, from heaven in Jesus name. Let Your fire and brimstone fall upon them just like the days of Sodom and Gomorrah.

7. For the Lord is righteous, He loves righteousness; the upright will behold His face.

7. You are a righteous God, Jehovah Tsidkenu and You love the righteous. Look upon me with Your grace. The guarantee of Your favour will continue to uphold me in Jesus name.

Psalm 12 ESV

The Psalm shows men can be unfaithful to one another and also towards God. It warns against words of men that will lead to destruction.

To the choirmaster: according to The Sheminith. A Psalm of David.

BIBLE

1. Save, O Lord, for the godly one is gone; for the faithful have vanished from among the children of man

PRAYER

1. I pray that Godly and faithful men will not cease to exist in our communities, our government and our nations in Jesus name. Purge us all of false-hood, deceit,

sycophancy, greed and corrupt-ion. Help me overcome the things that would challenge my faith. Help me Lord to maintain my stand and integrity, holding out for my faith in Jesus name. Lord help me to work with sincerity of purpose towards You and my fellow man.

	Psalm		Prayer
2.	Everyone utters lies to his neighbour; with flattering lips and a double heart they speak.	**2.**	Give me a heart that will always yearn to speak the truth, never flattering people to deceive them.
3.	May the Lord cut off all flattering lips, the tongue that makes great boasts,	**3.**	I pray that You will cut off flattering lips and tongues that lift people up only to pull them down thereafter.
4.	Those who say, "With our tongue we will prevail, our lips are with us; who is master over us?"	**4.**	The unfaithful feel they cannot be held to account for the things they say or do.
5.	"Because the poor are plundered, because the needy groan, I will now arise," says the Lord; "I will place him in the safety for which he longs.	**5.**	They oppress the poor; arise now and save all who are being destroyed by the falsehood of men.
6.	The words of the Lord are pure words, like silver refined in a furnace on the ground, purified seven times.	**6.**	Father as Your words are pure and like silver tried in a furnace and refined seven times, let Your words purify me, let my

7. You, O Lord, will keep them; you will guard us from this generation forever.
8. On every side the wicked prowl, as vileness is exalted among the children of man.

words be pure too. Lord cause me to think before I speak, making sure my words align with Your word.

7-8. Keep me O Lord from the wicked and preserve my generations forever, even as the wicked are all over me trying to steal, to kill and to destroy me. I will prevail because of Your love and protection. Your gift of Abundant Life will continue to be my portion in Jesus name.

Psalm 13 NASB

This Psalm is a cry for help from God, for deliverance and it also shows trust in God.

For the choir director. A Psalm of David.

BIBLE

1. How long, O Lord? Will You forget me forever? How long will You hide Your face from me?

2. How long shall I take counsel in my soul, having sorrow in my heart all the day? how long will my enemy be exalted over me?

PRAYER

1. Remember me O Lord; do not forget where I am. Let me see Your face; do not let it seem that You are hiding from me.
2. There is sorrow in my heart, and my enemies seem to be winning the battle. The One who answers prayers, how long would it take before You answer me?

3.	Consider and answer me, O Lord my God; enlighten my eyes, or I will sleep the sleep of death,	3.	Answer me speedily, wipe away my tears. Do not let me sleep the sleep of death.
4.	And my enemy will say, "I have overcome him," And my adversaries will rejoice when I am shaken.	4.	Do not allow my enemies say they have overcome me. Do not allow my enemies to rejoice when I am going through trials. Help me remain steadfast in You.
5.	But I have trusted in Your loving kindness; My heart shall rejoice in Your salvation.	5.	I trust in Your loving kindness. My heart will rejoice in Your salvation.
6.	I will sing to the Lord, Because He has dealt bountifully with me.	6.	I will sing to You Lord because You have done me well. Halleluiah

Psalm 14 NIV

The Psalm makes clear the foolishness of those who say there is no God.

For the director of music. Of David.

BIBLE		PRAYER	
1.	The fool says in his heart, "there is no God." They are corrupt, their deeds are vile; there is no one who does good.	1.	The foolish say there is no God; they do as they please. Lord I know You are God Almighty. Do not let me behave like a fool.
2.	The Lord looks down from heaven on all mankind to see if there are any who understand, any who seek God.	2-3.	You have looked down from heaven to see if any thirst for You and if any understand Your ways. As the people are

3. All have turned away, all have become corrupt; there is no one who does good, not even one.

4. Do all these evildoers know nothing? they devour my people as though eating bread; they never call on the Lord.

5. But there they are, overwhelmed with dread, for God is present in the company of the righteous.

6. You evildoers frustrate the plans of the poor, but the Lord is their refuge.

7. Oh, that salvation for Israel would come out of Zion! when the Lord restores his people, let Jacob rejoice and Israel be glad!

corrupt and do evil I ask that You give me a heart that will forever seek after You and a heart that will always do good.

4. The world is becoming filthier by the day. The wicked swallow the righteous with casual ease and have forgotten about God. Lord show Yourself on behalf of Your people. Let those who seek to oppress us tremble and stumble.

5. I ask for Your mercy to prevail. Thank You for the protection of the righteous.

6. You are my refuge and my protection.

7. Bring our land out of every form of captivity in Jesus name. As You restore us to Yourself our household will rejoice and our community will be glad in Jesus name.

Psalm 15 NIV

This Psalm shows those who want to enter into God's presence must be holy.

A Psalm of David.

BIBLE	PRAYER
1. Lord, who may dwell in Your sacred tent? Who may live on Your holy mountain?	**1.** I know I am sanctified by You, Jehovah Mekaddis-hkem through Jesus Christ. I want to be able to enter and stay in Your presence.
2. The one whose walk is blameless, who does what is righteous, who speaks the truth from their heart;	**2.** Help me walk with integrity in all that I say and do. Help me work in righteousness, taking care to obey You.
3. Whose tongue utters no slander, who does no wrong to a neighbour, and casts no slur on others;	**3.** Help me speak the truth directly from my heart not just from my lips. Help me to be straight with my neighbours, let backbiting be far from me. Help me to be clear and resolute in my mind, that I must not do evil to anyone.
4. Who despises a vile person but honours those who fear the Lord; who keeps an oath even when it hurts, and does not change their mind;	**4.** I pray that I will value men who fear You and honour men who love You. At the same time I pray that I will be able to give wicked and vile people the treatment they deserve.
5. Who lends money to the poor without interest;	**5.** Take greed away from my heart; help me not to

who does not accept a bribe against the innocent. Whoever does these things will never be shaken.

exploit the poor. Give me a heart that would help the poor and underprivileged.

Psalm 16 NASB

The Psalm makes clear faith in God and also thanksgiving to God for the many blessings.

A Mikhtam of David.

BIBLE

1. Preserve me, O God, for I take refuge in You.
2. I said to the Lord, "You are my Lord; I have no good besides You."
3. As for the saints who are in the earth, They are the majestic ones in whom is all my delight.
4. The sorrows of those who have bartered for another god will be multiplied; I shall not pour out their drink offerings of blood, Nor will I take their names upon my lips.
5. The Lord is the portion of my inheritance and my cup; You support my lot.

PRAYER

1. I commit myself to Your protection, all powerful God. I trust in no other but You.
2. You are my Lord and King.
3. I ask for the grace to be good in all ways to the excellent people You have surrounded me with.
4. I am certain that all who pursue other gods will be disappointed, their sorrows will multiply and offerings on such altars will come to nothing in Jesus name.
5. I declare You are my inheritance, not the material things of this world. I am completely

fulfilled in you.

	Psalm		Prayer
6.	The lines have fallen to me in pleasant places; indeed, my heritage is beautiful to me.	6.	All I receive from You refreshes my soul.
7.	I will bless the Lord who has counselled me; indeed, my mind instructs me in the night.	7.	Thank You for Your blessings. All You have blessed me with no one can take away. You counsel me at all times. By Your grace in my quiet moments I have made the right choices.
8.	I have set the Lord continually before me; Because He is at my right hand, I will not be shaken.	8.	I thank You Father for You have not left me alone. Jehovah Shammah, You have been with me at all times and I am stable in You.
9.	Therefore my heart is glad and my glory rejoices; My flesh also will dwell securely.	9.	I am glad that my confidence is in You. I rejoice that You are with me and I glorify You. I know that when it is time to depart this world, I shall be with You in heaven.
10.	For You will not abandon my soul to Sheol; Nor will You allow Your Holy One to undergo decay.	10.	I thank You because You will not abandon my soul in hell. My body will not see corruption.
11.	You will make known to me the path of life; In Your presence is fullness of joy; In Your right hand there are pleasures forever.	11.	Father show me the paths of life. Let me enjoy Your presence; fill my life with joy and pleasure. I thank You.

Psalm 17 NIV

The Psalm is a prayer of one in great danger who is obedient, but confident of deliverance from God.

A prayer of David

BIBLE	PRAYER
1. Hear me, Lord, my plea is just; listen to my cry. Hear my prayer— it does not rise from deceitful lips.	**1.** Hear me Father; answer me as I pray from my heart. Let my prayers be fruitful.
2. Let my vindication come from You; may Your eyes see what is right.	**2.** You are a righteous judge. Let justice be done. Deliver me from my enemies.
3. Though You probe my heart, though You examine me at night and test me, You will find that I have planned no evil; my mouth has not transgressed.	**3.** Visit me, look at my heart, examine the words of my mouth, I am determined not to use my mouth to transgress.
4. Though people tried to bribe me, I have kept myself from the ways of the violent through what Your lips have commanded.	**4-5.** Help me obey Your word, I must run away from evil people and their deeds. Help me not to do evil, rather help me do good.
5. My steps have held to Your paths; my feet have not stumbled.	
6. I call on You, my God, for You will answer me; turn Your ear to me and hear my prayer	**6.** I have come to You today because I know You will hear me.
7. Show me the wonders of Your great love, You who	**7.** Favour me my saviour, uphold me with Your

save by Your right hand those who take refuge in You from their foes.

8. Keep me as the apple of Your eye; hide me in the shadow of Your wings

9. From the wicked who are out to destroy me, from my mortal enemies who surround me.

10. They close up their callous hearts, and their mouths speak with arrogance.

11. They have tracked me down, they now surround me, with eyes alert, to throw me to the ground.

12. They are like a lion hungry for prey, like a fierce lion crouching in cover.

13. Rise up, Lord, confront them, bring them down; with Your sword rescue me from the wicked.

14. By Your hand save me from such people, Lord, from those of this world whose reward is in this life. May what you have stored up for the wicked fill their bellies; may their children gorge themselves on it, and may

righteous right hand, all my trust is in You. Protect me from all my enemies.

8. Lord keep me and hide me under Your wings.

9. Do not let the wicked destroy me for they have surrounded me.

10. The wicked are too proud to have the fear of God. Their wealth has clouded their senses.

11. The wicked are all over and their eyes are fixed on destruction. Let them be stopped in their tracks O God.

12. They are waiting for the opportunity to pounce on me.

13. Arise from the heavens and deliver me from the hands of the wicked. These men have no care for anybody but themselves.

14. You have allowed these men to afflict me. I ask that You deliver me from them all in Jesus name.

there be leftovers for their little ones.	
15. As for me, I will be vindicated and will see Your face; when I awake, I will be satisfied with seeing Your likeness.	**15.** I pray that in the end, I shall be with You and have rest in You.

Psalm 18 NASB

The Psalm is a cry for deliverance to God. It shows God would deliver one who he delights in. It also makes clear that the wicked will be destroyed. The Psalm gives glory to God for achievements.

For the choir director. A Psalm of David the servant of the Lord, who spoke to the Lord the words of this song in the day that the Lord delivered him from the hand of all his enemies and from the hand of Saul. And he said,

BIBLE	PRAYER
1. "I love You, O Lord, my strength."	**1.** Lord give me a heart that will love You completely with my spirit, soul and body. You are my strength, the source of my victory.
2. The Lord is my rock and my fortress and my deliverer, My God, my rock, in whom I take refuge; My shield and the horn of my salvation, my stronghold.	**2.** I declare that You are my rock and my fortress. I pray You will continue to keep me away from my enemies. You have delivered me from my enemies at all times and I pray that You will continue to deliver me in Jesus name. I do not have any other God but

	Psalm		Prayer
			You. You are my strength and I will continue to trust You. You are my buckler, You have not allowed the blows from the enemy to touch me. You are the horn of my salvation and my high tower. I depend on You to protect me.
3.	I call upon the Lord, who is worthy to be praised, and I am saved from my enemies.	**3.**	Thank you because I have access to You and I can call on You at all times. You are worthy to be praised and I thank you that I will be saved from my enemies.
4.	The cords of death encompassed me, and the torrents of ungodliness terrified me.	**4.**	I have seen death around me, the wickedness of ungodly men is overwhelming. I reject every arrow of death in Jesus name.
5.	The cords of Sheol surrounded me; the snares of death confronted me.	**5.**	Wherever fear has come from, let it go back to the ungodly in Jesus name.
6.	In my distress I called upon the Lord, and cried to my God for help; He heard my voice out of His temple, and my cry for help before Him came into His ears.	**6.**	When I call unto You, let my cry come unto You, hear me as I pray.
7.	Then the earth shook and quaked; and the foundations of the mountains were trembling	**7.**	Lord I ask that You show Your anger, let the earth shake and tremble, shake the foundations of

and were shaken, because He was angry.

8. Smoke went up out of His nostrils, and fire from His mouth devoured; Coals were kindled by it.

9. He bowed the heavens also, and came down with thick darkness under His feet.

10 He rode upon a cherub and flew; and He sped upon the wings of the wind.

11. He made darkness His hiding place, His canopy around Him, darkness of waters, thick clouds of the skies.

12. From the brightness before Him passed His thick clouds, Hailstones and coals of fire.

13. The Lord also thundered in the heavens, and the Most High uttered His voice, Hailstones and coals of fire.

14. He sent out His arrows, and scattered them, and lightning flashes in abundance, and routed them.

15. Then the channels of water appeared, and the foundations of the world

the hills for my sake.

8. Lord I ask that You put fear and dread into the heart of the wicked. Let the fire out of Your breath turn all my enemies into coal before You.

9. Come quickly my Lord, I know darkness can't stop You.

10. Fly on the wings of the wind O Lord.

11. I do not know how You move Lord but in the darkness, let the wicked know Your presence.

12. Send down hailstones and coals of fire upon my enemies.

13. Let them hear the thunder in Your voice I pray in Jesus name.

14-15. Let Your arrows pierce and scatter them, let lightning bolts destroy them in Jesus name. Lord I ask that You do everything to deliver me.

	were laid bare at Your rebuke, O Lord, at the blast of the breath of Your nostrils.		
16.	He sent from on high, He took me; He drew me out of many waters.	**16.**	Send help to me, I must not sink in Jesus name.
17.	He delivered me from my strong enemy, and from those who hated me, for they were too mighty for me.	**17.**	Thank You for delivering me from my strong enemy. Yes they hated me but You saw me through in my time of trouble.
18.	They confronted me in the day of my calamity, but the Lord was my stay.	**18.**	You are my protection. Thank you because You have given me freedom.
19.	He brought me forth also into a broad place; He rescued me, because He delighted in me.	**19.**	You delivered me by Your grace alone. I pray You will continue to take delight in me in Jesus name.
20.	The Lord has rewarded me according to my righteousness; according to the cleanness of my hands He has recompensed me.	**20.**	Thank you for delivering me, I told You that I had done nothing to deserve what the enemy was doing to me.
21.	For I have kept the ways of the Lord, and have not wickedly departed from my God.	**21.**	Help me continue to keep Your commandments.
22.	For all His ordinances were before me, and I did not put away His statutes from me.	**22.**	By Your grace I did according to Your word and did not depart from it.
23.	I was also blameless with Him, and I kept my-myself from my iniquity.	**23.**	Help me to be upright before You and keep away from sin.

24.	Therefore the Lord has recompensed me according to my righteousness, according to the cleanness of my hands in His eyes.	**24.**	Thank you for making me holy and enabling me to enter into Your presence.
25.	With the kind You show Yourself kind; with the blameless You show Yourself blameless;	**25.**	Help me show mercy to others even as You have promised You will be merciful unto me.
26.	With the pure You show Yourself pure, and with the crooked You show Yourself astute.	**26.**	Help me keep myself pure.
27.	For You save an afflicted people, but haughty eyes You abase.	**27.**	Lord I pray that the afflicted will be saved by You. Save me from myself, take pride away from me totally O Lord.
28.	For You light my lamp; the Lord my God illumines my darkness.	**28.**	When You bring light, darkness has no place. Light my candle O Lord.
29.	For by You I can run upon a troop; and by my God I can leap over a wall.	**29.**	By Your grace I have overcome every obstruction from the enemy; I have run through them like an army.
30.	As for God, His way is blameless; the word of the Lord is tried; He is a shield to all who take refuge in Him.	**30.**	You are a perfect God, You have not changed, and Your words have and will always come to pass. I pray that You will always protect me as I trust in You.
31.	For who is God, but the Lord? And who is a rock, except our God,	**31.**	LORD there is no other God but You; Thank You for giving us protection, stability and peace.

32.	The God who girds me with strength and makes my way blameless?	**32.**	My God I thank You for You have given me strength to live and to fight such that I could break a bow of steel.
33.	He makes my feet like hinds' feet, and sets me upon my high places.	**33.**	Thank you because You have put me in the high place of victory.
34.	He trains my hands for battle, so that my arms can bend a bow of bronze.	**34.**	You have taught my hands to war.
35.	You have also given me the shield of Your salvation, and Your right hand upholds me; and Your gentleness makes me great.	**35.**	Thank you for the shield of salvation. Your righteous right hand has upheld me and Your goodness and kindness has made me great.
36.	You enlarge my steps under me, and my feet have not slipped.	**36.**	My feet have been enlarged, big enough that rather than falling down I am steady.
37.	I pursued my enemies and overtook them, and I did not turn back until they were consumed.	**37.**	I have been able to pursue my enemies, I have overtaken them, and I did not turn back until they were consumed.
38.	I shattered them, so that they were not able to rise; they fell under my feet.	**38.**	Thank you because my enemies are totally destroyed and I will see them no more.
39.	For You have girded me with strength for battle; You have subdued under me those who rose up against me.	**39.**	Thank you for giving me the strength and courage for battle. I am successful because You have defeated them on my behalf.

40. You have also made my enemies turn their backs to me, and I destroyed those who hated me.
You have also made my enemies turn their backs to me, and I destroyed those who hated me.

41. They cried for help, but there was none to save, even to the Lord, but He did not answer them.

42. Then I beat them fine as the dust before the wind; I emptied them out as the mire of the streets.

43. You have delivered me frm the contentions of the people; You have placed me as head of the nations; a people whom I have not known serve me.

44. As soon as they hear, they obey me; foreigners submit to me.

45. Foreigners fade away, and come trembling out of their fortresses.

46. The Lord lives, and bless- ed be my rock;

40. You have given me the necks of my enemies not only to subdue them but also to destroy them and cut them off.

41. They have cried to You but it is in vain because You have not answered them.

42. The enemy is completely destroyed. Internal strife has been demolished from my home, my ministry and community.

43. The heathen will serve the righteous. You have made me head and not the tail. I pray that wherever I am, a people I have not known will serve me.

44. They will hear of me, they will obey me and they will submit to me and Your name will be glorified.

45. I pray that strangers around me, my house-hold and my community shall fade into oblivion never heard of again and fear shall come upon them in Jesus name.

46. My Lord and my God, You are immortal and I

	BIBLE		PRAYER
	and exalt- ed be the God of my sal- vation,		bless Your holy name. You who saved me Lord, I exalt and magnify You.
47.	The God who executes vengeance for me, and subdues peoples under me	**47.**	Thank you for avenging me and subduing my enemies.
48.	He delivers me from my enemies; surely You lift me above those who rise up against me; You rescue me from the violent man.	**48.**	Thank you for delivering me from my enemies, I was down but You lifted me up.
49.	Therefore I will give thanks to You among the nations, O Lord, and I will sing praises to Your name.	**49.**	As I testify of Your deeds in my life the world will come and appreciate You are indeed Almighty.
50.	He gives great delivera-nce to His king, and shows lovingkindness to His anointed, to David and his descendants forever.	**50.**	You delivered me; You showed mercy to me and to my future genera-tions.

Psalm 19 ESV

The Psalm shows the glory of the work of creation, the perfection and the power of the word of God.

To the choirmaster. A Psalm of David.

	BIBLE		PRAYER
1.	The heavens declare the glory of God, and the sky above proclaims His handiwork.	**1.**	Lord I look up to the heavens and I give glory to You. The stars, sun, moon and other planets co-exist without accident

	Scripture		Prayer
			You are indeed Almighty.
2.	Day to day pours out speech, and night to night reveals knowledge.	**2.**	You first divided light from darkness. From the beginning of time, day follows day and night follows night. It has never changed and it will never change, You are indeed an awesome God.
3.	There is no speech, nor are there words, whose voice is not heard.	**3.**	Lord there is nowhere in the world where the heavens do not show Your glory.
4.	Their voice goes out through all the earth, and their words to the end of the world. In them He has set a tent for the sun,	**4.**	All throughout the earth, the heavens are seen and appreciated by men, the heavens show You are God.
5.	Which comes out like a bridegroom leaving his chamber, and, like a strong man, runs its course with joy.	**5.**	The sun has a special place in the heavens and comes out always like a bridegroom coming out of his bedroom.
6.	Its rising is from the end of the heavens, and its circuit to the end of them, and there is nothing hidden from its heat.	**6.**	The sun moves from one part of the heavens to the other and no part of the earth escapes the heat generated. You are indeed a glorious God.
7.	The law of the Lord is perfect, reviving the soul; the testimony of the Lord is sure, making wise the simple;	**7.**	Your commandments are perfect. Help me abide in them. Help me become a soul winner as my acts and my words testify of who You are.
8.	The precepts of the Lord	**8.**	Help me study Your word

are right, rejoicing the heart; the commandment of the Lord is pure, enlightening the eyes;

9. The fear of the Lord is clean, enduring forever; the rules of the Lord are true, and righteous altogether

10. More to be desired are they than gold, even much fine gold; sweeter also than honey and drippings of the honeycomb.

11. Moreover, by them is Your servant warned; in keeping them there is great reward.

12. Who can discern his errors? Declare me innocent from hidden faults.

13. Keep back Your servant also from presumptuous sins; let them not have dominion over me! Then I shall be blameless, and innocent of great transgression.

and as I do so let it bring rejoicing to my heart. I also pray that the word will bring enlightenment to my eyes giving me direction at all times.

9. I pray that I will not depart from fearing the Lord. I know the judgments of the Lord are righteous because He himself is righteous.

10. I pray that obeying Your commandments will be more desirable to me than gold and sweeter than honey and the honeycomb.

11. I pray that I would see the warnings in the word of God and my heart would willingly obey and by His grace I will receive the rewards in Jesus name.

12. You know everything O God. I ask that You cleanse me from secret faults; faults I have that I do not identify as faults.

13. I ask that in Your power You will help me by stopping me from being presumptuous, knowingly doing things that are wrong and damning the consequences. Let these sins not have dominion over me. Let me walk in victory over sin. Help me so that I can stand upright before You at all times.

14. Let the words of my mouth and the meditation of my heart be acceptable in Your sight, O Lord, my rock and my redeemer.	**14.** Teach me to meditate on Your word and let the words of my mouth and the meditation of my heart be acceptable to You. You are my strength and I pray You will continue to be my LORD and my God.

Psalm 20 ESV

The Psalm is an intercession on behalf of the king and shows God is always dependable.

To the choirmaster. A Psalm of David.

BIBLE	PRAYER
1. May the Lord answer you in the day of trouble! May the name of the God of Jacob protect you!	**1.** My Lord hear me when I call You. Keep me and protect me from all that trouble me. I call on the name that is above all names to defend me.
2. May He send you help from the sanctuary and give you support from Zion!	**2.** Send me help from heaven. Release fire from heaven on my adversaries.
3. May He remember all your offerings and regard with favour your burnt sacrifices! Selah	**3.** Let all my offerings and sacrifices be acceptable to You in Jesus name. Let them touch Your heart and stir You to hear

my cry.

4. May He grant you your heart's desire and fulfil all your plans!

4. Let all my desires be according to Your will, and as I ask answer me speedily.

5. May we shout for joy over your salvation, and in the name of our God set up our banners! May the Lord fulfil all your petitions!

5. As You deliver us, we will rejoice. The heavens and the whole world will know that You are a good God and You are a prayer answering God.

6. Now I know that the Lord saves His anointed; He will answer him from His holy heaven with the saving might of His right hand.

6. I know because I am anointed by You, You will not fail me; You will not put me to shame. You will hear my prayers and You will deliver now.

7. Some trust in chariots and some in horses, but we trust in the name of the Lord our God.

7. Those who trust in weapons and their abilities will always fail. I pray that I will always remember Your name and my trust will solely be on Your name.

8. They collapse and fall, but we rise and stand upright.

8. I pray that I will always remember what You have done in the past. Therefore I will stand firm, never shaken in Jesus name.

9. O Lord, save the king! May He answer us when we call.

9. I pray again, my Lord and King, hear us whenever we call.

Psalm 21 NIV

The Psalm is a thanksgiving for success after the blessings of God.

For the director of music. A Psalm of David.

BIBLE		PRAYER	
1.	The king rejoices in Your strength, Lord. How great is his joy in the victories You give!	1.	I rejoice in Your strength and I thank You for saving me.
2.	You have granted him his heart's desire and have not withheld the request of his lips.	2.	I thank You because You have heard my prayers.
3.	You came to greet him with rich blessings and placed a crown of pure gold on his head.	3.	In Your loving kindness you have blessed me so much that my heart is fixed upon You. Thank You for the victories You have given me, they are like crowns of gold on my head.
4	He asked You for life, and You gave it to him—length of days, for ever and ever.	4.	Lord grant me long life and eternal life too.
5.	Through the victories You gave, his glory is great; You have bestowed on him splendour and majesty.	5.	You have honoured me by saving me. It has not caused me anything but it caused You Your Son; I am now part of the family of God. All glory and honour to You my Lord and king.
6.	Surely You have granted him unending blessings	6.	I thank You for the blessings which make

	Psalm		Prayer
	and made him glad with the joy of Your presence.		me glad at all times and have changed my countenance forever.
7.	For the king trusts in the Lord; through the unfailing love of the Most High he will not be shaken.	**7.**	Help me continue to trust in You, I pray that by Your mercy I will not be moved. My salvation is permanent and my blessings will not be taken away in Jesus name.
8.	Your hand will lay hold on all Your enemies; Your right hand will seize Your foes.	**8.**	I pray that no matter how far my enemies run, Your hand shall find them; Your right hand of power shall destroy them in Jesus name.
9.	When You appear for battle, You will burn them up as in a blazing furnace. The Lord will swallow them up in His wrath, and His fire will consume them.	**9.**	I ask that You destroy my enemies as if they were burnt in an oven. Show Your anger, swallow them in Your wrath and let Your fire destroy them all.
10.	You will destroy their descendants from the earth, their posterity from mankind.	**10.**	Let their offspring be destroyed too.
11.	Though they plot evil against You and devise wicked schemes, they cannot succeed.	**11.**	I ask that every evil intended against my household and my community be nullified in Jesus name. Every evil imagination against me shall not succeed in Jesus name. Lord make it impossible for them to rise up against me.

12. You will make them turn their backs when You aim at them with drawn bow.	**12.** Let them stay defeated such that they would not be able to rise up against me in Jesus name.
13. Be exalted in Your strength, Lord; we will sing and praise Your might.	**13.** Be exalted O Lord in Your power and majesty, I will praise You forever-rmore.

Psalm 22 NASB

The Psalm is a picture of the crucifixion of Jesus Christ using that as a base it shows the complaints of man and the power of the enemy. It is also request to God for deliverance and the exaltation of Christ.

For the choir director; upon Aijeleth Hashshahar.
A Psalm of David.

BIBLE	**PRAYER**
1. My God, my God, why have You forsaken me? Far from my deliverance are the words of my groaning. **2.** O my God, I cry by day, but You do not answer; and by night, but I have no rest. **3.** Yet You are holy, O You who are enthroned upon the praises of Israel.	**1.** Lord just as Jesus Christ cried on the cross, I pray do not forsake me. Do not abandon me to my enemies. **2-3.** I cry day and night, hear me out Father. Even though I have not seen answers, You are holy and I will continue to praise You. You have been merciful to me even when I am undeserving.
4. In You our fathers trusted; they trusted and You delivered them.	**4.** I have trusted You in the past and I will always trust You.

5. To You they cried out and were delivered; In You they trusted and were not disappointed.

6. But I am a worm and not a man, a reproach of men and despised by the people.

7. All who see me sneer at me; They separate with the lip, they wag the head, saying,

8. "Commit yourself to the Lord; let Him deliver him; Let Him rescue him, because He delights in him."

9. Yet You are He who brought me forth from the womb; You made me trust when upon my mother's breasts.

10. Upon You I was cast from birth; You have been my God from my mother's womb.

11. Be not far from me, for trouble is near; For there is none to help.

12. Many bulls have surrounded me; Strong bulls of Bashan have encircled me.

13. They open wide their mouth at me, as a ravening and a roaring lion.

5. You have delivered me in the past; I trust You will do it again.

6-7. People around me pour scorn on me because of my faith in You.

8. They say vile things but I trust that You are a great deliverer.

9. Lord You have kept me from my birth up until this day, You have not changed and You can never change.

10. You are my God and You will always be.

11. Do not be far from me for I have no one to call on but You in times of trouble.

12. Many surround me looking to destroy me.

13. Let all looking at me with wide open mouths have such mouths shut up permanently in Jesus

			name.
14.	I am poured out like water, and all my bones are out of joint; My heart is like wax; It is melted within me.	**14.**	The attacks from the enemy are vicious. I ask for help O God.
15.	My strength is dried up like a potsherd, and my tongue cleaves to my jaws; And You lay me in the dust of death.	**15.**	I am without strength. I cannot fight back, I cannot talk.
16.	For dogs have surrounded me; A band of evildoers has encompassed me; They pierced my hands and my feet.	**16.**	The men who surround me are like dogs, seeking to devour me.
17.	I can count all my bones. They look, they stare at me;	**17.**	My enemies look at me with contempt. Let every evil eyes be blinded in Jesus name.
18.	They divide my garments among them, and for my clothing they cast lots.	**18.**	They try to distribute my assets, as if I am no more.
19.	But You, O Lord, be not far off; O You my help, hasten to my assistance.	**19.**	Do not be far away from me, arise and fight for me O God.
20.	Deliver my soul from the sword, my only life from the power of the dog.	**20.**	Lord deliver me from the snare of the wicked.
21.	Save me from the lion's mouth; From the horns of the wild oxen You answer me.	**21.**	Save me from the mouth of the lion.
22.	I will tell of Your name to my brethren; In the midst of the assembly I will praise You.	**22.**	Help me declare Your name on the rooftop, in the midst of the people help me to give You

23. You who fear the Lord, praise Him; All you descendants of Jacob, glorify Him, and stand in awe of Him, all you descendants of Israel.

24. For He has not despised nor abhorred the afflictiion of the afflicted; Nor has He hidden His face from him; But when he cried to Him for help, He heard.

25. From You comes my praise in the great assembly; I shall pay my vows before those who fear Him.

26. The afflicted will eat and be satisfied; Those who seek Him will praise the Lord. Let your heart live forever!

27. All the ends of the earth will remember and turn to the Lord, and all the families of the nations will worship before You.

28. For the kingdom is the Lord's and He rules over the nations.

praise.

23. Give me a heart that would fear You, praise You and glorify You at all times.

24. Thank You for I called and You answered, You always show up when Your children call on You.

25. I will worship in the presence of Your children.

26. I pray that Your blessings upon all who seek You, upon those who are afflicted will bring satisfaction and prosperity in Jesus name.

27. I pray that all who seek You shall find You and shall recognise You are worthy to be praised. I pray that all who come to You shall enjoy eternal life with You.

28. I pray that all people who have turned away from worshiping You shall remember there is none like You. They shall accept the error of their ways, come back to You and worship You.

29. All the prosperous of the earth will eat and worship, all those who go down to the dust will bow before Him, even he who cannot keep his soul alive.

29. The earth is Yours and all that are in it. The rich and the poor, the weak and the strong shall worship You; people of all races shall bow down and worship You.

30. Posterity will serve Him; It will be told of the Lord to the coming generation

30. I pray that my children and generations to come will serve You. None shall depart from Your presence in Jesus name.

31. They will come and will declare His righteousness to a people who will be born, that He has performed it.

31. I pray that the present generation and the future shall continue to proclaim the gospel and its righteousness until Jesus Christ shall come. Amen.

Psalm 23 ESV

The Psalm expresses the appreciation of God's goodness and man's dependence upon him.

A Psalm of David.

BIBLE

1. The Lord is my shepherd; I shall not want.

PRAYER

1. I gladly come to You as Your sheep. Thank You for being my shepherd. According to Your loving kindness I shall not lack any good thing. I shall not want for good health,

provision and protection.

2. He makes me lie down in green pastures. He leads me beside still waters.

2. Thank You for the green pastures in Your word, where all Your promises reside. You lead me beside the still waters. The waters provide comfort when I am thirsty. The waters calm me when I am pressured.

3. He restores my soul. He leads me in paths of righteousness for His name's sake.

3. When I stray out of Your presence, You restore me when I come back. You lead me in righteousness; I pray I will continue following You, never looking away.

4. Even though I walk through the valley of the shadow of death, I will fear no evil, for You are with me; Your rod and Your staff, they comfort me.

4. Thank You Father for being with me when I walk through the valley of the shadow of death. As You are with me, I will not stay in the shadows of death, I will always overcome all that come my way. I do not fear evil. Your rod and Your staff comfort me.

5. You prepare a table before me in the presence of my enemies; You anoint my head with oil; my cup overflows.

5. All I need You have provided. My enemies will be alive to watch my victory parade. Thank You for the anointing that runs over in my life, the anointing to excel, to achieve and to prosper in all that I do, Father I

6. Surely goodness and mercy shall follow me all the days of my life, and I shall dwell in the house of the Lord forever.

am grateful.

6. My shepherd, with all that You have done and with all that You are doing, I know that Your goodness and mercies will follow me all the days of my life. By Your grace I will settle, rest and live in Your presence forever more.

Psalm 24 ESV

The Psalm shows Christ as King and lets us know the attributes of His subjects.

A Psalm of David.

BIBLE

1. The earth is the Lord's and the fullness thereof, the world and those who dwell therein,
2. For He has founded it upon the seas and established it upon the rivers.
3. Who shall ascend the hill of the Lord? And who shall stand in His holy place?
4. He who has clean hands and a pure heart, who does not lift up his soul to what is false and does

PRAYER

1. You own the whole earth and everything in it including me. You own all that I am and all that I have.
2. You created the earth on the waters and till this day we see Your handiwork.
3. You are holy, You are pure and You are perfect. The filthy in heart cannot come into Your presence.
4. Help me to be upright, help me to be clean. Help me keep my heart pure, give me a heart

	not swear deceitfully.		that hates idol worship and a heart that is not vain. Help me speak the truth at all times. I ask that You release the Holy Spirit to work a new work in me in Jesus name.
5.	He will receive blessing from the Lord and righteousness from the God of his salvation.	**5.**	I ask for every blessing from You, fill me with favour and grace. Thank You for the free gift of salvation and my righteousness which I have received through Jesus Christ.
6.	Such is the generation of those who seek Him, who seek the face of the God of Jacob. Selah	**6.**	I recognise that I do not have any power of my own. I pray that You will grant me the grace to seek You at all times.
7.	Lift up your heads, O gates! And be lifted up, O ancient doors, that the King of glory may come in.	**7.**	Lord I open the gate of my heart to You, I open my household to You, and I open all that I am associated with to You.
8.	Who is this King of glory? The Lord, strong and mighty, the Lord, mighty in battle!	**8.**	Let Your glory fill my life.
9.	Lift up your heads, O gates! And lift them up, O ancient doors, that the King of glory may come in.	**9.**	I pray that the everlasting doors of heaven will be open to me and all that is mine in Jesus name. I ask that every door shut against me by the enemy be opened now in Jesus name. Let Your might and Your

power cause all gates shut against me be opened now in Jesus name.

10. Who is this King of glory? The Lord of hosts, he is the King of glory! Selah	**10.** You are the king of glory; the hosts of heaven are subject to You. I worship You. Amen.

Psalm 25 NASB

The Psalm shows a desire for direction, help from enemies, repentance, affection and trust in God.

A Psalm of David.

BIBLE	PRAYER
1. To You, O Lord, I lift up my soul.	**1.** Lord I lift my soul up to You in thanksgiving. I worship and honour You. Lord I lift my soul up to You in thanksgiving. I worship and honour You.
2. O my God, in You I trust, do not let me be ashamed; Do not let my enemies exult over me.	**2.** I commit my life into Your hands Father because I trust You. Anyway there is no one I can turn to.
3. Indeed, none of those who wait for You will be ashamed; Those who deal treacherously without cause will be ashamed.	**3.** Let me not be ashamed because I trust You. Let me not live a life that is different from the faith I have in You. Do not let my enemies triumph over me. Let all who sin be ashamed.
4. Make me know Your ways, O Lord; Teach me Your paths.	**4-5.** I ask that You show me and teach me the ways of life so that I would not

go the wrong way.
You are responsible for keeping me away from danger. I am totally dependent on You at all times.

5. Lead me in Your truth and teach me, for You are the God of my salvat-tion; for You I wait all the day.

6. Remember, O Lord, Your compassion and Your lovingkindnesses, for they have been from of old.

6. I pray that You remem-ber Your compassion of old towards me, continue to favour and help me Father. Show me Your mercy and lovingkindness.

7. Do not remember the sins of my youth or my transgressions; accord-ing to Your lovingkind-ness remember me, for Your goodness' sake, O Lord.

7. Have mercy on me, remember me for good. My sins You have promised You will remember no more as I seek forgiveness.

8. Good and upright is the Lord; Therefore He instructs sinners in the way.

8. You are a good and righteous God. You do not want any to perish. I ask that You teach me Your ways.

9. He leads the humble in justice, and He teaches the humble His way.

9. Help me to be meek and guide me in Your righteous judgement.

10. All the paths of the Lord are loving kindness and truth to those who keep His covenant and His testimonies.

10. Help me walk along the paths of mercy and truth at all times. Give me a heart that will obey You.

11. For Your name's sake, O Lord, pardon my iniquity, for it is great.

11. I ask for forgiveness of all my sins O God. Help me live in awe of You. I voluntarily decide to follow the path that You

12. Who is the man who fears the Lord? He will instruct him in the way he should choose.

13. His soul will abide in prosperity, and his descendants will inherit the land.

14. The secret of the Lord is for those who fear Him, and He will make them know His covenant.

15. My eyes are continually toward the Lord, for He will pluck my feet out of the net.

16. Turn to me and be gracious to me, for I am lonely and afflicted.

17. The troubles of my heart are enlarged; Bring me out of my distresses.

18. Look upon my affliction and my trouble, and forgive all my sins.

19. Look upon my enemies, for they are many, and they hate me with violent hatred.

have chosen for me. Help me to be steadfast in it.

12. As I follow the path You have chosen by Your grace, grant me a life of peace.

13. I pray that my seed will enjoy the benefits of God's goodness in Jesus name.

14. I pray the fear of God will be paramount in my heart and as I reverence You Lord, You will grant me access to Your secrets in Jesus name. Help me understand the covenant You have with me.

15. I look up to You; keep my feet from every trap the enemy has laid for me.

16. Do not hide Your face from me, have mercy on me as I am alone and afflicted.

17. The enemies are increasing in number; deliver me from every negative situation confronting me.

18. Look upon my pain and troubles and forgive me all my sins.

19. No matter how many enemies are after me, do not let them be victorious over me. Deliver me from danger.

20. Guard my soul and deliver me; Do not let me be ashamed, for I take refuge in You.

21. Let integrity and uprightness preserve me, for I wait for You.

22. Redeem Israel, O God, out of all his troubles.

20. Deliver me and let me not be ashamed, my trust is in You.

21. Help me to be upright and let my life be preserved.

22. I ask that You will redeem Your children all over the world from every trouble that is facing them.

Psalm 26 NASB

The Psalm shows that we must walk in integrity.

A Psalm of David.

BIBLE

1. Vindicate me, O Lord, for I have walked in my integrity, and I have trusted in the Lord without wavering.

2. Examine me, O Lord, and try me; test my mind and my heart.

3. For Your lovingkindness is before my eyes, and I have walked in Your truth.

4. I do not sit with deceitful

PRAYER

1. Help me Lord to live with integrity. Help me trust in You and as I do so I will not fail in Jesus name.

2. Lord I ask that You test my heart and where there are failings, correct and uphold me in Jesus name.

3. Thank you because You have caused me to see and experience Your lovingkindness. Help me walk in Your truth.

4-5. Help me run away from

men, nor will I go with pretenders.	sitting with evil people or going about with people who have evil intentions.
5. I hate the assembly of evildoers, and I will not sit with the wicked.	
6. I shall wash my hands in innocence, and I will go about Your altar, O Lord,	**6-7.** Help me to be conscious of the cleansing I have already received through the blood of Jesus as I come into Your presence to give thanks and testify of Your goodness.
7. That I may proclaim with the voice of thanksgiving and declare all Your wonders.	
8. O Lord, I love the habitation of Your house and the place where Your glory dwells.	**8.** I pray that You put an unquenchable love for Your house on me and that the love of Your presence will always consume me.
9. Do not take my soul away along with sinners, nor my life with men of bloodshed,	**9.** Do not let me be associated with men who have blood on their hands, men who partake in mischief and those who pervert justice.
10. In whose hands is a wicked scheme, and whose right hand is full of bribes.	**10-11.** Help me walk in integrity and I ask that You redeem me from troubles that come my way.
11. But as for me, I shall walk in my integrity; redeem me, and be gracious to me.	
12. My foot stands on a level place; in the congregations I shall bless the Lord.	**12.** You are my firm foundation. Keep me stable in You O Lord. I will bless You forever.

Psalm 27 NASB

The Psalm shows that God will never leave us nor forsake us. In the midst of troubles He is always there for us.

A Psalm of David.

BIBLE	PRAYER
1. The Lord is my light and my salvation; Whom shall I fear? The Lord is the defence of my life; Whom shall I dread?	**1.** Thank You Lord for You are my light. Thank You for moving me out of the darkness of failure, sin, lack, separation from You and all forms of affliction. Thank You for enlightening me. Thank You for saving me. Thank You for helping me conquer fear. As You are my light and my strength, there is no more reason to be afraid of the devil and his agents.
2. When evildoers came upon me to devour my flesh, my adversaries and my enemies, they stumbled and fell.	**2.** Thank You for protecting me when the wicked attacked me, setting traps for me wanting to devour me, Your presence caused them to stumble and fall.
3. Though a host encamp against me, my heart will not fear; Though war arise against me, In spite of this I shall be confident.	**3.** Thank You for causing Your angels to encamp round about me; therefore I can be confident of victory over any attacks from the agents of wickedness.
4. One thing I have asked	**4.** Help me achieve my

from the Lord, that I shall seek: That I may dwell in the house of the Lord all the days of my life, to behold the beauty of the Lord and to meditate in His temple.

5. For in the day of trouble He will conceal me in His tabernacle; In the secret place of His tent He will hide me; He will lift me up on a rock.

6. And now my head will be lifted up above my enemies around me, and I will offer in His tent sacrifices with shouts of joy; I will sing, yes, I will sing praises to the Lord.

7. Hear, O Lord, when I cry with my voice, and be gracious to me and answer me.

8. When You said, "Seek My face," my heart said to You, "Your face, O Lord, I shall seek."

9. Do not hide Your face from me, do not turn Your servant away in anger; You have been

desire to seek after You in prayer and tarrying until You answer. Help me dwell in Your presence, to want to be involved in the things of God, to have a heart longing for You. Help me appreciate Your beauty, rendering worship and giving praise all the days of my life.

5. Thank You for hiding me where enemies can't get at me, on a rock that is higher than I.

6. Thank You because You have lifted my head over my enemies. Help me bring sacrifices of joy every day to the temple, and help me sing praises to Your holy name.

7. Lord whenever I cry to You, show me mercy by delivering me from my troubles.

8. You have said I should seek Your face, as long as I live, help me obey You. I will seek Your face.

9. However do not hide Your face from me, do not leave me alone, I pray do not send me

my help; Do not abandon me nor forsake me, O God of my salvation!	away from Your presence. Thank You my Father for saving me.
10. For my father and my mother have forsaken me, but the Lord will take me up.	**10.** People will disappoint me, I know You have never and You will never disappoint me.
11. Teach me Your way, O Lord, and lead me in a level path because of my foes.	**11.** Teach me O God the path of truth and the path of holiness so I would not fall back into the hands of my enemies.
12. Do not deliver me over to the desire of my adversaries, for false witnesses have risen against me, and such as breathe out violence.	**12.** My enemy wants to kill, to steal and to destroy me. I ask do not deliver me into his hands.
13. I would have despaired unless I had believed that I would see the goodness of the Lord in the land of the living.	**13.** Thank You because my hope in You sustained me when the enemy rose against me. My portion is in the land of the living and not in the land of the dead.
14. Wait for the Lord; Be strong and let your heart take courage; Yes, wait for the Lord.	**14.** Give me the strength to wait on You, never ever giving up.

Psalm 28 NASB

The Psalm shows persistence in heartfelt prayer.

A Psalm of David.

BIBLE

1. To You, O Lord, I call; My rock, do not be deaf to me, for if You are silent to me, I will become like those who go down to the pit.

2. Hear the voice of my supplications when I cry to You for help, when I lift up my hands toward Your holy sanctuary.

3. Do not drag me away with the wicked and with those who work iniquity, who speak peace with their neighbours, while evil is in their hearts.

4. Requite them according to their work and according to the evil of their practices; Requite them according to the deeds of their hands; Repay them their recompense.

5. Because they do not regard the works of the Lord nor the deeds of His hands, He will tear them down and not build them up.

PRAYER

1. Hear my cry O God my rock and support. Answer me now, take notice of my prayer. Do not let me be like those in distress that do not have any help.

2. Hear my cry as I lift up my hands to You.

3. I ask that You protect me from wicked people who say one thing but mean the opposite, wolves in sheep's clothing.

4. You are a just God. Do not let the wicked go unpunished.

5. They do not appreciate You, neither do they give You the glory You deserve, let them be destroyed by Your mighty hands.

	Bible		Prayer
6.	Blessed be the Lord, because He has heard the voice of my suplication.	**6.**	Thank You for answerring my prayers.
7.	The Lord is my strength and my shield; my heart trusts in Him, and I am helped; Therefore my heart exults, and with my song I shall thank Him.	**7.**	You are my strength and my shield. All my trust is on You. Thank You for helping me out of all my troubles. Let my heart sing songs of praise to You.
8.	The Lord is their strength, and He is a saving defence to His anointed	**8-9.**	Thank You O my Saviour, thank You for the many blessings, provisions and protection.
9.	Save Your people and bless Your inheritance; Be their shepherd also, and carry them forever.		

Psalm 29 NIV

The Psalm shows us the great things the voice of the Lord does and should lead us giving glory to God.

A Psalm of David.

BIBLE		PRAYER	
1.	Ascribe to the Lord, you heavenly beings, ascribe to the Lord glory and strength.	**1.**	Help me give unto You the glory and honour that You deserve. I acknowledge who You are, all You have done from the beginning till date. Power resides in You my Lord and my God.
2.	Ascribe to the Lord the glory due His name; worship the Lord in the	**2.**	Help me ascribe honour to Your name, for in Your name is love, grace,

splendour of His holiness.

mercy, power, favour and wisdom. Open my eyes to see You seated in splendour and majesty. I worship You as I bow my heart to You.

3. The voice of the Lord is over the waters; the God of glory thunders, the Lord thunders over the mighty waters.

3. I ask that as You speak into every situation, let the waters respond and obey You.

4. The voice of the Lord is powerful; the voice of the Lord is majestic.

4. Let the power in Your voice and the power behind Your voice break every opposition even to the bone and marrow in Jesus name.

5. The voice of the Lord breaks the cedars; the Lord breaks in pieces the cedars of Lebanon.

6 He makes Lebanon leap like a calf, Sirion like a young wild ox.

5-6. Lord just as the waters obey You, let Your voice break through the toughest cedars and bring surrender to You in Jesus name.

7. The voice of the Lord strikes with flashes of lightning.

7. Let the fire hear You as Your voice cuts through and shows You are indeed God Almighty. Let Your voice enable us to discern the tangible and the intangible

8. The voice of the Lord shakes the desert; the Lord shakes the Desert of Kadesh.

8. Let every forest tremble at the sound of Your voice in Jesus name.

9. The voice of the Lord twists the oaks and

9. Let Your voice bring fear into every being hiding

strips the forests bare. And in His temple all cry, "Glory!"

from You in Jesus name. Let Your voice compel every barren situation in my life to turn around just as it makes the oaks and the forests respond. Teach me and all who hear Your voice to give You glory due to You.

10. The Lord sits enthroned over the flood; the Lord is enthroned as King forever.

10. I thank You and I give You praise because no matter the storm or the wind or the fire, You are in charge. All storms respond to Your voice. Halleluiah

11. The Lord gives strength to His people; the Lord blesses His people with peace.

11. Thank You God for giving me strength, for seeing me through every adversity. Thank You for blessing me with Your peace.

Psalm 30 ESV

This is a Psalm of forgiveness and thanksgiving. The Psalmist encourages us to extol (lift up) God who is the only One who lifts us up.

A Psalm of David. A song at the dedication of the temple

BIBLE

1. I will extol You, O Lord, for You have drawn me up and have not let my foes rejoice over me.

PRAYER

1. Help me give You the praise that You deserve. Without You I cannot do anything. I lift You up above my life, my family,

2. O Lord my God, I cried to You for help, and You have healed me.

3. O Lord, You have brought up my soul from Sheol ; You restored me to life from among those who go down to the pit.

4. Sing praises to the Lord, O you his saints, and give thanks to His holy name.

5. For His anger is but for a moment, and His favour is for a lifetime. Weeping may tarry for the night, but joy comes with the morning.

6. As for me, I said in my

schooling, business, church etc. You have been simply wonderful to me. You have not given my enemies any reason to rejoice over me.

2. Thank You Father for in my times of despair I cried to You and You answered me. I was ill and You healed me. All glory to You.

3. Thank You for You did not allow me to die; I am alive to continue praising You.

4. I thank You with all my heart as I remember Your holiness, loving kindness and Your mercy when I was in trouble. Help me as I call on other saints to join in my praise to You.

5. Thank You Lord for when You are angry, it does not last long. Thank You for Your mercy, rather than giving me the death that I deserve, You favour me with life. Thank You Lord because joy will always overtake any moment of weeping.

6. Help me to continually

prosperity, "I shall never be moved."

depend on You, never falling into the deception that my success is of my making.

7. By Your favour, O Lord, You made my mountain stand strong; You hid Your face; I was dismayed.

7. I ask that You strengthen me and support me for I do not have any help but You. Without You I will be in great trouble. If I allow pride into my life, my blessing will turn into mourning. Therefore I reject pride in Jesus' name.

8. To You, O Lord, I cry, and to the Lord I plead for mercy:

8. I cry unto You, never leave me O Lord.

9. "What profit is there in my death, if I go down to the pit? Will the dust praise You? Will it tell of Your faithfulness?

9. Lord, if You allow me to die, I would not be in a position to praise You.

10. Hear, O Lord, and be merciful to me! O Lord, be my helper!"

10. Hear me O God as I call on You. Have mercy on me; help me out of my troubles.

11. You have turned for me my mourning into dancing; you have loosed my sackcloth and clothed me with gladness,

11. Thank You for hearing my prayers, You have turned my mourning into dancing and my sorrow into joy.

12. That my glory may sing Your praise and not be silent. O Lord my God, I will give thanks to You forever!.

12. Help me praise You always. Give me a heart of thanksgiving O God. Halleluiah, Halleluiah, Halleluiah, Halleluiah, Halleluiah, Halleluiah, Halleluiah.

Psalm 31 NASB

This Psalm teaches us that even when we are in trouble we should have trust and be confident that God will deliver us. It ends with praises to God.

For the choir director. A Psalm of David.

BIBLE

1. In You, O Lord, I have taken refuge; Let me never be ashamed; In Your righteousness deliver me.

2. Incline Your ear to me, rescue me quickly; Be to me a rock of strength, A stronghold to save me.

3. For You are my rock and my fortress; For Your name's sake You will lead me and guide me.

4. You will pull me out of the net which they have secretly laid for me, for You are my strength.

5. Into Your hand I commit my spirit; You have ransomed me, O Lord,

PRAYER

1. In You and You only do I put my trust. Deliver me in Your righteousness and mercy out of the hands of my enemies. Do not let them defeat me, let me not be ashamed.

2. Help me so my faith would not fail. Deliver me speedily O Lord. You are my rock. I know I am safe in You, yes I am secure, and nothing can take me out of Your security.

3. Lead me and guide me through the traps that have been laid for me. Let Your name be glorified.

4. Sometimes I feel weak, I ask that You give me strength to fight. I also ask that You use Your strength on my behalf, Almighty God.

5. My life is in Your hands, You will do what is best for me. You have

	Psalm		Prayer
	God of truth.		redeemed me; You have already paid a price for me. You are the God of truth, You have never failed and You will never fail.
6.	I hate those who regard vain idols, but I trust in the Lord.	**6.**	I trust in none other but You.
7.	I will rejoice and be glad in Your lovingkindness, because You have seen my affliction; You have known the troubles of my soul.	**7.**	I am glad when You show your mercy. Look at my situation; I am truly dependent on You to deliver me.
8.	And You have not given me over into the hand of the enemy; You have set my feet in a large place.	**8.**	Do not leave me in the hands of my enemies.
9.	Be gracious to me, O Lord, for I am in distress; My eye is wasted away from grief, my soul and my body also.	**9.**	This situation is painful, it is causing me sorrow, have mercy on me.
10.	For my life is spent with sorrow and my years with sighing; My strength has failed because of my iniquity, and my body has wasted away.	**10.**	My troubles have continued for a long time. Sin and unbelief have weighed me down. I need Your help.
11.	Because of all my adversaries, I have become a reproach, especially to my neighbours, and an object of dread to my acquaintances; Those who see me in the street flee from me.	**11.**	Lord I do not want to become a reproach, help me O God. Friends and family have deserted me.

12. I am forgotten as a dead man, out of mind; I am like a broken vessel.

13. For I have heard the slander of many, terror is on every side; While they took counsel together against me, they schemed to take away my life.

14. But as for me, I trust in You, O Lord, I say, "You are my God."

15. My times are in Your hand; Deliver me from the hand of my enemies and from those who persecute me.

16. Make Your face to shine upon Your servant; Save me in Your lovingkindness.

17. Let me not be put to shame, O Lord, for I call upon You; Let the wicked be put to shame, let them be silent in Sheol.

18.` Let the lying lips be mute, which speak arrogantly against the righteous with pride and contempt.

19. How great is Your goodness, which You have stored up for those who fear You, which You

12. I have been slandered, many are waiting for my downfall, and they have ganged up against me.

13. In Your mercy, arise against every gathering against me, my household and my community and put confusion amongst them in Jesus name.

14. I declare again and again that my trust is in You. I have no other God but You.

15. Deliver me from the hands of my enemies.

16. You are the only One who can help me. My life is in Your hands.

17. Do not allow me to suffer shame. My enemies deserve shame. They want me to die, but they should die in my place.

18. They have spoken vile things against me.

19. You are a good God; I will always fear You and I will always trust You.

have wrought for those who take refuge in You, before the sons of men!

20. You hide them in the secret place of Your presence from the conspiracies of man; You keep them secretly in a shelter from the strife of tongues.

20. I ask that You hide and protect me from every form of danger. Hide me in Your secret place where evil can't have access to me.

21. Blessed be the Lord, for He has made marvellous His loving kindness to me in a besieged city.

21. I bless You my Lord and King, continue to show me Your lovingkindness.

22. As for me, I said in my alarm, "I am cut off from before Your eyes"; Nevertheless You heard the voice of my supplications when I cried to You.

22. In my worry I thought I had lost the battle; I thank You because You heard my cry. Your goodness proved me wrong and restored me.

23. O love the Lord, all you His godly ones! The Lord preserves the faithful and fully recompenses the proud doer.

23. Give me a heart that will always love You. Lord release rewards to the faithful.

24. Be strong and let your heart take courage, all you who hope in the Lord.

24. Thank You Father for deliverance, I have no other but You.

Psalm 32 ESV

The Psalm is a Psalm of repentance, instruction from God and rejoicing after being pardoned by God.

A Maskil of David.

BIBLE	PRAYER
1. Blessed is the one whose transgression is forgiven, whose sin is covered.	**1.** Thank You for forgiving me of all my sins.
2. Blessed is the man against whom the Lord counts no iniquity, and in whose spirit there is no deceit.	**2.** Thank You because You have sent Your Son Jesus Christ to die for my sins and You don't remember them anymore. I am no longer guilty; I am free from the clutches of sin.
3. For when I kept silent, my bones wasted away through my groaning all day long.	**3.** Lord make me uneasy when I have done wrong, so I will have no choice but to come to You, confess and repent.
4. For day and night Your hand was heavy upon me; my strength was dried up as by the heat of summer. Selah	**4.** Your hand is heavy on me and every moisture and ease is being dried up. I plead for mercy for Your mercy triumphs over judgement.
5. I acknowledged my sin to You, and I did not cover my iniquity; I said, "I will confess my transgressions to the Lord," and You forgave the iniquity of my sin. Selah	**5.** As long as I have breath in me, I will always thank You that in Your goodness, You will always hear me.

6.	Therefore let everyone who is godly offer prayer to You at a time when You may be found; surely in the rush of great waters, they shall not reach him.	6.	I know all who come to You, will not be stopped by the assaults and obstacles of life, for You are our protector. I declare that these ungodly floods of great waters will not reach me, my household and my community in Jesus name.
7.	You are a hiding place for me; You preserve me from trouble; You surround me with shouts of deli deliverance. Selah	7.	Lord hide me from evil; keep me from the troubles that have blighted me in the past.
8.	I will instruct you and teach you in the way you should go; I will counsel you with my eye upon you.	8.	Give me a heart that will take instructions, help me follow Your directions.
9.	Be not like a horse or a mule, without understanding, which must be curbed with bit and bridle, or it will not stay near you.	9.	Give me the spirit of understanding; help me use all the abilities You have endowed me with. Do not let me go the way of horses and mules, having to be restrained permanently.
10.	Many are the sorrows of the wicked, but steadfast love surrounds the one who trusts in the Lord.	10.	Let all who perpetuate wickedness meet with sorrow all the days of their lives. On the other hand I pray that all who trust You shall experience Your mercies in Jesus name.
11.	Be glad in the Lord, and	11.	I will be glad and

rejoice, O righteous, and shout for joy, all you upright in heart!	rejoicing shall have a home in my heart in Jesus name.

Psalm 33 NASB

The Psalm shows many reasons why we should praise God

BIBLE	PRAYER
1. Sing for joy in the Lord, O you righteous ones; Praise is becoming to the upright.	1. Rejoicing fills my heart. Thank You Lord because You created me to praise You. I will praise You from my heart and I know You will receive it with joy.
2. Give thanks to the Lord with the lyre; Sing praises to Him with a harp of ten strings.	2. I will praise You with any instrument I can lay my hands upon.
3. Sing to Him a new song; Play skilfully with a shout of joy.	3. Every day when I wake up my heart will sing a new song of praise unto You.
4. For the word of the Lord is upright, and all His work is done in faithfulness.	4. There is no error in my words; You are the same, yesterday, today and forever.
5. He loves righteousness and justice; The earth is full of the lovingkindness of the Lord.	5. You are a righteous and just God. I look around, and everything is the evidence of Your goodness.
6. By the word of the Lord the heavens were made, and by the breath of His	6. You said let there be, and there was.

mouth all their host.

7. He gathers the waters of the sea together as a heap; He lays up the deeps in storehouses.

8. Let all the earth fear the Lord; Let all the inhabitants of the world stand in awe of Him.

9. For He spoke, and it was done; He commanded, and it stood fast.

10. The Lord nullifies the counsel of the nations; He frustrates the plans of the peoples.

11. The counsel of the Lord stands forever, the plans of His heart from generation to generation.

12. Blessed is the nation whose God is the Lord, the people whom He has chosen for His own inheritance.

13. The Lord looks from heaven; He sees all the sons of men;

14. From His dwelling place He looks out on all the inhabitants of the earth,

15. He who fashions the

7. You put all the waters together, reservoirs of wealth You put under the ground.

8. I stand this day in reverential awe of Your Being.

9. What You created in the beginning has stood the test of time. You are indeed Almighty.

10. Every evil counsel and plan against You comes to nothing.

11. Therefore every gathering against me will come to nothing in Jesus mighty name. Your judgement is forever.

12. You will continue to be our God and we will continue to be Your people. You have chosen me as Your child and all benefits of being a member of Your Household shall accrue to me in Jesus name.

13-14. From Your throne in the heavens, there is nothing that passes You by.

15. You turn the hearts of

hearts of them all, He who understands all their works.

16. The king is not saved by a mighty army; a warrior is not delivered by great strength.

17. A horse is a false hope for victory; Nor does it deliver anyone by its great strength.

18. Behold, the eye of the Lord is on those who fear Him, on those who hope for His lovingkindness,

19. To deliver their soul from death and to keep them alive in famine.

20. Our soul waits for the Lord; He is our help and our shield.

21. For our heart rejoices in Him, because we trust in His holy name.

22. Let Your lovingkindness, O Lord, be upon us, according as we have hoped in You.

men whichever way You want. I am dependent on You.

16-17. Help me walk in Your strength as I have no power of my own.

18. Let Your eye be upon me. I pray I will live in reverential awe of You at all times, always hoping in Your mercy.

19. Deliver me from the clutches of death, and let me blossom and flourish even in times of famine, Jehovah Jireh.

20. You will forever be my help and shield.

21. I pray that rejoicing will fill my heart because I trust in You.

22. My hope is that Your mercy will be upon me and all that concerns me in Jesus name.

Psalm 34 ESV

The Psalm teaches that we should praise God for his goodness and shows that God favours the righteous and shows his displeasure to the wicked.

Of David, when he changed his behaviour before Abimelech, so that he drove him out, and he went away.

	BIBLE		PRAYER
1.	I will bless the Lord at all times; His praise shall continually be in my mouth.	**1.**	I have every reason to praise You. Every moment of my life I will bless Your holy name. I will praise You openly and the whole world will know You are a good God.
2.	My soul makes its boast in the Lord; let the humble hear and be glad.	**2.**	I pray that my testimonies of the goodness of God will encourage all who hear and it will bring gladness into their hearts.
3.	Oh, magnify the Lord with me, and let us exalt His name together!	**3.**	I will magnify the Lord forever and I pray my testimonies will cause people to exalt God Almighty with me.
4.	I sought the Lord, and He answered me and delivered me from all my fears.	**4.**	I thank God because in my times of trouble I looked for God and in His grace He heard me and He delivered me from all the fears that had tormented my soul.
5.	Those who look to Him are radiant, and their	**5.**	I pray that at all times when I look unto God,

faces shall never be ashamed.	His glory will shine upon me, fear and terror will disappear in Jesus name.
6. This poor man cried, and the Lord heard him and saved him out of all his troubles.	6. Lord Your promise is that all who call upon You, You will answer and deliver out of trouble. Yes nothing is too hard for You to do.
7. The angel of the Lord encamps around those who fear Him, and delivers them.	7. As I fear the Lord in His glory, I ask Father that the angel of the Lord encamp round about me, my family, my business and all that concerns me from this moment in Jesus name. Let Your angel fight for me and deliver me in Jesus name.
8. Oh, taste and see that the Lord is good! Blessed is the man who takes refuge in Him!	8. I declare that the Lord is good and I appreciate You Father because all those who trust You are blessed.
9. Oh, fear the Lord, you His saints, for those who fear Him have no lack!	9. Lord I do not want to live in want. Teach me how to fear You.
10. The young lions suffer want and hunger; but those who seek the Lord lack no good thing.	10. There are benefits to fearing You my Lord. As I do so, I will not lack anything good in Jesus name.
11. Come, O children, listen to me; I will teach you the fear of the Lord.	11. I ask that all people around me come together and hear me. Grant me the grace to

	teach the fear of the Lord.
12. What man is there who desires life and loves many days, that he may see good?	**12.** I pray that all who desire long life will see the goodness of God in Jesus name.
13. Keep your tongue from evil and your lips from speaking deceit.	**13.** Help me keep my tongue from speaking evil and from being deceitful.
14. Turn away from evil and do good; seek peace and pursue it.	**14.** When I see evi attempt-l ing to lure me into its bosom, teach me to run away at every opportunity. Let doing good at all times be my priority.
15. The eyes of the Lord are toward the righteous and His ears toward their cry.	**15** I ask that Your eyes be upon me at all times, and Your ears are open to my cry.
16. The face of the Lord is against those who do evil, to cut off the memory of them from the earth.	**16.** Let Your face be against all evil doers ensuring that they are totally cut off and there is no help for them.
17. When the righteous cry for help, the Lord hears and delivers them out of all their troubles.	**17.** As the righteous cry, hear them and deliver them from every affliction in Jesus name.
18. The Lord is near to the brokenhearted and saves the crushed in spirit.	**18.** Let my heart be contrite and humble at all times, I ask that You come near to me, do not leave me nor forsake me.
19. Many are the afflictions of the righteous, but the Lord delivers him out of them all.	**19.** Thank You for total deliverance from all afflictions in Jesus name.
20. He keeps all his bones;	**20.** Thank You for total phys-

not one of them is broken.

21. Affliction will slay the wicked, and those who hate the righteous will be condemned.

22. The Lord redeems the life of His servants; none of those who take refuge in Him will be condemed.

ical and spiritual protection.

21. All evil doers will be slayed by the evil they plant for the righteous in Jesus name.

22. I thank You Father for redeeming me and my trust in You will never be in vain.

Psalm 35 ESV

This Psalm is a prayer for God

BIBLE

1. Contend, O Lord, with those who contend with me; fight against those who fight against me!

2. Take hold of shield and buckler and rise for my help!

3. Draw the spear and javelin against my pursuers! Say to my soul, "I am your salvation!"

4. Let them be put to shame and dishonour who seek after my life! Let them be turned back and disappointed who devise evil against me!

PRAYER

1. You are a Man of war. Fight for me against all who are arrayed against me.

2. You are my shield and buckler. I ask that You defend me from my enemies.

3. I ask that You use all You are to defend me, be a wall of fire around me. I am confident that You are my salvation.

4. Let confusion be released into the midst of my enemies. Let their retreat be in shame.

5. Let them be like chaff before the wind, with the angel of the Lord driving them away!

6. Let their way be dark and slippery, with the angel of the Lord pursuing them!
7. For without cause they hid their net for me; without cause they dug a pit for my life.
8. Let destruction come upon him when he does not know it! And let the net that he hid ensnare him; let him fall into it—to his destruction!
9. Then my soul will rejoice in the Lord, exulting in His salvation.
10. All my bones shall say, "O Lord, who is like you, delivering the poor from him who is too strong for him, the poor and needy from him who robs him?"
11. Malicious witnesses rise up; they ask me of things that I do not know.
12. They repay me evil for good; my soul is bereft.
13. But I, when they were sick—I wore sackcloth; I afflicted myself with fasting; I prayed with head bowed on my chest.

5. Release a strong wind to blow them into nothingness. Let Your angel chase and scatter them permanently.

6. As they retreat, let them stumble and fall never to get up.

7-8. Let them fall into the traps they have set for me. Set them up for utter destruction.

9. Let my deliverance bring joy into my life.

10. I do not have any power of my own. My Lord, You are the only one who can deliver me.

11-12. False things have been said against me. Help me continue doing as You have taught me.

13-14. Grant me the grace to pray in the face of adversity.

14. I went about as though I grieved for my friend or my brother; as one who laments his mother, I bo bowed down in mourning.

15. But at my stumbling they rejoiced and gathered; they gathered together against me; wretches whom I did not know tore at me without ceasing;

16. Like profane mockers at a feast, they gnash at me with their teeth.

17. How long, O Lord, will You look on? Rescue me from their destruction, my precious life from the lions!

18. I will thank You in the great congregation; in the mighty throng I will praise You.

19. Let not those rejoice over me who are wron wrongfully my foes, and let not those wink the eye who hate me without cause.

20. For they do not speak peace, but against those who are quiet in the land they devise words of deceit.

21. They open wide their mouths against me; they say, "Aha, Aha! Our eyes

15-16. Expose every evil gang up against me. As they gather together, rise up against them.

17. Do not delay. Rescue me from the destruction planned by my enemies.

18. LORD I will come out and testify of Your power, deliver me speedily.

19. Do not let my enemies be victorious. Let joy be far away from them.

20-21. They do not have anything good to say about an anyone, neither do they see anything good in anybody. Shut them up permanently O LORD.

have seen it!"

22. You have seen, O Lord; be not silent! O Lord, be not far from me!

23. Awake and rouse yourself for my vindication, for my cause, my God and my Lord!

24. Vindicate me, O Lord, my God, according to Your righteousness, and let them not rejoice over me!

25. Let them not say in their hearts, "Aha, our heart's desire!" Let them not say, "We have swallowed him up."

26. Let them be put to shame and disappointed altogether who rejoice at my calamity! Let them be clothed with shame and dishonour who magnify themselves against me!

27. Let those who delight in my righteousness shout for joy and be glad and say evermore, "Great is the Lord, who delights in the welfare of His servant!"

28. Then my tongue shall tell of Your righteousness and of Your praise all the day long.

22. Do not be silent. Do not leave me alone for the enemy to continue attacking me.

23-24. Arise O Lord and execute instant judgement on my behalf. Let Your righteousness be seen by the world.

25. Let them not have the opportunity to say I am defeated.

26. Let all who rejoice at my hurt be covered in shame, confusion and dishonour.

27. Let the righteous shout for joy. Let all who favour me celebrate. Let Your name be magnified all over the earth for You delight in the peace and prosperity of Your children.

28. I want to praise You forever and ever. Help me do so. Amen.

Psalm 36 NASB

The Psalm contrasts the lovingkindness of God which extends everywhere with the character of the wicked.

For the choir director.

A Psalm of David the servant of the Lord.

BIBLE

1. Transgression speaks to the ungodly within his heart; There is no fear of God before his eyes.

2. For it flatters him in his own eyes concerning the discovery of his iniquity and the hatred of it.

3. The words of his mouth are wickedness and deceit; He has ceased to be wise and to do good.

4. He plans wickedness upon his bed; He sets himself on a path that is not good; He does not despise evil.

5. Your lovingkindness, O Lord, extends to the heavens, Your faithfulness reaches to the skies.

PRAYER

1. Help me guard my heart so that sin will not speak to me. Give me a heart that will live and walk in the fear of God.

2. Help me never to forget that anything I have or have achieved is by Your grace. I must never deceive myself by thinking I have arrived.

3. Help me so I do not speak wickedness and deceit. Give me a heart that wants to do good at all times. I ask You for wisdom to live day by day O God.

4. Help me control my mind. Give me a heart that will not think evil thoughts, a heart that will hate evil and not partake of anything evil.

5. I thank You for Your lovingkindness and faithfulness which extends from the earth to the heavens.

6. Your righteousness is like the mountains of God; Your judgments are like a great deep. O Lord, You preserve man and beast.
7. How precious is Your lovingkindness, O God! And the children of men take refuge in the shadow of Your wings.
8. They drink their fill of the abundance of Your house; And You give them to drink of the river of Your delights.
9. For with You is the fountain of life; In Your light we see light.
10. O continue Your lovingkindness to those who know You, and Your righteousness to the upright in heart.
11. Let not the foot of pride come upon me, and let not the hand of the wicked drive me away.
12. There the doers of iniquity have fallen; They

6. I pray You would preserve me, protect me and provide for me. I praise You who judges in righteousness.
7. Help me put my trust in You.
8. Thank You for divine provision and also for allowing me to enjoy Your pleasures. Thank you for Your love and grace that abounds towards me.
9. LORD You are Alpha and Omega, that is, the beginning and the end, thank You for all life flows out of You.
10. In Your grace I pray You will continue to shower me with Your lovingkindness. Help me live a life of uprightness so I will benefit from Your righteousness.
11. Help me so I do not succumb to pride in any form. I pray that every plan of the wicked to destroy me will come to nothing in Jesus name.
12. Thank You Father because I know that the wick-

have been thrust down and cannot rise.

ed will not be spared and the wicked will be destroyed totally in Jesus mighty name.

Psalm 37 NASB

The Psalm teaches us how the righteous should live and the promises of God to the righteous and at the same time reveals the punishment for the wicked.

A Psalm of David.

BIBLE	PRAYER
1. Do not fret because of evildoers, be not envious toward wrongdoers.	**1.** By Your grace I will not be worried about the successes of evil doers.
2. For they will wither quickly like the grass and fade like the green herb.	**2.** I ask that You cut them down speedily. Let their joy be short lived.
3. Trust in the Lord and do good; Dwell in the land and cultivate faithfulness.	**3.** Help me trust You and You alone. Help me desire to do good at all times. Let me live in peace and also enjoy Your blessings in the position You have placed me.
4. Delight yourself in the Lord; And He will give you the desires of your heart.	**4.** Let me continually find joy in everything about You. Your faithfulness and lovingkindness. I pray that as You have promised You will give me the desires of my heart.
5. Commit your way to the Lord, Trust also in Him,	**5.** My life is in Your hands; let Your perfect will for

and He will do it.

me be done in Jesus name.

6. He will bring forth your righteousness as the light and your judgment as the noonday.

6. Let my righteousness show forth as clear as light for the world to see.

7. Rest in the Lord and wait patiently for Him; Do not fret because of him who prospers in his way, because of the man who carries out wicked schemes.

7. Help me rest in You with confidence knowing You are more than able to see me through. The seeming prosperity of the wicked will have no impact on me in Jesus name.

8. Cease from anger and forsake wrath; Do not fret; it leads only to evildoing.

8. Help me not to live under any form of anger. I pray restlessness must not lead me to do or cooperate with evil in Jesus name.

9. For evildoers will be cut off, but those who wait for the Lord, they will inherit the land.

9. Let every evil doer be cut off from Your goodness. I pray for a heart of patience, knowing You will always come good in Jesus name.

10. Yet a little while and the wicked man will be no more; And you will look carefully for his place and he will not be there.

10. Let the wicked and their wickedness be as nothing, ending swiftly in Jesus name.

11. But the humble will inherit the land and will delight themselves in abundant prosperity.

11. Give me a heart that is humble and as I live a life of humility, let me dominate all You have created. Let the battles come to an end. Let me enjoy peace all the days

of my life too.

12. The wicked plots against the righteous and gnashes at him with his teeth.	**12.** Let every plan of the wicked against me backfire in Jesus name.
13. The Lord laughs at him, for He sees his day is coming.	**13.** Let the devices and schemes of the wicked end in confusion by Your mighty power.
14. The wicked have drawn the sword and bent their bow to cast down the afflicted and the needy, to slay those who are upright in conduct.	**14-15.** The wicked are ever ready to attack. Let their weapons be turned against them, bringing destruction upon them in Jesus name.
15. Their sword will enter their own heart, and their bows will be broken.	
16. Better is the little of the righteous than the abundance of many wicked.	**16.** Help me to be contented with what I have.
17. For the arms of the wicked will be broken, but the Lord sustains the righteous.	**17.** Uphold me and strengthen me O Lord. Let the wicked become helpless before You.
18. The Lord knows the days of the blameless, and their inheritance will be forever.	**18.** You are my Lord, You know my end, I pray I will fulfil my destiny in Jesus name.
19. They will not be ashamed in the time of evil, and in the days of famine they will have abundance.	**19.** I pray in challenging times, I will not be ashamed for all my needs will be provided by You in Jesus name.
20. But the wicked will perish; And the enemies of the Lord will be like the glory of the pastures,	**20.** Let every wicked one be consumed by their evil deeds. Answer each and every enemy by fire such

they vanish—like smoke they vanish away.

21. The wicked borrows and does not pay back, but the righteous is gracious and gives.

22. For those blessed by Him will inherit the land, but those cursed by Him will be cut off.

23. The steps of a man are established by the Lord, and He delights in his way.

24. When he falls, he will not be hurled headlong because the Lord is the One who holds his hand.

25. I have been young and now I am old, yet I have not seen the righteous forsaken or his descendants begging bread.

26. All day long he is gracious and lends, and his descendants are a blessing.

27. Depart from evil and do good, so you will abide forever.

that they will be no more in Jesus name.

21. I pray for a heart that will give to the needy at all times. Help me pay my debts so I will not bring shame to myself and to You.

22. Help me walk as one who is blessed and will inherit all that You have created. Let the wicked be cut off in Jesus name.

23. I ask that You order my steps O God and as I am blessed and favoured by You, I pray that I will always be a delight to You.

24. I ask that You be my shield and buckler. Whenever I am about to fall, I pray Your mighty hands will continually uphold me in Jesus name.

25. I thank You for continuous protection and provision. By Your grace I will never beg for bread in Jesus name.

26. I pray all my future generations will be blessed by You.

27. Help me depart from every evil. Let all my actions be good in Your sight.

28. For the Lord loves justice and does not forsake His godly ones; they are preserved forever, but the descendants of the wicked will be cut off.

28. Keep me and mine away from the clutches of satan. Let the evil ones and their offspring be cut off from You forever.

29. The righteous will inherit the land and dwell in it forever.

29. Thank You for making me a part of Your family. I will forever partake of my inheritance.

30. The mouth of the righteous utters wisdom, and his tongue speaks justice.

30. I pray for wisdom Lord. Help me exhibit wisdom both in speech and in deed.

31. The law of his God is in his heart; His steps do not slip.

31. Help me put and retain Your word in my heart. Let me never fall into the way of sin.

32. The wicked spies upon the righteous and seeks to kill him.

33. The Lord will not leave him in his hand or let him be condemned when he is judged.

32-33. Lord I pray for protection from the wicked ones as they look for avenues to attack me.

34. Wait for the Lord and keep His way, and He will exalt you to inherit the land; When the wicked are cut off, you will see it.

34. Help me wait on You and obey You with all my heart. I ask that You lift me up so high that the wicked will see Your glory upon me.

35. I have seen a wicked, violent man spreading himself like a luxuriant tree in its native soil.

36. Then he passed away, and lo, he was no more; I

35-36. Let the end of the wicked be as swift as they rose up. Let their posterity be wiped off the face of the earth.

sought for him, but he could not be found.

37. Mark the blameless man, and behold the upright; For the man of peace will have a posterity.

38. But transgressors will be altogether destroyed; The posterity of the wicked will be cut off.

39. But the salvation of the righteous is from the Lord; He is their strength in time of trouble.

40. The Lord helps them and delivers them; He delivers them from the wicked and saves them, because they take refuge in Him.

37. I pray that I will be upright and perfect in You. I pray that Your peace shall envelope me all the days of my life.

38. Let destruction come upon every single transgressor of Your word who refuses to turn away from their evil deeds.

39-40. Thank You for delivering me. You are my strength in times of trouble. You have promised You will never leave me or forsake me. You are my helper. Help me put all my trust in You forever.

Psalm 38 NASB

The Psalmist sings that his sickness has been caused by his sin. He confesses and asks for God's grace and His help.

A Psalm of David, for a memorial.

BIBLE

1. O Lord, rebuke me not in Your wrath, and chasten me not in Your burning anger.

2. For Your arrows have

PRAYER

1. Lord be gentle with me, I say do not be angry with me when You chastise me Lord. Please be merciful O God.

2. Have mercy on me. Your

sunk deep into me, and Your hand has pressed down on me.

3. There is no soundness in my flesh because of Your indignation; There is no health in my bones because of my sin.

4. For my iniquities are goe over my head; as a heavy burden they weigh too much for me.

5. My wounds grow foul and fester because of my folly.

6. I am bent over and greatly bowed down; I go mourning all day long.

7. For my loins are filled with burning, and there is no soundness in my flesh.

8. I am benumbed and badly crushed; I groan because of the agitation of my heart.

9. Lord, all my desire is before You; And my sighing is not hidden from You.

10. My heart throbs, my

rebuke hurts, for Your words are like arrows sticking deep into my soul and Your hand is heavy upon me too.

3. I ask for Your mercy, I am in pain all over my body and I am in distress. I have brought this upon myself because I sinned against You.

4. Lord my sins threaten to swallow me, the shame and the guilt are too much for me to bear. Help me O God.

5. My foolishness led me to sin; the impact is like a big wound. I need healing.

6. Lord intervene in my situation, I am troubled and utterly cast down, lift me up my Lord and my God.

7. I cry to You for help, my body is weak and my spirit is weighed down by my sin.

8. Lord I am weakened by my affliction and my heart is heavy. Have mercy on me Lord.

9. Lord do not hide Yourself away from me, have mercy on me and deliver me from all my troubles.

10. My heart is full of grief, I

strength fails me; And the light of my eyes, even that has gone from me.

11. My loved ones and my friends stand aloof from my plague; And my kinsmen stand afar off.

12. Those who seek my life lay snares for me; And those who seek to injure me have threatened destruction, and they devise treachery all day long.

13. But I, like a deaf man, do not hear; And I am like a mute man who does not open his mouth.

14. Yes, I am like a man who does not hear, And in whose mouth are no arguments.

15. For I hope in You, O Lord; You will answer, O Lord my God.

16. For I said, "May they not rejoice over me, who, when my foot slips, would magnify themselves against me."

17. For I am ready to fall, And my sorrow is continually before me.

18. For I confess my iniquity; I am full of anxiety because of my sin.

am worried. I am now weak both physically and spiritually; Do not let my light go dim.

11. I do not have any other help but You. Friends will always abandon one another but You are steadfast and sure.

12. Enemies have also joined in, speaking lies and laying traps. Let the traps laid catch those who laid them.

13-14. Help me take no notice of what is said about me.

15. I call on You my Lord and my God, let Your mercy prevail over me.

16. Hear me and answer me, do not let my enemies rejoice over me.

17. Lord I am ready to stop sinning, help me, and keep me away from sin.

18. Lord there is nothing to hide from You, Jehovah El Roi, the One who sees all things. I ask for forgiveness of my sins.

19. But my enemies are vigorous and strong, and many are those who hate me wrongfully.

19. My enemies are many even though I have not offended anybody.

20. And those who repay evil for good, they oppose me, because I follow what is good.

20. Help me in continuing to follow You and obeying You. My enemies continue to repay my good deeds with evil.

21. Do not forsake me, O Lord; O my God, do not be far from me!

21. Do not forsake me Lord; I have nowhere to turn to. My friends have abandoned me.

22. Make haste to help me, O Lord, my salvation!

22. I am desperate for Your help, thank You for being my salvation.

Psalm 39 ESV

The Psalmist filled with thoughts of unbelief and prays for help from God.

To the choirmaster: to Jeduthun. A Psalm of David.

BIBLE

1. I said, "I will guard my ways, that I may not sin with my tongue; I will guard my mouth with a muzzle, so long as the wicked are in my prense-nce."

2. I was mute and silent; I held my peace to no avail, and my distress

PRAYER

1. Help me to be careful about my conduct and the things I say so that I would not sin against You. Help me so that I do not give my enemies any opportunity to speak evil of me.

2. Help me remain silent so that I do not say stuff contrary to Your will.

	grew worse.		
3.	My heart became hot within me. As I mused, the fire burned; then I spoke with my tongue:	**3.**	As excited as I can be, grant me the grace to come to You and You alone in prayer to express my thoughts to You.
4.	"O Lord, make me know my end and what is the measure of my days; let me know how fleeting I am!	**4.**	Lord You are the one who knows when this suffering will come to an end. I ask that You let me know so my heart will be at rest.
5.	Behold, You have made my days a few handbreadths, and my lifetime is as nothing before You. Surely all mankind stands as a mere breath! Selah	**5.**	My life is in Your hands. You know the beginning and the end.
6.	Surely a man goes about as a shadow! Surely for nothing they are in turmoil; man heaps up wealth and does not know who will gather!	**6.**	I pray that all I do here on earth will stand the test of time. Help me to seek You first at all times with the knowledge that all other things will be added on to me.
7.	"And now, O Lord, for what do I wait? My hope is in You.	**7.**	I pin all my hopes on You. Help me O Lord.
8.	Deliver me from all my transgressions. Do not make me the scorn of the fool!	**8.**	I ask that You forgive my sins.
9.	I am mute; I do not open my mouth, for it is You who have done it.	**9.**	Help me surrender completely to You, keeping quiet when I am expected to and believ-

ing that You are able to see me through.

10. Remove Your stroke from me; I am spent by the hostility of Your hand.

10. In Your mercy let every affliction come to an end.

11. When You discipline a man with rebukes for sin, You consume like a moth what is dear to him; surely all mankind is a mere breath! Selah

11. Give me a heart that will accept correction for it is those whom You love that You correct.

12. "Hear my prayer, O Lord, and give ear to my cry; hold not Your peace at my tears! For I am a sojourner with You, a guest, like all my fathers.

12. I pray from the depths of my heart, hear me speedily for I am Your child.

13. Look away from me, that I may smile again, before I depart and am no more!"

13. Heal me completely O God. Do not let me die in my situation. Thank You for You are a prayer answering God.

Psalm 40 ESV

The Psalm shows we can triumph and God answers our prayers.

To the choirmaster. A Psalm of David.

BIBLE

1. I waited patiently for the Lord; He inclined to me and heard my cry.

2. He drew me up from the pit of destruction, out of

PRAYER

1. Help me wait patiently for You Lord. Thank You for I know my cry to You will not be in vain.

2. Thank You Lord for no matter how horrible the

	the miry bog, and set my feet upon a rock, making my steps secure.		pit is You will lift me up. Thank You for putting me on solid ground in every area of my life. Thank You for ensuring that there is no danger of me going back to where I was in the past.
3.	He put a new song in my mouth, a song of praise to our God. Many will see and fear, and put their trust in the Lord.	**3.**	Thank You Lord for changing my story. Help me continue in my praise to You. By Your grace I will testify and many will see what You have done. I pray that what You have done will put fear in their hearts and they will worship You and put their trust in You.
4.	Blessed is the man who makes the Lord his trust, who does not turn to the proud, to those who go astray after a lie!	**4.**	Help me put all my trust in You and I will receive Your blessings. Give me a heart that will hate lying.
5.	You have multiplied, O Lord my God, Your wondrous deeds and Your thoughts toward us; none can compare with You! I will proclaim and tell of them, yet they are more than can be told.	**5.**	Thank You for the uncountable works that You have done for me, those that I know about and many that I am unaware of. I thank You for the thoughts of good that You have for me. Give me a heart that is bold enough to speak about Your goodness all the time and every-everywhere.
6.	In sacrifice and offering	**6.**	Thank You Father for

	You have not delighted, but You have given me an open ear. Burnt offering and sin offering You have not required.		You no longer require sacrifices and offerings from me. You have given Your Son Jesus as the supreme sacrifice.
7.	Then I said, "Behold, I have come; in the scroll of the book it is written of me:	**7.**	Thank You for the blood that was shed on cavalry by Jesus Christ. The work is done, it is finished.
8.	I delight to do Your will, O my God; Your law is within my heart."	**8.**	Give me a heart that will delight to do Your will. Teach me how to keep Your law within my heart.
9.	I have told the glad news of deliverance in the great congregation; behold, I have not restrained my lips, as You know, O Lord.	**9-10.**	Help me live a life of righteousness and witnessing everywhere I go. Give me the grace to share with the world the lovingkindness You have shown to me.
10.	I have not hidden Your deliverance within my heart; I have spoken of Your faithfulness and Your salvation; I have not concealed Your steadfast love and Your faithfulness from the great congregation.		
11.	As for You, O Lord, You will not restrain Your mercy from me; Your steadfast love and Your faithfulness will ever preserve me!	**11.**	Let Your mercies flow towards me, for without Your mercy I am lost.
12	For evils have encompassed me beyond number; my iniquities have	**12.**	Lord sometimes I remember my past sins and my heart is heavy. I

overtaken me, and I cannot see; they are more than the hairs of my head; my heart fails me.	pray that You'd help me focus on my future rather my past in Jesus name.
13. Be pleased, O Lord, to deliver me! O Lord, make haste to help me!	**13.** Lord do not let me be enveloped by sorrow. Deliver me O God.
14. Let those be put to shame and disappointed altogether who seek to snatch away my life; let those be turned back and brought to dishonour who delight in my hurt!	**14-15.** Let all who seek my failure and destruction fail and be destroyed. Yes let them be ashamed. All they wish me let it come upon them.
15. Let those be appalled because of their shame who say to me, "Aha, Aha!"	
16. But may all who seek You rejoice and be glad in You; may those who love Your salvation say continually, "Great is the Lord!"	**16.** Lord put gladness and rejoicing in my heart. Be magnified in the heavens and on earth.
17. As for me, I am poor and needy, but the Lord takes thought for me. You are my help and my deliverer; do not delay, O my God!	**17.** Thank You for being my help and deliverer. Thank You for providing all my needs.

Psalm 41 ESV

The Psalm gives the benefits of being merciful, the extent of the wickedness of the enemies and the comfort we find in the grace of God.

To the choirmaster. A Psalm of David.

BIBLE	PRAYER
1. Blessed is the one who considers the poor! In the day of trouble the Lord delivers him;	**1.** Give me a heart that will show compassion to the poor spiritually, poor in health and those who are financially poor. Give me a heart that would respect them, a heart that would go all lengths to provide for them and a heart that would speak and stand up for them. I pray Lord that whenever I am in trouble You will deliver me.
2. The Lord protects him and keeps him alive; he is called blessed in the land; You do not give him up to the will of his enemies.	**2.** I pray that You will preserve me; You will protect me when the enemy comes my way. I pray that the will of my enemies will not prevail over me because You will not allow them. In Your goodness, I will be blessed on every side and in every area of my life.
3. The Lord sustains him on his sickbed; in his illness You restore him to full health.	**3.** Lord I pray that You will strengthen me when-whenever I am ill and You will restore me to full

4. As for me, I said, "O Lord, be gracious to me; heal me, for I have sinned against You!"

5. My enemies say of me in malice, "When will he die, and his name perish?"

6. And when one comes to see me, he utters empty words, while his heart gathers iniquity; when he goes out, he tells it abroad.

7. All who hate me whisper together about me; they imagine the worst for me.

8. They say, "A deadly thing is poured out on him; he will not rise again from where he lies."

9. Even my close friend in whom I trusted, who ate my bread, has lifted his heel against me.

10. But You, O Lord, be gracious to me, and raise me up, that I may repay them!

11. By this I know that You delight in me: my enemy

health as You have promised me.

4. You are the great healer, Jehovah Rapha have mercy upon me and forgive me of my sins.

5. My enemies speak evil about me; even people who I thought were my friends.

6. I ask that You shut their mouths up permanently in Jesus name.

7. My enemies are putting me down and all they want is to hurt me.

8. They speak of imaginary illnesses and they wish me dead. Lift me up and let them be disappointed forever.

9. Trusted friends that I have supported in many ways have joined in as well. My prayer is that You help me identify who my real friends are.

10. My Lord I ask that in Your mercy lift me up so they will be disappointed. By Your grace I will repay them with good rather than evil.

11. Favour me Father; let Your name be glorified.

	will not shout in triumph over me.		
12.	But You have upheld me because of my integrity, and set me in Your presence forever.	**12.**	ord I bless You for upholding me; I am standing by Your grace and Your grace alone. It is Your grace that enables me to come into Your presence.
13.	Blessed be the Lord, the God of Israel, from everlasting to evarlasting! Amen and Amen.	**13.**	From everlasting to everlasting You are God and You will continue to be God. Blessed be Your holy name.

BOOK 2

Psalm 42 ESV

The Psalm reveals a deep thirst for God no matter the situation. God always comes good for His children.

To the choirmaster. A Maskil of the Sons of Korah.

BIBLE

1. As a deer pants for flowing streams, so pants my soul for You, O God.
2. My soul thirsts for God, for the living God. When shall I come and appear before God?
3. My tears have been my food day and night, while they say to me all the day long, "Where is your God?"
4. These things I remember, as I pour out my soul: how I would go with the throng and lead them in procession to the house of God with glad shouts and songs of praise, a multitude keeping festival.
5. Why are you cast down, O my soul, and why are you in turmoil within me? Hope in God; for I shall again praise Him, my salvation.

PRAYER

1. Lord I thirst for You, let me enjoy Your presence O God.
2. I want to meet with You, my Father and my God.

3 Let my tears speak to You my Lord. Do not let the enemy gloat, where is my God?

4. I remember my past experiences of Your presence; it was always a time of praise and worship of Your awesomeness.
5. I refuse to be cast down in my soul; my hope is stayed on You my Lord. As I praise You, I know You will lighten my soul.

	Scripture		Prayer
6.	And my God. My soul is cast down within me; therefore I remember You from the land of Jordan and of Hermon, from Mount Mizar.	**6.**	I remember the acts of Your goodness and kindness to me in times past. Do something new today my Father.
7.	Deep calls to deep at the roar of Your waterfalls; all Your breakers and Your waves have gone over me.	**7.**	Trouble seems to follow trouble, but I know that Your thoughts towards me are of good and not of evil. Therefore they shall all pass away in Jesus name.
8.	By day the Lord commands His steadfast love, and at night His song is with me, a prayer to the God of my life.	**8.**	I receive Your loving-kindness and songs of praise and prayer will continually be in my mouth.
9.	I say to God, my rock: "Why have You forgotten me? Why do I go mourning because of the oppression of the enemy?"	**9.**	You are my rock, I know Lord You will not leave me or forsake me. Yes the enemy is trying to oppress me; I know You have not forgotten me.
10.	As with a deadly wound in my bones, my adversaries taunt me, while they say to me all the day long, "Where is your God?"	**10.**	The reproach from the enemy is hard and they continue to challenge my faith in my God. Father I ask that You answer them by lifting me up. Let me become a testimony of Your grace and favour.
11.	Why are you cast down, O my soul, and why are you in turmoil within me? Hope in God; for I shall again praise Him, my	**11.**	I am not cast down Lord for my hope is in You. You will lighten my countenance in Jesus name.

salvation and my God.

Psalm 43 NASB

The Psam is dominated with questions that arise out of heaviness in the heart of the writer. It aflfirms that when we walk in the light we will have cause to praise God.

BIBLE

1. Vindicate me, O God, and plead my case against an ungodly nation; O deliver me from the deceitful and unjust man!

2. For You are the God of my strength; why have You rejected me? Why do I go mourning because of the oppression of the enemy?

3. O send out Your light and Your truth, let them lead me; Let them bring me to Your holy hill and to Your dwelling places.

4. Then I will go to the altar of God, to God my exceeding joy; And upon the lyre I shall praise You, O God, my God.

5. Why are you in despair, O my soul? And why are

PRAYER

1. Lord I want You to judge me for You know I have done no wrong. Then defend me against my enemies. They accuse me unjustly and they are deceitful.

2. You are the source of my strength. Do not cast me away; I have nowhere to turn to. I will not mourn, for I pray that the oppression from my enemies will become victory for me in Jesus name.

3. Let Your light shine upon me, and lead me back to where I should be: Your presence.

4. In Your presence I know I will find joy and Your praise will not cease in my mouth.

5. My hope is in You and my countenance will be

you disturbed within me? Hope in God, for I shall again praise Him, the help of my countenance and my God.

lightened forever in Jesus name.

Psalm 44 NASB

The Psalmist remembers past victories over enemy nations, expresses faith in God and wonders why the nation is in the situation they are at the time. It ends with a call for God to arise and help them.

For the choir director. A Maskil of the sons of Korah.

BIBLE		PRAYER	
1.	O God, we have heard with our ears, our fathers have told us the work that You did in their days, in the days of old.	1.	Thank you for the great and mighty things You have done both in my life and in the world at large. As my ancestors have passed on to me their testimonies, help me preserve Your works by passing my testimonies to my children and grandchildren.
2.	You with Your own hand drove out the nations; Then You planted them; You afflicted the peoples, the You spread them abroad.	2-3.	You have driven away my enemies and afflicted them with different types of punishment. Thank you for favouring me. Your light has shone around me and darkness has disappeared. I have not put in any effort but Your right hand of righteousness has deli-
3.	For by their own sword they did not possess the land, and their own arm did not save them, but Your right hand and Your		

	arm and the light of Your presence, for You favoured them.		vered me from my enemies.
4.	You are my King, O God; Command victories for Jacob.	**4.**	I humble myself before You, my King and my Maker. It is within Your power to command Your angels to fight on my behalf. I ask that You do so now in Jesus name.
5.	Back our adversaries; Through Your name we will trample down those who rise up against us.	**5-6.**	I do not have any powers of my own to fight my enemies. I thank you because with You on my side I shall tread on all who have risen against me.
6.	For I will not trust in my bow, nor will my sword save me.		
7.	But You have saved us from our adversaries, and You have put to shame those who hate us.	**7.**	Thank You for saving me from my enemies. Let them be put to shame never to rise again in Jesus name.
8.	In God we have boasted all day long, and we will give thanks to Your name forever. Selah.	**8.**	By Your grace I will boast of Your faithfulness all day long. Give me the words that will do You justice when I open my mouth to speak about You. Let me praise You continually until I die because You deserve it.
9.	Yet You have rejected us and brought us to dishonour, and do not go out with our armies.	**9.**	Do not cast me off and put me to shame as without You I am defeated by the agents of the enemy.
10.	You cause us to turn back from the adversary;	**10.**	I do not want to be cowardly by giving up in

And those who hate us have taken spoil for themselves.

11. You give us as sheep to be eaten and have scattered us among the nations.

12. You sell Your people cheaply, and have not profited by their sale.

13. You make us a reproach to our neighbours, a scoffing and a derision to those around us.

14. You make us a byword among the nations, a laughingstock among the peoples.

15. All day long my dishonour is before me and my humiliation has overwhelmed me,

16. Because of the voice of him who reproaches and reviles, because of the presence of the enemy and the avenger.

17. All this has come upon us, but we have not forgotten You, and we have not dealt falsely

battle. Do not let me be overrun by the enemy.

11. Do not allow me to become mincemeat for the enemy to do as they please.

12 I pray Father that You will not deliver me into the hands of the enemy for punishment as You sometimes did to the Israelites. Do not let the enemy think that I am not valuable in Your sight. Help me O Lord.

13-14. Do not allow the enemy to turn me into an object of ridicule as if I am no longer Your child. Lord do not allow the enemy to trample on me any longer.

15. My situation sometimes makes me wonder and ask, Lord are You there when bad things happen?

16. Do not allow the enemy to continue to blaspheme Your holy name.

17. Grant me the grace to stay steadfast in faith when the enemy bombards me with

with Your covenant.

18. Our heart has not turned back, and our steps have not deviated from Your way,

19. Yet You have crushed us in a place of jackals and covered us with the shadow of death.

20. If we had forgotten the name of our God or extended our hands to a strange god,

21. Would not God find this out? For He knows the secrets of the heart.

22. But for Your sake we are killed all day long; We are considered as sheep to be slaughtered.

23. Arouse Yourself, why do You sleep, O Lord? Awake, do not reject us forever.

24. Why do You hide Your face and forget our affliction and our oppression?

25. For our soul has sunk down into the dust; our body cleaves to the

temptation.

18. Help me guard my heart so that unbelief will not creep in and cause me to turn away from my faith.

19. The attacks have been fierce and a death like darkness has sometimes been overwhelming, I thank You for sufficient grace.

20-21 Lord, if I think of turning to the camp of the devil You will know because You are the all-knowing God. I pray by Your grace nothing will ever shake my confidence in You. Help me remember at all times the work Your son, Jesus did on the cross.

22. Your children are being persecuted all over the world because they will not worship lesser gods.

23. Arise O Lord God, let Your enemies be scattered. Deliver us speedily for You have the power to do so.

24. Show up now O God. Do not hide Your face away from me.

25. At the moment I am weak and tired. Have mercy on me.

earth.

26. Rise up, be our help, and redeem us for the sake of Your lovingkindness.

26. Arise my Father, help me because You are a merciful God. Thank You Father in Jesus name.

Psalm 45 NASB

The Psalm is a song showing love to Christ and a showering of praise to Him.

For the choir director; according to the Shoshannim.
A Maskil of the sons of Korah. A Song of Love.

BIBLE

1. My heart overflows with a good theme; I address my verses to the King; My tongue is the pen of a ready writer.

2. You are fairer than the sons of men; Grace is poured upon Your lips; Therefore God has blessed You forever.

3. Gird Your sword on Your thigh, O Mighty One, in Your splendour and Your

PRAYER

1. I pray my heart will be moved by the Holy Spirit to speak to my King and my Maker, the LORD Jesus Christ. As the thoughts come to me, let the words flow out of me like the pen of a ready writer.

2. My King, You are beautiful and none can be compared with You. I bless You for the words of life that You speak. May Your grace be passed on to all Your children in Jesus name. Thank You for enabling me partake of the blessings that are in You.

3. You have never lost a battle. Let Your sword come down heavily on

	Psalm		Prayer
	majesty!		the wicked destroying those who would not surrender and convicting those who open the doors of their heart.
4.	And in Your majesty ride on victoriously, for the cause of truth and meekness and righteousness; Let Your right hand teach You awesome things.	**4-5.**	As the gospel makes inroads into the hearts of men, let the attributes of truth, meekness and righteousness make a difference in the lives of all who encounter You. Let Your right hand of righteousness destroy Your enemies and at the same time bring conviction into the hearts of all who receive You. Let the arrows of Your words go directly into the hearts of those that are convicted and let those who refuse Your reign over them be damned.
5.	Peoples fall under You; Your arrows are in the heart of the King's enemies.		
6.	Your throne, O God, is forever and ever; A sceptre of uprightness is the sceptre of Your kingdom.	**6.**	My LORD and King, You reign over Your creation and Your government is forever.
7.	You have loved righteousness and hated wickedness; Therefore God, Your God, has anointed You with the oil of joy above Your fellows.	**7.**	Help me imitate You my Lord Jesus Christ, loving righteousness and hating wickedness. I ask that You anoint me with the oil of gladness that has been given to You by Your Father in heaven.
8.	All Your garments are	**8.**	By Your grace I pray that

fragrant with myrrh and aloes and cassia; Out of ivory palaces stringed instruments have made You glad.

9. Kings' daughters are among Your noble ladies; At Your right hand stands the queen in gold from Ophir.

10. Listen, O daughter, give attention and incline your ear: Forget your people and your father's house;

11. Then the King will desire your beauty. Because He is your Lord, bow down to Him.

12. The daughter of Tyre will come with a gift; The rich among the people will seek your favour.

13. The King's daughter is all glorious within; Her clothing is interwoven with gold.

14. She will be led to the King in embroidered work; The virgins, her companions who follow

when I depart from this world I will enjoy the splendour of Your throne room in heaven.

9. Thank you for the blood of Jesus that has cleansed me and given me access to come into Your presence.

10. Help me forget my past that I may submit completely to You, and live within the instructions in Your word to me.

11. Help me prove my love to You by worshipping You with all my heart and genuinely forsaking all others in Jesus name.

12. Let me find favour with all that are around me. I ask that You cause all my needs to be met miraculously in Jesus name.

13. Let Your glory rest upon me both internally and externally. I pray that the words that come out of my mouth and my thoughts will reveal the glory of God continuously in Jesus name.

14. I can't see You without being clean and pure. My prayer is that nothing will make me miss my

her, will be brought to You.

15. They will be led forth with gladness and rejoicing; They will enter into the King's palace.

16. In place of your fathers will be your sons; You shall make them princes in all the earth.

17. I will cause Your name to be remembered in all generations; Therefore the peoples will give You thanks forever and ever.

destiny, which is to reign with You in heaven.

15. When the trumpet sounds, there will be rejoicing and I will be a partaker of all that happens in Your palace.

16-17. I pray that I will fulfil my purpose and by God's grace I am able to pass on my faith onto my future generations. Your praise shall continually be on my lips forever in Jesus name.

Psalm 46 ESV

The Psalm teaches that we should be happy because no matter the situation, God is always present with us.

To the choirmaster. Of the Sons of Korah.
According to Alamoth. A Song.

BIBLE

1. God is our refuge and strength, a very present help in trouble.

2. Therefore we will not fear though the earth gives way, though the mountains be moved into the heart of the sea,

PRAYER

1. Thank You Father because You are always there for me, I have nowhere or nobody to turn to apart from You. In troubling times You are always there.

2. Lord because of my confidence in You, I will not fear neither will I be afraid. Volcanoes can erupt, earthquakes can

bring destruction and bushes can catch fire, my confidence will always be You.

	Scripture		Prayer
3.	Though its waters roar and foam, though the mountains tremble at its swelling. Selah	**3.**	Tsunamis or floods can cause devastation, I will not fear for You are my refuge.
4.	There is a river whose streams make glad the city of God, the holy habitation of the Most High.	**4.**	I pray that even as storms rage around me, I will enjoy peace like a river and gladness will fill my heart.
5.	God is in the midst of her; she shall not be moved; God will help her when morning dawns.	**5.**	Thank You Father for You are always with me, therefore I cannot be moved. You are my very present help in times of need.
6.	The nations rage, the kingdoms totter; He utters His voice, the earth melts.	**6.**	Let every rage, every commotion from the heathen come to an end in the name of Jesus. By Your grace I will not be moved from my position. As You speak concerning my situation let the enemy crumble and melt down permanently in Jesus mighty name.
7.	The Lord of hosts is with us; the God of Jacob is our fortress. Selah	**7.**	Thank You Father because You are with us and You are also in us.
8.	Come, behold the works of the Lord, how He has brought desolations on the earth.	**8.**	I thank You because You are the only one who could have delivered me. The destruction You have wroth on the

enemy is the testimony of Your great power.

9. He makes wars cease to the end of the earth; He breaks the bow and shatters the spear; He burns the chariots with fire.

9. You are able to put a stop to every war by giving me victory over the enemy, I ask that by Your mighty power all wars against me come to an end in the name of Jesus.

10. "Be still, and know that I am God. I will be exalted among the nations, I will be exalted in the earth!"

10. Teach me how to be still in Your presence so that I can hear what You are saying to me. Draw my heart to the fact that indeed You are God. As I exalt You, let the unbeliever see Your mighty works and worship You.

11. The Lord of hosts is with us; the God of Jacob is our fortress. Selah

11. I thank You for being with me at all times, for fighting for me and overcoming the enemy. Halleluiah

Psalm 47 NASB

The Psalm is about praising God for being the great King of all the earth.

For the choir director. A Psalm of the sons of Korah.

BIBLE

1. O clap your hands, all peoples; Shout to God with the voice of joy.

PRAYER

1. Lord I make a joyful noise unto You. I shout with joy at Your awesome power, I also shout for the world to know that

			You are God Almighty.
2.	For the Lord Most High is to be feared, a great King over all the earth.	**2.**	Lord You are the King of kings, You have never lost a battle, You are all powerful and there is no king like You.
3.	He subdues peoples under us and nations under our feet.	**3.**	You sit in the heavens and Your footstool reaches the earth. All nations are under Your feet.
4.	He chooses our inheritance for us, the glory of Jacob whom He loves. Selah.	**4.**	I thank You that You have given me the whole earth as my inheritance.
5.	God has ascended with a shout, the Lord, with the sound of a trumpet.	**5.**	I praise You Lord for what You have done for me. You are worthy to be praised.
6.	Sing praises to God, sing praises; Sing praises to our King, sing praises.	**6-7.**	I pray that from today the songs I sing to You must minister directly from my heart to You. Let me sing praises with an understanding of Your greatness. Let my spirit be aligned with the Holy Spirit as I worship You.
7.	For God is the King of all the earth; Sing praises with a skilful Psalm.		
8.	God reigns over the nations, God sits on His holy throne.	**8.**	Jehovah Adonai, the Sovereign Lord You reign over all the earth. Sin cannot reside in Your presence. You are holy.
9.	The princes of the people have assembled themselves as the people of the God of Abraham, for the shields of	**9.**	Everything and everrybody is subject to You. You are high and lifted up. I exalt You forever.

the earth belong to God; He is highly exalted.	

Psalm 48 ESV

This is a song of praise to the God of Zion.

A Song. A Psalm of the Sons of Korah.

BIBLE	PRAYER
1. Great is the Lord and greatly to be praised in the city of our God! His holy mountain,	1. I praise You O LORD my God for You are great and there is none like You. You are greater than the greatest.
2. Beautiful in elevation, is the joy of all the earth, Mount Zion, in the far north, the city of the great King	2. Let Your beauty O God distinguish us before the whole world.
3. Within her citadels God has made Himself known as a fortress.	3. Thank You for being my refuge. Thank You for the assurance that You will always protect me for I do not have any power of my own.
4. For behold, the kings assembled; they came on together. 5. As soon as they saw it, they were astounded; they were in panic; they took to flight.	4-5. Let Your glory rest upon the church and let all who gang up against the church of God disappear and become nothing in Jesus name.
6. Trembling took hold of them there, anguish as of a woman in labour.	6. I ask that You put fear and torment into every enemy in Jesus name.
7. By the east wind You shattered the ships of	7. I ask that You blow away every adversary with

Tarshish.

8. As we have heard, so have we seen in the city of the Lord of hosts, in the city of our God, which God will establish forever. Selah

9. We have thought on Your steadfast love, O God, in the midst of Your temple.

10. As Your name, O God, so Your praise reaches to the ends of the earth. Your right hand is filled with righteousness.

11. Let Mount Zion be glad! Let the daughters of Judah rejoice because of Your judgments!

12. Walk about Zion, go around her, number her

Your mighty east wind in Jesus name.

8. Thank You for Your goodness. I praise You for I am alive to experience and enjoy all Your goodness which I have heard about. Halleluiah. I have seen Your power and You have protected me. I pray that all You have done will be permanent in Jesus name.

9. Help me to regularly reflect on Your lovingkindness, understanding that I have not done anything to deserve all that You have blessed me with. You have only showed me Your loving-Kindness.

10. Let the world know that You are Almighty; I ask that You focus their minds on Your sovereingnty so that praise will be given to You even by the unbeliever. I bless You for Your righteousness in everything that You do.

11. Let rejoicing fill our hearts. Let there be gladness as we appreciate all You have done for us.

12. Let me continue to see the evidence of Your

towers,

13. Consider well her ramparts, go through her citadels, that you may tell the next generation

14. That this is God, our God forever and ever. He will guide us forever.

majesty and power all around me.

13. Help me pass on to future generations all my experiences of Your greatness and faithfulness.

14. Thank You Lord for You have said You will be my God and I will be Your child. I ask that You guide me until I die in Jesus name.

Psalm 49 NASB

The Psalm is a reminder that the ways of worldly people will always end in folly. The folly at the end of the life of the ungodly contrasts with the end of the righteous man.

For the choir director. A Psalm of the sons of Korah.

BIBLE

1. Hear this, all peoples; Give ear, all inhabitants of the world,

2. Both low and high, rich and poor together.

3. My mouth will speak wisdom, and the meditation of my heart will be understanding.

PRAYER

1. Lord help me hear Your word. I ask that You incline my heart to long for instructions from You.

2. I pray that whatever my situation in life is, it will not diminish my faith in You.

3. Help me speak with wisdom so that those I am speaking to will receive what I am saying. I also ask that You help me meditate on Your word. Give me und-

4. I will incline my ear to a proverb; I will express my riddle on the harp.

5. Why should I fear in days of adversity, When the iniquity of my foes surrounds me,

6. Even those who trust in their wealth and boast in the abundance of their riches?

7. redeem his brother or give to God a ransom for him—
8. For the redemption of his soul is costly, and he should cease trying forever—
9. That he should live on eternally, that he should not undergo decay.
10. For he sees that even wise men die; The stupid and the senseless alike perish and leave their wealth to others.
11. Their inner thought is that their houses are forever and their dwelling places to all genera-

erstanding too in Jesus name.

4. Help me understand what You teach me so I will be able to teach others too.
5. Help me so I do not succumb to fear when trouble comes my way. Help me remember that Jesus Christ has paid the supreme price for my sins.
6. Help me put my trust in You alone. Rather than boast about what I have, let me be thankful of the blessings that have come my way.
7-9. Thank You Father for giving up Your Son, Jesus Christ to pay a price to redeem me from death. I have not done anything to deserve this gift. Blessed be Your holy name.

10-11. Help me live without fear of physical death because every man, rich or poor, wise or foolish will die. I must live with the understanding that I came naked into this world and I cannot take anything with me when I

tions; They have called their lands after their own names.

12. But man in his pomp will not endure; He is like the beasts that perish.

13. This is the way of those who are foolish, and of those after them who approve their words. Selah.

14. As sheep they are appointed for Sheol; Death shall be their shepherd; And the upright shall rule over them in the morning, and their form shall be for Sheol to consume so that they have no habitation.

15. But God will redeem my soul from the power of Sheol, for He will receive me. Selah.

16. Do not be afraid when a man becomes rich, when the glory of his house is increased;

17. For when he dies he will carry nothing away; His

die.

12. Let every honour that You bestow upon me be permanent in Jesus name. My prayer is that I will fulfil the number of my days in Jesus name.

13. May the path of folly never be my choice in Jesus name.

14. Lord You have promised me eternal life, therefore death has no power to feed on me in Jesus name. By Your grace I will live a life of dominion in Jesus mighty name. With what I am being taught about what happens when the wicked die, my prayer is that my Lord will help me live a life of holiness in Jesus name.

15. You have promised that heaven is my home. This will be so when I die in Jesus name.

16-17. By Your grace I will have no reason to envy the rich, knowing that their riches are temporary and the righteousness of Jesus Christ in me will

glory will not descend after him.

18. Though while he lives he congratulates himself— And though men praise you when you do well for yourself—

19. He shall go to the generation of his fathers; They will never see the light.

20. Man in his pomp, yet without understanding, is like the beasts that perish.

give me a better ending.

18. Every blessing that comes my way will be from the Almighty God. By the grace of God I will be a blessing to others in Jesus name. The praise of men will have no impact on me in Jesus name.

19-20. Help me understand all that You teach me. Help me heed all the warnings that are available. By Your grace I will not end up in dishonour in Jesus name.

Psalm 50 NIV

The Psalm teaches the type of worship that is not acceptable to God and ends with a call for men to repent.

A Psalm of Asaph.

BIBLE

1. The Mighty One, God, the Lord, speaks and summons the earth from the rising of the sun to where it sets.

2. From Zion, perfect in beauty, God shines forth.

3. Our God comes and will

PRAYER

1. The Almighty God, You have spoken. Let the world come to attention when You speak.

2. May You continue to shine throughout the universe.

3. Do not keep silent my

not be silent; a fire devours before Him, and around Him a tempest rages.

Lord. Whenever You speak help me hear Your voice. As You appear, come in Your power to judge the wicked in Jesus name. As You are a consuming fire, let Your presence consume every trace of wickedness in my life in Jesus name.

4. He summons the heavens above, and the earth, that He may judge His people:

4. As judgement starts in Your house, my prayer is that I will not be found wanting in Jesus name.

5. "Gather to Me this consecrated people, who made a covenant with Me by sacrifice."

5. Thank you for Jesus Christ has made the supreme sacrifice on my behalf. Therefore as You call for a gathering of the saints, nothing will stop me from being part of it in Jesus name.

6. And the heavens proclaim His righteousness, for He is a God of justice.

6. Thank you Lord for You will only judge in righteousness. Unrighteousness can never be found in You.

7. "Listen, My people, and I will speak; I will testify against You, Israel: I am God, Your God.

7. Help me to be ready when You speak to me. Give me a heart that will accept correction for You only chastise those that You love.

8. I bring no charges against you concerning your sacrifices or concerning your burnt offerings,

8. Let my heart understand and accept that I am owned by You; therefore all I have is actually

which are ever before me.

9. I have no need of a bull from your stall or of goats from your pens,

10. For every animal of the forest is mine, and the cattle on a thousand hills.

11. I know every bird in the mountains, and the insects in the fields are mine.

12. If I were hungry I would not tell you, for the world is mine, and all that is in it.

13. Do I eat the flesh of bulls or drink the blood of goats?

14. "Sacrifice thank offerings to God, fulfil your vows to the Most High,

15. And call on Me in the day of trouble; I will deliver you, and you will honour Me."

Yours. I therefore pray that I will not find it difficult to bring stuff to You out of what You have blessed me with.

9-11. Let it settle in my spirit that I cannot bribe You or Your Ministers with any material gifts for You are richer than the richest man and bigger than the best man.

12-13. I honour and revere You my Lord for You are genuinely all sufficient and there is nothing I can bring into Your presence that You cannot do without.

14. Give me a thankful heart that will continually give sacrifices of praise and thanksgiving to You. Help me pay my vows with the knowledge that whatever I promise, I must go the extra mile to fulfil in Jesus name.

15. I am praying that You must always be my first port of call in times of trouble. Let the desire to seek human counsel be subject to your leading only; Let every desire to take short cuts be non-existent in me in Jesus name. Thank You for I know that You are more than able to deliver me.

16. But to the wicked person, God says: "What right have you to recite My laws or take My covenant on your lips?

17. You hate My instruction and cast My words behind you.

18. When you see a thief, you join with him; you throw in your lot with adulterers.

19. You use your mouth for evil and harness your tongue to deceit.

20. You sit and testify against your brother and slander your own mother's son.

21. When you did these things and I kept silent,

16. Help me become both a hearer and doer of Your commandments. Let hypocrisy be far away from me in Jesus name.

17. Give me a humble heart so that I am able to take instructions and correction with ease. Let every form of arrogance within me die immediately in Jesus name.

18. I pray for boldness to be able to speak the truth without fear at all times. Let the spirit of the fear of God reign in me rather than me fearing men.

19. Let the lying spirit be far away from me from this moment in Jesus name. I refuse to be deceitful from this moment in Jesus name.

20. Rather than speak against my brother, help me obey Your commandment which says I should love my neighbour as myself.

21. Do not be silent where I am concerned. I ask for

you thought I was exactly like you. But I now arraign you and set my accusations before you.

22. "Consider this, you who forget God, or I will tear you to pieces, with no one to rescue You:

23. Those who sacrifice thank offerings honour Me, and to the blameless I will show My salvation."

forgiveness of all my sins. Help me accept all correction that You send my way.

22. Help me continue to improve my relationship with You, obeying at all times such that I will never forget You.

23. Let all that I do glorify You. Let my praise be acceptable in Your sight. Let the words of my mouth always show that I am a saved child in Jesus name.

Psalm 51 NASB

This is a Psalm of confession, repentance of sin, a request for forgiveness and gratitude to God.

For the choir director. A Psalm of David, when Nathan the prophet came to him, after he had gone in to Bathsheba.

BIBLE

1. Be gracious to me, O God, according to Your lovingkindness; According to the greatness of Your compassion blot out my transgressions.

PRAYER

1. I have sinned. My Lord and my God have mercy on me. Pardon my sin by wiping it out completely. I ask that the blood of Jesus wash my sins away. Have mercy on me. I do not come to remind You of the great things I have done for You. I am appealing to the lovingkindness of

Your heart.

2. Wash me thoroughly from my iniquity and cleanse me from my sin.

2. Wash me thoroughly till every stain is gone. Wash me till the guilt is no more on my conscience. Cleanse me so I'll be able to come into Your presence.

3. For I know my transgressions, and my sin is ever before me.

3. I remember my sins all the time. As You forgive me and You forget, help me forget so I am not permanently crippled by my sins.

4. Against You, You only, I have sinned and done what is evil in Your sight, so that You are justified when You speak and blameless when You judge.

4. You are aware of all I have done because there is nothing hidden from You. I have sinned against You. I know I am guilty, be lenient with me O God.

5. Behold, I was brought forth in iniquity, and in sin my mother conceived me.

5. I was born with a natural tendency to sin, hotwithstanding I ask for forgiveness from You.

6. Behold, You desire truth in the innermost being, and in the hidden part You will make me know wisdom.

6. I pray that falsehood will be far away from me. Help me to be truthful at all times. I ask for wisdom Lord, for it will keep me from going back to my past sins.

7. Purify me with hyssop, and I shall be clean; Wash me, and I shall be whiter than snow.

7. Let the blood of Jesus cleanse me removing every trace of my sins.

8. Make me to hear joy and gladness, let the bones

8. Let joy and gladness come into my heart to

	which You have broken rejoice.		replace the pain of my sins.
9.	Hide Your face from my sins and blot out all my iniquities.	**9.**	My Father, do not remember my sins when relating to me. I ask that You remove them completely from my heavenly account.
10.	Create in me a clean heart, O God, and renew a steadfast spirit within me.	**10.**	I ask that You remove the old heart of sin and give me a new heart. Let my old nature be transformed by the entrance of Your spirit into me.
11.	Do not cast me away from Your presence and do not take Your Holy Spirit from me.	**11.**	Let Your presence be with me at all times. Do not cast me out of Your presence. I will be empty and vulnerable without the Holy Spirit in me so I ask that Your Spirit be retained in me.
12.	Restore to me the joy of Your salvation and sustain me with a willing spirit.	**12.**	The joy of being Your child has gone from me. I ask that You restore the joy of salvation to me. Let Your forgiveness of my sins bring me peace. Let Your spirit uphold me from falling again in Jesus name.
13.	Then I will teach transgressors Your ways, and sinners will be converted to You.	**13.**	Help me teach sinners to come back to You in repentance so that they shall be liberated from the power of satan.
14.	Deliver me from blood guiltiness, O God, the	**14.**	Deliver me from the guilt of shedding innocent

	Psalm		Prayer
	God of my salvation; Then my tongue will joyfully sing of Your righteousness.		blood. Help me praise Your righteousness forever.
15.	O Lord, open my lips, that my mouth may declare Your praise.	**15.**	Open the lips that have been shut by guilt. Let Your praises fill my heart in Jesus name.
16.	For You do not delight in sacrifice, otherwise I would give it; You are not pleased with burnt offering.	**16.**	Thank You Lord for Jesus Christ has already been sacrificed in the place of every burnt offering I might ever need.
17.	The sacrifices of God are a broken spirit; A broken and a contrite heart, O God, You will not despise.	**17.**	Help me approach You in humility and with sorrow for sin whenever I have to come to You in repentance as this is the only remedy that You have prescribed.
18.	By Your favour do good to Zion; Build the walls of Jerusalem.	**18.**	I pray that You remember Your church, do good to Your children everywhere. Bless the church with favour and protection in Jesus name.
19.	Then You will delight in righteous sacrifices, in burnt offering and whole burnt offering; Then young bulls will be offered on Your altar.	**19.**	As You bless Your children, they will come back to You with sacrifices of praise and thanksgiving. I pray You alone will be glorified in Jesus mighty name.

Psalm 52 ESV

This Psalm should stir a hatred for lying and an appreciation that those who lie will be destroyed by God.

To the choirmaster. A Maskil of David, when Doeg, the Edomite, came and told Saul, "David has come to the house of Ahimelech."

BIBLE

1. Why do you boast of evil, O mighty man? The steadfast love of God endures all the day.
2. Your tongue plots destruction, like a sharp razor, you worker of deceit.
3. You love evil more than good, and lying more than speaking what is right. Selah
4. You love all words that devour, O deceitful tongue.
5. But God will break you down forever; He will snatch and tear you from

PRAYER

1. Give me a heart that will not partake in mischief, talk less of boasting about it. Thank You Father for Your goodness and Your faithfulness. Your character contrasts heavily against that of the wicked that continually do evil.
2. Help me bridle my tongue so I won't use it to cause mischief.
3. Teach me to love being good rather than doing evil and telling the truth at all times even when it might seem inconvenient.
4. Help me watch what I say at all times, not saying things that would hurt people on purpose and never being deceitful.
5. For every act of mischief by the wicked, I ask that You destroy them, cut

your tent; He will uproot you from the land of the living. Selah

6. The righteous shall see and fear, and shall laugh at him, saying,

7. "See the man who would not make God his refuge, but trusted in the abundance of his riches and sought refuge in his own destruction!"

8. But I am like a green olive tree in the house of God. I trust in the steadfast love of God forever and ever.

9. I will thank You forever, because You have done it. I will wait for Your name, for it is good, in the presence of the godly.

them off and utterly root them out in Jesus name.

6. With my eyes I will see the punishment of the wicked and appreciate Your awesome power

7. Help me to be dependent on You as I acknowledge I do not have any strength of my own. Help me not to put my trust in material wealth but to understand that all I am and all I have are from You.

8. As You help me dwell in Your house I will be like a green olive tree nourished by You in Your mercy.

9. I pray that I will continue to praise You forever and ever. Help me wait on You forever for the supply of my needs which shall be my testimony in the presence of the saints.

Psalm 53 ESV

The Psalm shows the corruption of man, it should stir us to hate sin and at the same time raise our confidence that God will deliver us.

To the choirmaster: according to Mahalath.
A Maskil of David.

BIBLE	PRAYER
1. The fool says in his heart, "There is no God." They are corrupt, doing abominable iniquity; there is none who does good.	**1.** Lord take foolishness away from me. Take away every corrupt attitude and spirit that can lead me to deny You. Those spirits must not have a place in my life.
2. God looks down from heaven on the children of man to see if there are any who understand, who seek after God.	**2.** Help me seek You at all times, give me the understanding that I must do as You say for my own good.
3. They have all fallen away; together they have become corrupt; there is none who does good, not even one.	**3.** Help me so I do not go back to the life I have left behind. Help me deal with every form of filthiness that I might want to cling to.
4. Have those who work evil no knowledge, who eat up my people as they eat bread, and do not call upon God?	**4.** Lord cause everyone who has eaten anything that belongs to me to vomit them now in Jesus name.
5. There they are, in great terror, where there is no terror! For God scatters the bones of him who encamps against you; you put them to shame,	**5.** Father put fear in the hearts of all who surro-und me seeking my life. I ask that You scatter them, put confusion into their midst and destroy

for God has rejected them.

6. Oh, that salvation for Israel would come out of Zion! When God restores the fortunes of His people, let Jacob rejoice, let Israel be glad.

them totally in Jesus name.

6. Deliver me speedily; let joy fill my heart in Jesus name

Psalm 54 NASB

The Psalm is an urgent call to God for deliverance.
The Psalmist thanks God after God has heard his prayers.

For the choir director; on stringed instruments. A Maskil of David, when the Ziphites came and said to Saul, "Is not David hiding himself among us?"

BIBLE	**PRAYER**
1. Save me, O God, by Your name, and vindicate me by Your power.	1. Lord I ask that You save me by Your name because Your name is a strong tower. Your name tells me that You are all powerful and all knowing. I ask that You declare judgement in my favour in Jesus name.
2. Hear my prayer, O God; Give ear to the words of my mouth.	2. Hear me Lord, I ask that You deliver me from those who seek my hurt, who are out to betray me.
3. For strangers have risen against me and violent men have sought my life; They have not set God before them. Selah.	3. Lord I am surrounded by enemies who want to destroy my soul. They act as if they can get away with whatever they

	do to me.
4. Behold, God is my helper; The Lord is the sustainer of my soul.	**4.** I ask for Your help, I have no power to fight. Fight for me O God. Thank You for giving me friends who support my cause.
5. He will recompense the evil to my foes; Destroy them in Your faithfulness.	**5.** I ask that You deal with my enemies as they are dealing with me. You have said You will recompense.
6. Willingly I will sacrifice to You; I will give thanks to Your name, O Lord, for it is good.	**6.** Give me a thankful heart and I pray that my sacrifice of praise will be acceptable to You.
7. For He has delivered me from all trouble, and my eye has looked with satisfaction upon my enemies.	**7.** Thank You for showing me mercy and delivering me, thank You that I am alive to see judgement on my enemies.

Psalm 55 ESV

The Psalmist cries to God for vengeance against his enemies.

To the choirmaster: with stringed instruments.
A Maskil of David.

BIBLE	PRAYER
1. Give ear to my prayer, O God, and hide not Yourself from my plea for mercy!	**1.** I lift up my heart to You in prayer O God. I ask that You hear my fervent prayers, do not hide Yourself from me.
2. Attend to me, and answer me; I am restless in	**2.** Give me Your attention O God for I need You to

my complaint and I moan,	answer me now. Lord my soul is heavy at this time.
3. Because of the noise of the enemy, because of the oppression of the wicked. For they drop trouble upon me, and in anger they bear a grudge against me. **4.** My heart is in anguish within me; the terrors of death have fallen upon me.	**3-4.** My enemies are waging war against me. At every turn I face oppression, I have not done anything to deserve the hatred being shown against me. At the moment I am very worried and overwhelmed by what is going on around me. I need Your help Father.
5. Fear and trembling come upon me, and horror overwhelms me.	**5.** I know You have not given me a spirit of fear, but honestly I am so fearful that I tremble whenever I remember my situation.
6. And I say, "Oh, that I had wings like a dove! I would fly away and be at rest; **7.** Yes, I would wander far away; I would lodge in the wilderness; Selah	**6-7.** Make a way of escape for me. Let Your angels lift me up so I can fly where I will not be troubled.
8. I would hurry to find a shelter from the raging wind and tempest.	**8.** Help me escape all who want a pound of my flesh.
9. Destroy, O Lord, divide their tongues; for I see violence and strife in the city.	**9.** jehovah Saboath the Commander in chief of heavenly armies, I call on You to fight on my behalf and destroy my enemies. Put confusion in their midst by dividing their tongues. Let them all start to misunder-

stand one another.

10. Day and night they go around it on its walls, and iniquity and trouble are within it;
11. Ruin is in its midst; oppression and fraud do not depart from its marketplace.

12. For it is not an enemy who taunts me—then I could bear it; it is not an adversary who deals insolently with me—then I could hide from him.
13. But it is you, a man, my equal, my companion, my familiar friend.
14. We used to take sweet counsel together; within God's house we walked in the throng.
15. Let death steal over them; let them go down to Sheol alive; for evil is in their dwelling place and in their heart.
16. But I call to God, and the Lord will save me.

17. Evening and morning and at noon I utter my complaint and moan, and He hears my voice.

18. He redeems my soul in

10. The mischief makers do not rest. They are at it every waking moment of the day.
11. Deceit an und unfaithfulness is perpetuated against me by people who are meant to be friends with me. Help me I pray.
12-14. My friends have joined my enemies. I am exposed as all my secrets are out in the open. By Your grace I pray I will not betray my own friends in Jesus name.

15. Let all who wish me dead die in my place by fire in Jesus name. Let hell be their final resting place.

16. Help me call on You at all times. Out of Your grace I know You will save me in Jesus name.
17. Help me pray without ceasing and with the fervency that will cause You to respond immediately.
18. Thank You for fighting for

safety from the battle that I wage, for many are arrayed against me.

me and delivering me from the hands of my enemies. My enemies are outnumbered by the hosts of heaven. Glory and honour to Your name my Lord.

19. God will give ear and humble them, He who is enthroned from of old, Selah because they do not change and do not fear God.

19. I ask that You destroy every evil voice that has risen against me. The wicked have lived their lives as if You do not exist. There is no fear of God in them. I ask that You expose their foolishness by showing that You are the Almighty.

20. My companion stretched out his hand against his friends; he violated his covenant.

20. The traitors have broken the covenant of friendship with me without any reasons. Let their violence come before You.

21. His speech was smooth as butter, yet war was in his heart; his words were softer than oil, yet they were drawn swords.

21. Their words were smooth but they had ulterior motives. Give me a discerning spirit so I'll know those who are actually for me in future.

22. Cast your burden on the Lord, and He will sustain you; He will never permit the righteous to be moved.

22. As I cast my burdens unto You, help me leave them at Your feet rather than holding on to issues I cannot solve myself. Thank You for I know You are more than able to see me through.

23. But you, O God, will cast them down into the pit of

23. Let the men with blood on their hands and those

destruction; men of blood and treachery shall not live out half their days. But I will trust in You.

who are deceitful end up as You have programmed for them in hell. Help me live my life in complete trust of Your faithfulness in Jesus name.

Psalm 56 NASB

The Psalm teaches that even when in danger we should continue to praise God.

For the choir director; according to Jonath elem rehokim. A Mikhtam of David, when the Philistines seized him in Gath.

BIBLE	PRAYER
1. Be gracious to me, O God, for man has trampled upon me; Fighting all day long he oppresses me.	**1.** Have mercy on me O God, the enemy wants to take my life for there is war on many fronts.
2. My foes have trampled upon me all day long, for they are many who fight proudly against me.	**2.** Many agents of my enemy gang up against me. You are the Most High God, higher than the highest seeing everything that is happening to me.
3. When I am afraid, I will put my trust in You.	**3.** Lord sometimes I am afraid of my enemies, afraid of my own mistakes, but help me trust in You for You are faithful and You are merciful.
4. In God, whose word I praise, in God I have put my trust; I shall not be afraid. What can mere	**4.** Help me praise Your word, You have spoken to me and I hold on to all You have said. Help me

man do to me?

5. All day long they distort my words; All their thoughts are against me for evil.

6. They attack, they lurk, they watch my steps, as they have waited to take my life.

7. Because of wickedness, cast them forth, in anger put down the peoples, O God!

8. You have taken account of my wanderings; Put my tears in Your bottle. Are they not in Your book?

9. Then my enemies will turn back in the day when I call; This I know, that God is for me.

10. In God, whose word I praise, in the Lord, whose word I praise,

11. In God I have put my trust, I shall not be afraid. What can man do to me?

12. Your vows are binding upon me, O God; I will render thank offerings to You.

13. For You have delivered my soul from death,

focus on You so I will not be afraid of any man.

5. At all times my words are used against me, intervene and help me my Lord. The thoughts of my enemies are evil.

6. Lord they gather together, watching my every step and waiting for my soul.

7. Do not let them go unpunished. Put confusion in their midst, bring them down and destroy them my God.

8. Lord I have experienced different troubles, remember my tears O God.

9. Help me as I cry unto You, arise on my behalf and let my enemies turn away from me.

10. I have received Your word, my Lord and my God I praise You.

11. Teach me to trust You Almighty God, for with You on my side, no man can hurt me.

12. Help me keep my vows to You, I have promised to praise You.

13. Thank You for delivering me from death. I know

indeed my feet from stumbling, so that I may walk before God in the light of the living.

You are able to keep me from falling and from failing. Out of Your mercy and favour I will continue to enjoy Your presence.

Psalm 57 ESV

The Psalmist asks for the mercy of God and declares God to be his refuge. He describes the acts of his enemies and concludes by thanking God for His loving kindness.

To the choirmaster: according to Do Not Destroy.
A Miktam of David, when he fled from Saul, in the cave.

BIBLE	PRAYER
1. Be merciful to me, O God, be merciful to me, for in You my soul takes refuge; in the shadow of Your wings I will take refuge, till the storms of destruction pass by.	**1.** I ask for Your mercy, help me O God for I do not have anyone to turn to. I trust in You. Protect me under Your wings as You stop the attacks from my enemies.
2. I cry out to God Most High, to God who fulfils His purpose for me.	**2.** I cry to You the Most High; You are higher than all things. Thank You for I know You will perfect all that concerns me.
3. He will send from heaven and save me; He will put to shame him who tramples on me. Selah God will send out his steadfast love and his faithfulness!	**3.** Thank You as You answer from heaven, release Your angels and deliver me from every reproach that has been programmed by the enemy. Let me experience Your mercy and Your

			truth.
4.	My soul is in the midst of lions; I lie down amid fiery beasts—the children of man, whose teeth are spears and arrows, whose tongues are sharp swords.	**4.**	The men around me are like lions, their teeth are like spears and arrows, their tongues like spears.
5.	Be exalted, O God, above the heavens! Let Your glory be over all the earth!	**5.**	Be exalted in the heavens; let Your glory be above all the earth.
6.	They set a net for my steps; my soul was bowed down. They dug a pit in my way, but they have fallen into I themselves. Selah	**6.**	My enemies have prepared a net to catch my feet; they have dug a pit so I can fall into it. Have mercy on me; send help to me, O God. Thank You Lord because those who dug a pit for me fell into it just as Haman hung in the gallows prepared for Mordecai.
7.	My heart is steadfast, O God, my heart is steadfast! I will sing and make melody!	**7.**	No matter what I am going through, no matter where I am, I will always praise You. Give me a heart that is steadfast in my appreciation of Your loving kindness.
8.	Awake, my glory! Awake, O harp and lyre! I will awake the dawn!	**8.**	Let my soul awaken within me; let my worship be like sweet music in Your ears my Lord and my God. Help me give my best to You early in the morning.
9.	I will give thanks to You,	**9.**	Help me lift Your name

	O Lord, among the peoples; I will sing praises to You among the nations.		with boldness; let the joy in my heart be seen by all the people; help me as I lift Your name on high.
10.	For Your steadfast love is great to the heavens, Your faithfulness to the clouds.	**10.**	So apparent is Your love towards me, that it is recognised in the heavens and on earth.
11.	Be exalted, O God, above the heavens! Let Your glory be over all the earth! steadfast! I will sing and make melody!	**11.**	Be exalted in the heave-heavens; let us all continue to behold Your glory here on earth. Thank You Father.

Psalm 58 ESV

The Psalm is a prayer for the defeat of ungodly men.

To the choirmaster: according to Do Not Destroy.
A Miktam of David.

	BIBLE		**PRAYER**
1.	Do you indeed decree what is right, you gods? Do you judge the children of man uprightly?	**1.**	Lord give us rulers at every level of society that will make the right decisions.
2.	No, in your hearts you devise wrongs; your hands deal out violence on earth.	**2.**	Lord I ask that You stop the people in authority all over the world from inflicting violence on the people. Let governmental wickedness come to an end. You are our defence O God.
3.	The wicked are estranged from the womb; they go astray from birth,	**3.**	Lord every man was born in sin, I thank You for finding me. For those

speaking lies.

4. They have venom like the venom of a serpent, like the deaf adder that stops its ear,

5. So that it does not hear the voice of charmers or of the cunning enchanter.

6. O God, break the teeth in their mouths; tear out the fangs of the young lions, O Lord!

7. Let them vanish like water that runs away; when he aims his arrows, let them be blunted.

8. Let them be like the snail that dissolves into slime, like the stillborn child who never sees the sun.
9. Sooner than your pots

who continue to live a life of sin, growing further apart from You, I pray O Lord that all their efforts will come to nothing. The wicked speak poisonous words; they refuse to hear Godly counsel. I pray I will not partake of any form of wickedness in Jesus name.
4. You are the All-powerful God. Let their poisonous words and arrows go back to their origins in Jesus name.
5. Let every enchantment and divination against my household and my community come to nothing in Jesus name.
6. Lord I ask that You render the wicked ineffective, break their teeth and let them be utterly destroyed I pray.
7. Lord unsettle the wicked and let them become dispirited. Move them out of their comfort zone. Let them melt in their sins. Destroy all their weapons of war.
8. Let them all pass away such that Your children will no longer be disturbed.
9. Lord, before they try to

can feel the heat of thorns, whether green or ablaze, may he sweep them away!

bite again, let Your whirlwind blow them away.

10. The righteous will rejoice when he sees the vengeance; he will bathe his feet in the blood of the wicked.

10. Let me rejoice when I see Your judgement on the wicked.

11. Mankind will say, "Surely there is a reward for the righteous; surely there is a God who judges on earth."

11. pray the righteous will reap the fruits of their righteousness in Jesus name.

Psalm 59 NASB

The Psalm is a prayer of David asking God to deliver him from his enemies.

For the choir director; set to Al-tashheth. A Mikhtam of David, when Saul sent men and they watched the house in order to kill him.

BIBLE

1. Deliver me from my enemies, O my God; Set me securely on high away from those who rise up against me.

PRAYER

1. I ask that You deliver me from my enemies. Protect me from all who rise up against me. I ask that You instruct the hosts of heaven to keep me from all harm instigated by my enemies.

2. Deliver me from those who do iniquity and save me from men of bloodshed.

2. I ask that You deliver me from agents of the devil whose only purpose is to stop me from fulfilling my

3. For behold, they have set an ambush for my life; Fierce men launch an attack against me,not for my transgression nor for my sin, O Lord,

4. For no guilt of mine, they run and set themselves against me. Arouse Yourself to help me, and see!

5. You, O Lord God of hosts, the God of Israel, awake to punish all the nations; Do not be gracious to any who are treacherous in iniquity. Selah.

6. They return at evening, they howl like a dog, and go around the city.

7. Behold, they belch forth with their mouth; Swords are in their lips, for, they say, “Who hears?”

8. But You, O Lord, laugh at

purpose in life. These people are violent and have innocent blood on their hands.

3. They are a multitude gathered against me. I have not done anything to warrant what is being done to me. Let every gang up against me come to nothing in Jesus name.

4. Lord arise and fight for me. Come down in all Your power. Let Your name be glorified. There are too many people waiting to pounce on me.

5. My Lord, do not let the wicked get away scot-free. Visit them with the might of heaven and let them know that You are God.

6. Their search for me day and night both physically and spiritually shall be in vain. Their words which come out of their mouths as if they are dogs will always be futile.

7. They speak with so much venom about what they will do if they catch me. Let them swallow their words.

8. They laugh at me now

Scripture	Prayer
them; You scoff at all the nations.	but I know You will laugh at them. Yes You will put them to shame in Jesus name. They will all become figures of ridicule as soon as You move against them.
9. Because of His strength I will watch for You, for God is my stronghold.	**9.** You are stronger than the strongest, that is why I rely on You as my defence. The righteous run to You and they are safe.
10. My God in His lovingkindness will meet me; God will let me look trumphantly upon my foes.	**10.** In Your mercy I know You will arise on my behalf. I thank You because You will let me see my desire on my enemies.
11. Do not slay them, or my people will forget; Scatter them by Your power, and bring them down, O Lord, our shield.	**11.** My enemies deserve to die, but do not kill them. I ask that You scatter them by Your power. Let them know that I am a child of the all-powerful God. Let them live so they'll see me fulfil my destiny. Others who follow them will now see the futility of attacking me. Thank You for being my shield and protection.
12. On account of the sin of their mouth and the words of their lips, let them even be caught in their pride, and on account of curses and	**12-13.** For their sins which include lying lips, arrogance and cursing without restraint, let Your wrath fall upon them; I ask that You consume

lies which they utter.

13. Destroy them in wrath, destroy them that they may be no more; That men may know that God rules in Jacob to the ends of the earth. Selah.

them in wrath. Let them fall into ruin in such a way that they would know that it is an act of God. Let all the earth come to the realisation that You are the God of heaven and the earth.

14. They return at evening, they howl like a dog, and go around the city.

15. They wander about for food and growl if they are not satisfied.

14-15. Let the wicked become nothing such that they will have to scavenge for food before eating like dogs without owners.

16. But as for me, I shall sing of Your strength; Yes, I shall joyfully sing of Your lovingkindness in the morning, for You have been my stronghold and a refuge in the day of my distress.

16. Yes I will sing of Your power for I will always experience it. You will continually give me victory over my enemies. All day long, until I die, help me acknowledge Your mercy over me. Help me give enough praise to show my appreciation for You being my defence. In my season of trouble, I pray I will always run to You for safety for You are Master over all seasons

17. O my strength, I will sing praises to You; For God is my stronghold, the God who shows me lovingkindness

17. My prayer is that You will continue to strengthen me. In Your strength I will sing praises of You being a merciful God. Lord help me tarry in the place of prayer.

Psalm 60 NASB

The Psalm is a prayer of deliverance from our enemies.
For the choir director; according to Shushan Eduth.
A Mikhtam of David, to teach; when he struggled with Aram-naharaim and with Aram-zobah, and Joab returned, and smote twelve thousand of Edom in the Valley of Salt.

BIBLE		PRAYER	
1.	O God, You have rejected us. You have broken us; You have been angry; O, restore us.	**1.**	Lord I ask that You do not let go of me. Do not show Your displeasure with me by allowing the enemy to scatter me and defeat me
2.	You have made the land quake, You have split it open; Heal its breaches, for it totters.	**2.**	Lord when natural disasters happen, we are afraid. I ask that You heal our land. Take us back to the times of peace O God
3.	You have made Your people experience hardship; You have given us wine to drink that makes us stagger.	**3.**	Help me through the trials that I experience, help me to endure all that come my way.
4.	You have given a banner to those who fear You, that it may be displayed because of the truth. Selah.	**4.**	Thank You for being our banner and our shield. Help us as we display the banner for the world to see at all times.
5.	That Your beloved may be delivered, save with Your right hand, and answer us!	**5.**	I pray in the name of Your Son Jesus Christ, hear me and deliver me from my enemies.
6.	God has spoken in His holiness: "I will exult, I	**6-7.**	Thank You Father for I know that all You have

will portion out Shechem and measure out the valley of Succoth.

7. "Gilead is Mine, and Manasseh is Mine; Ephraim also is the helmet of My head; Judah is My sceptre.

8. "Moab is My washbowl; Over Edom I shall throw My shoe; Shout loud, O Philistia, because of Me!"

9. Who will bring me into the besieged city? Who will lead me to Edom

10. Have not You Yourself, O God, rejected us? And will You not go forth with our armies, O God?

11. O give us help against the adversary, for deliverance by man is in vain.

12. Through God we shall do valiantly, and it is He who will tread down our adversaries

spoken will come to pass. I will rejoice.

8. Thank You Lord for I will triumph over every enemy. They are all under my feet, with my feet crushing their necks.

9-10. I ask that the hosts of heaven be released to fight on my behalf.

11. Help me Lord for I have nowhere else to turn to.

12. Thank You Father for giving Your children complete victory over our enemies.

Psalm 61 NKJV

The Psalm leads us to where we will find strength in times of pain and challenges.

To the Chief Musician. On a stringed instrument. A Psalm of David.

	BIBLE		PRAYER
1.	Hear my cry, O God; Attend to my prayer.	1.	I have no other God but You. Consider my petitions my God and my King. I come to You desperate for answers.
2.	From the end of the earth I will cry to You, when my heart is overwhelmed; Lead me to the rock that is higher than I.	2.	No matter where I am, I will still cry to You. The situation is challenging but I know You are the solution. I need to be at a higher and better place than where I am now. You are the way to that place. When You open the door, no man can shut it. Hold me by the hand, lead me now in Jesus name.
3.	For You have been a shelter for me, a strong tower from the enemy.	3.	Thank You that You have always been there for me, sheltering and protecting me from the enemy.
4.	I will abide in Your tabernacle forever; I will trust in the shelter of Your wings. Selah	4.	Yes Your presence is a source of peace and joy for me and I will abide in it for ever. Let me find rest in You forever.
5.	For You, O God, have heard my vows; You	5.	Help me make vows that I can keep. As I make the

have given me the heritage of those who fear Your name.

vows hear them and by Your grace let them be fulfilled in Jesus name. I want to be part of those, whom You have given a heritage to, give me a heart that fears You. Let me live in Your light and in the abundance of grace in Jesus name.

6. You will prolong the king's life, His years as many generations.

6. Grant me long life. Help me fulfil the number of my days. Let nothing cut my destiny short in Jesus name.

7. He shall abide before God forever. Oh, prepare mercy and truth, which may preserve him!

7. I pray that I dwell in Your presence forever. I pray that mercy and truth will be hung round my neck and that I shall walk in them all the days of my life.

8. So I will sing praise to Your name forever, that I may daily perform my vows.

8. I will praise You forever and by Your grace I will pay all my vows in Jesus name

Psalm 62 NIV

The Psalm shows confidence and dependence on God even in times of trial.

For the director of music. For Jeduthun. A Psalm of David.

BIBLE

1. Truly my soul finds rest in God; my salvation

PRAYER

1. I wait on You without any doubt. Help me wait

comes from Him.

patiently for You. You are the only One who can save me. I look nowhere else but unto You.

2. Truly He is my rock and my salvation; He is my fortress, I will never be shaken.

2. Let my eyes be continually open to the fact that You are my rock. You are more than able to save me, You are my salvation. I pray You will be my defence from all adversaries, therefore I will not be moved from my rightful place.

3. How long will you assault me? Would all of you throw me down—this leaning wall, this tottering fence?

3. I pray that every mischief done against me is nullified in Jesus name. I pray that all who delight in lies will receive the vengeance of God in Jesus name.

4. Surely they intend to topple me from my lofty place; they take delight in lies. With their mouths they bless, but in their hearts they curse.

4. Help me discern the intent behind the words that I hear in Jesus name. All who are against me will slay one another in Jesus name. As they fight one another, I pray that they all totter and fall in Jesus name.

5. Yes, my soul, find rest in God; my hope comes from Him.

5. I pray that anytime I waver the Lord will uphold me in Jesus name. Help me wait in assurance because You are more than able to

see me through. My faith will not shake.

6. Truly He is my rock and my salvation; He is my fortress, I will not be shaken.

6. You are my defence and nothing that comes my way will move me out of Your bosom.

7. My salvation and my honour depend on God; He is my mighty rock, my refuge.

7. Lord I am yours and all I have is in You and You alone; My salvation, my refuge, my glory are all in You.

8. Trust in Him at all times, you people; pour out your hearts to Him, for God is our refuge.

8. Help me continue to trust in You and I pray that people will come to You and know that You are worthy to be trusted. I pray that people will come to You and pour out their hearts to You and You will sustain them.

9. Surely the lowborn are but a breath, the high-born are but a lie. If weighed on a balance, they are nothing; together they are only a breath.

9. Help me remember at all times that men, high or low are not worthy to be trusted.

10. Do not trust in extortion or put vain hope in stolen goods; though your riches increase, do not set your heart on them.

10. Lord I ask for the grace to respect fellow human beings not acting in oppression against the less privileged. I pray that I will not be motivated by money and I will realise that money cannot buy trust.

11. One thing God has spoken, two things I

11. Lord give me listening ears, as You speak let

have heard: "Power belongs to You, God,

me hear and let what I hear stay with me forever. Let my heart accept that You are Almighty and all power resides in You. Let this fact increase my trust in You.

12. And with You, Lord, is unfailing love"; and, "You reward everyone according to what they have done."

12. I pray that You will have mercy on me and on all that is mine.

Psalm 63 ESV

This Psalm is written as David is in flight from his enemies. In this distressing situation there is a deep desire and love for God.

A Psalm of David, when he was in the wilderness of Judah.

BIBLE		PRAYER	
1.	O God, You are my God; earnestly I seek You; my soul thirsts for You; my flesh faints for You, as in a dry and weary land where there is no water.	**1.**	You are my God. I thirst for You. I will always seek You in the quietness and freshness of the morning. Help me know You better; I am in a dry situation. There is no other that can provide succour for me but You.
2.	So I have looked upon You in the sanctuary, beholding Your power and glory.	**2.**	I long to behold Your power and glory as I have experienced in the past.
3.	Because Your steadfast love is better than life,	**3.**	I praise You O God as I revel in Your loving

my lips will praise You.

4. So I will bless You as long as I live; in Your name I will lift up my hands.
5. My soul will be satisfied as with fat and rich food, and my mouth will praise You with joyful lips,
6. When I remember You upon my bed, and meditate on You in the watches of the night;
7. For You have been my help, and in the shadow of Your wings I will sing for joy.
8. My soul clings to You; Your right hand upholds me.
9. But those who seek to destroy my life shall go down into the depths of the earth
10. They shall be given over to the power of the sword; they shall be a portion for jackals
11. But the king shall rejoice

kindness which is better than life itself.

4. The dead cannot praise You O Lord. As long as I live I will praise and I will worship You.
5. My soul will be satisfied with the love You have for me and I will praise You from the depths of my heart and with my mouth.
6. Help me remember Your ways and Your acts, show me how to meditate on Your word during the night.
7. As I meditate and because You have helped me I will ride on Your wings and I will rejoice.
8. I pray that You will uphold me with Your righteous right hand, and as You do so, I pray I will continue to follow after You; I will not turn away from You.
9. I pray that all who seek after my soul to destroy me shall receive Your wrath and die.
10. Since they are of the sword they will fall by the sword of the angelic hosts of heaven in Jesus name.
11. As I am Your child and

in God; all who swear by Him shall exult, for the mouths of liars will be stopped.

You are the King of Kings, I am a King here on earth, I will rejoice continually. My allegiance is totally to You and I pray that I will partake of Your glory. I ask that all who speak lies against me be stopped permanently in Jesus name.

Psalm 64 NASB

This Psalm is a cry to God for protection from enemies and shows the wicked are marked for ruin and failure because of their character.

For the choir director. A Psalm of David.

BIBLE

1. Hear my voice, O God, in my complaint; Preserve my life from dread of the enemy.

2. Hide me from the secret counsel of evildoers, from the tumult of those who do iniquity,

3. Who have sharpened their tongue like a sword.

PRAYER

1. My God I ask that You hear me as I call on You. I ask that You preserve my life from the enemy that has surrounded me.

2. The wicked have ganged up against me. I ask that You hide me from their wicked counsel. Let them not remember me in Jesus name. They always have devious plans. I ask that You protect me from all such plans in Jesus name.

3. The wicked use their tongues like swords **and**

They aimed bitter speech as their arrow,

4. To shoot from concealment at the blameless; Suddenly they shoot at him, and do not fear.

5. They hold fast to themselves an evil purpose; They talk of laying snares secretly; They say, "Who can see them?"

6. They devise injustices, saying, "We are ready with a well-conceived plot"; For the inward thought and the heart of a man are deep.

7. But God will shoot at them with an arrow; Suddenly they will be wounded.

8. So they will make him stumble; Their own tongue is against them; All who see them will shake the head.

9. Then all men will fear, and they will declare the work of God, and will consider what He has done.

10. The righteous man will

arrows aimed at shooting me down.

4. They lay ambush trying to destroy the perfect man. They are not bothered at the damage they cause.

5. Let Your fire scatter every evil gang up against my family and my community in Jesus name.

6. Let the wicked fall into every snare they have laid for me in Jesus name.

7. Shoot at all who have shot at me, wound them, such that they would be unable to shoot at me in the future.

8. As confusion arose during the building of the Tower of Babel, let them all be confused in Jesus name.

9. I pray that all men shall see the result of what You have done to those who have ganged up against me. Your fear shall enter into them and Your name shall be glorified.

10. I pray that the righteous

be glad in the Lord and will take refuge in Him; And all the upright in heart will glory.

would see Your mighty works and their trust in You would be greatly increased in Jesus name.

Psalm 65 NIV

The Psalm shows how to approach God and how God responds by the performance of wonders through his protection and provision.

For the director of music. A Psalm of David. A song.

BIBLE	PRAYER
1. Praise awaits You, our God, in Zion; to You our vows will be fulfilled.	1. Help me praise You at all times. Help me make and keep my vows.
2. You who answer prayer, to You all people will come.	2. Thank You for You always hear and answer my prayers. Incline my heart to approach You at all times.
3. When we were overwhelmed by sins, You forgave our transgressions.	3. I thank You for my sins do not count against me any longer; I am forgiven. Glory to You O God.
4. Blessed are those You choose and bring near to live in Your courts! We are filled with the good things of Your house, of Your holy temple.	4. Thank You for choosing me; for bringing me out of darkness into Your marvellous light.
5. You answer us with awesome and righteous deeds, God our Saviour, the hope of all the ends	5. Lord You answer prayer whichever way You like for You are sovereign. I am certain that all Your

of the earth and of the farthest seas,

6. Who formed the mountains by Your power, having armed Yourself with strength,

7. Who stilled the roaring of the seas, the roaring of their waves, and the turmoil of the nations.

8. The whole earth is filled with awe at Your wonders; where morning dawns, where evening fades, You call forth songs of joy.

9. You care for the land and water it; You enrich it abundantly. The streams of God are filled with water to provide the people with grain, for so You have ordained it.

10. You drench its furrows and level its ridges; You soften it with showers and bless its crops.

11. You crown the year with Your bounty, and Your carts overflow with abundance.

12. The grasslands of the wilderness overflow; the hills are clothed with gladness.

13. The meadows are cover-

answers will work for my good in Jesus name.

6-8. You who set the mountains and still the seas, there is nothing too hard for You to do. Have mercy on me.

9. I ask that You visit me and meet my needs, for whereverYou go, there is always blessing left behind.

10. Thank You for making me fruitful in every area of my life.

11. When You visit there is fertility, crown every day of my life with your inexhaustible goodness.

12. I pray You will touch the hearts of those who are far away from You. Let there be rejoicing in such hearts as a result of the encounter with You.

13. Let there be reason for

covered with flocks and the valleys are mantled with grain; they shout for joy and sing.

me to shout for joy forever and ever. Amen

Psalm 66 NKJV

This is a Psalm of praise to God for His wonderful works of deliverance and protection.

To the Chief Musician. A Song. A Psalm.

BIBLE	PRAYER
1. Make a joyful shout to God, all the earth!	**1.** Help me develop a loving affection for You that would cause me to praise You at all times. Help me make a joyful noise to You both in public and privately too.
2. Sing out the honour of His name; Make His praise glorious.	**2.** Let my praise be heartfelt, let it be like a sweet smelling aroma in Your ears. Your name is worthy to be praised. Help me sing and sing well too in Jesus name.
3. Say to God, "How awesome are Your works! Through the greatness of Your power Your enemies shall submit themselves to You.	**3.** Your power has always brought forth great and mighty works. Let the greatness of Your power cause Your enemies to surrender completely to You in Jesus name.
4. All the earth shall worship You and sing praises to You; They	**4.** May all the earth worship You, not out of compulsion but out of joy. May

shall sing praises to Your name." Selah

songs of praise of the Almighty God be heard in every corner of the earth.

5. Come and see the works of God; He is awesome in His doing toward the sons of men.

5. Let the remembrance of Your great and mighty deeds throughout all generations bring forth praise in Jesus name.

6. He turned the sea into dry land; They went through the river on foot. There we will rejoice in Him.

6. As You made a way in the sea for the people of Israel, I ask that You make a way for me through every obstruction that stands between me and my blessing. As I walk through the difficulties, praise and worship will flow out of my mouth in Jesus name.

7. He rules by His power forever; His eyes observe the nations; Do not let the rebellious exalt themselves. Selah

7. Thank You for You have been in charge of Your creation. Nothing happens without Your consent for Your eyes are over all nations. Your kingdom is forever. Rebels against Your kingdom are subdued forever in Jesus name.

8. Oh, bless our God, you peoples! And make the voice of His praise to be heard,

8. Help me praise You with all my heart. I bless You O God and my prayer is that I will continue to partake of Your goodness in Jesus name.

9. Who keeps our soul

9. I ask that You continue to

among the living, and does not allow our feet to be moved.

preserve my life. Do not let me fall to the delight of my enemies. My feet will not be moved from where You have planted me in Jesus name.

10. For You, O God, have tested us; You have refined us as silver is refined.

10. I ask that You see me through every trial and temptation that comes my way. I pray that You will remove every impurity in me and at the end of the day, I will be no different from refined silver.

11. You brought us into the net; You laid affliction on our backs.

11. I ask that You see through every affliction that comes my way for You have promised You will never leave me nor forsake me.

12. You have caused men to ride over our heads; We went through fire and through water; But You brought us out to rich fulfilment.

12. Thank You for You are with me through every trial and tribulation. I thank You for You have promised that my end will be better than my beginning. Thank You for enabling me enjoy times of refreshing in Your presence.

13. I will go into Your house with burnt offerings; I will pay You my vows,

14. Which my lips have uttered and my mouth has spoken when I was in trouble.

13-14. Lord for delivering me, I will bring sacrifices of praise continually to Your house. Help me pay my vows promptly in Jesus name.

15. I will offer You burnt sacrifices of fat animals, with the sweet aroma of rams; I will offer bulls with goats. Selah	**15.** Let every sacrifice I offer to You be acceptable to You in Jesus name.
16. Come and hear, all you who fear God, and I will declare what He has done for my soul.	**16.** Help me testify of everything that You have done for me. As I testify let all who hear of my testimony be drawn to You in Jesus name.
17. I cried to Him with my mouth, and He was extolled with my tongue.	**17.** Teach me how to pray effectively to You O God. Let my cry continually come unto You. Let my tongue speak of Your goodness and love to me at all times.
18. If I regard iniquity in my heart, The Lord will not hear.	**18.** Help me guard against iniquity in my heart. Please remind me of my sin so that I can repent of them immediately. I do not want sin to be a barrier to You answering my prayer.
19. But certainly God has heard me; He has attended to the voice of my prayer.	**19.** Thank You for Your faithfulness. Thank You for hearing and answering my prayers.
20. Blessed be God, who has not turned away my prayer, nor His mercy from me!	**20.** Thank You for extending Your mercy to me. I bless and magnify Your holy name.

Psalm 67 NKJV

The Psalm prays for blessings for the church and salvation for those who have not yet received the Saviour.

To the Chief Musician. On stringed instruments.
A Psalm. A Song.

BIBLE	PRAYER
1. God be merciful to us and bless us, and cause His face to shine upon us, Selah	**1.** I ask that You show Your children mercy, bless us with all Your promises which come out of Your love. I pray that Your grace and loving kindness will continue to abound towards us. Lord cause Your face to shine upon us, let us receive favour on a daily basis from You.
2. That Your way may be known on earth, Your salvation among all nations.	**2.** Let all You do for us draw men to the saving grace of the gospel of Jesus Christ. Help me spread the good news of the gospel with all my heart.
3. Let the peoples praise You, O God; Let all the peoples praise You.	**3.** As the gospel is preached and received let the people start to praise You.
4. Oh, let the nations be glad and sing for joy! For You shall judge the people righteously, and govern the nations on earth. Selah	**4.** Let gladness fill the hearts of the nations; Cause them to sing for joy in their salvation. You are a righteous judge and the nations will be better for it as they submit to Your autho-

rity.

5. Let the peoples praise You, O God; Let all the peoples praise You.
6. Then the earth shall yield her increase; God, our own God, shall bless us.
7. God shall bless us, and all the ends of the earth shall fear Him

5. Yes let there be continuous praise on the lips of Your people.
6. Thank You for the increase, thank You for the blessings.
7. Help us worship You with reverential fear.

Psalm 68 ESV

This is a Psalm of triumphant praise and jubilation. We are called to praise God for His greatness and foe His goodness.

To the choirmaster. A Psalm of David. A Song.

BIBLE

1. God shall arise, His enemies shall be scattered; and those who hate Him shall flee before Him!
2. As smoke is driven away, so You shall drive them away; as wax melts before fire, so the wicked shall perish before God!
3. But the righteous shall be glad; they shall exult before God; they shall be jubilant with joy!
4. Sing to God, sing praises to His name; lift up a song to Him who rides

PRAYER

1. Let Your enemies vanish into thin air, just as smoke disappears.
2. As You drive them away, let them melt just as wax melts in fire. Show up O Lord and at Your appearance let the wicked perish before You.
3. Let Your presence bring joy and gladness to my heart.
4. Out of my heart will I sing sweet songs to You. I pray O God that I will lift

through the deserts; His name is the Lord; exult before Him!

5. Father of the fatherless and protector of widows is God in His holy habitation.

6. God settles the solitary in a home; He leads out the prisoners to prosperity, but the rebellious dwell in a parched land.

7. O God, when You went out before Your people, when You marched through the wilderness, Selah

8. The earth quaked, the heavens poured down rain, before God, the One of Sinai, before God, the God of Israel.

9. Rain in abundance, O God, You shed abroad; You restored Your inheritance as it languished;

10. Your flock found a

You up and extol Your holy name.

5. Thank You my Lord because You are the Father to the Fatherless. It is Your nature to stand up for the widow.

6. Thank You for raising families whose foundations are in You, the bound and the oppressed are delivered by You. All who rebel against Your name will be desolate in Jesus name. Thank You for what you did in the past leading the people out of bondage.

7. You are the same God; I thank You for going before me and leading me through the wilderness.

8. I pray Lord as the earth shook in the days of old, let the world today stand still at Your presence.

9. Let there be a rain of the Holy Spirit on the world this day, giving strength to the weary and turning our hearts back to You. Thank You for divine provision at all times.

10. Thank You Lord for Your

	dwelling in it; in Your goodness, O God, You provided for the needy.		mercies towards us, You enable the poor to partake of Your goodness.
11.	The Lord gives the word; the women who announce the news are a great host:	11.	You have given the word, enable me to preach the good news at all times and to all people. I pray that as the good news spreads, all who have been bound by the kingdom of darkness will be loosed into the marvellous light of God.
12.	"The kings of the armies—they flee, they flee!" The women at home divide the spoil—	12.	As the enemies flee, let all Your children enjoy every promise You have given through Your word in Jesus name.
13.	Though you men lie among the sheepfolds—the wings of a dove covered with silver, its pinions with shimmering gold.	13.	I pray that as I reign in victory the glory of God will rest upon me.
14.	When the Almighty scatters kings there, let snow fall on Zalmon.	14.	The reign of evil must come to an end as the Almighty scatters the kings
15.	O mountain of God, mountain of Bashan; O many-peaked mountain, mountain of Bashan!	15.	I pray that the church worldwide shall be known as the hill where God is permanently resident.
16.	Why do you look with hatred, O many-peaked mountain, at the mount that God desired for His	16.	I pray that arrogance and pride in self-achievement will come to an end within the body of Christ.

abode, yes, where the Lord will dwell forever?

17. The chariots of God are twice ten thousand, thousands upon thousands; the Lord is among them; Sinai is now in the sanctuary.

18. You ascended on high, leading a host of captives in Your train and receiving gifts amo- ng men, even among the rebellious, that the Lord God may dwell there.

19. Blessed be the Lord, who daily bears us up; God is our salvation. Selah

20. Our God is a God of salvation, and to God, the Lord, belong deliverances from death.

21. But God will strike the heads of His enemies, the hairy crown of him who walks in his guilty ways.

22. The Lord said, "I will bring them back from

17. You are the winner of all battles; the Commander in chief of the heavenly hosts and You have at your service thousands and thousands of thousands of chariots and angels.

18. You ascended on high, thank You because what held Your children captive has now been arrested and is now held permanently captive in Jesus name. Thank You for victory over the enemy, Your name is glorified.

19. I bless You my Lord and my God, I appreciate the daily blessings, physical and spiritual that You load me with.

20. You are my God, thank You for giving me salvation, delivering me from the clutches of the evil one.

21. Thank You Lord for breaking, destroying and bruising the head of the enemy, his schemes and designs against me in Jesus name.

22. Thank You as You bring me up from the depths

Bashan, I will bring them back from the depths of the sea,

23. That you may strike your feet in their blood, that the tongues of your dogs may have their portion from the foe."

24. Your procession is seen, O God, the procession of my God, my King, into the sanctuary—

25. The singers in front, the musicians last, between them virgins playing tambourines:

26. "Bless God in the great congregation, the Lord, O you who are of Israel's fountain!"

27. There is Benjamin, the least of them, in the lead, the princes of Judah in their throng, the princes of Zebulun, the princes of Naphtali.

28. Summon Your power, O God, the power, O God, by which You have worked for us.

29. Because of Your temple

that the enemy me to.

23. I will walk in victory and all will know that my Lord has done great things for me.

24. I pray that the whole world will give You glory for what You have done, what You are doing and what You will do.

25. Let the joy in the messa-ge of salvation lead to singing and dancing by Your children in Jesus name.

26. We proclaim You are God forever. You are great and greatly to be praised. I join hands with all from the seed of Abraham to bow before You and declare You are God Almighty. Jehovah El Gibbo

27. Let the big and the small, poor and rich, old and young join hands together in worship and adoration of Your holy name.

28. Thank You for fighting for Your children. Thank You for strength to tarry in the place of prayer.

29. Incline my heart never to

	Scripture		Prayer
	at Jerusalem kings shall bear gifts to You.		forget the source of my blessings. Let my gifts be acceptable in Your sight in Jesus name.
30.	Rebuke the beasts that dwell among the reeds, the herd of bulls with the calves of the peoples. Trample underfoot those who lust after tribute; scatter the peoples who delight in war.	**30.**	I rebuke every agent of the devil on assignment against me. Let them come to their senses and repent of the evil being done against Your kingdom here on earth.
31.	Nobles shall come from Egypt; Cush shall hasten to stretch out her hands to God.	**31.**	Let every nation that is opposed to the preaching of the gospel of Jesus Christ suddenly surrender in Jesus name.
32.	O kingdoms of the earth, sing to God; sing praises to the Lord, Selah	**32.**	I bless You my LORD and my God, creator of heaven and earth. Be magnified in the heavens, be magnified here on earth.
33.	To Him who rides in the heavens, the ancient heavens; behold, He sends out His voice, His mighty voice.	**33.**	As You reign in heaven, may Your voice continue to be heard here on earth. May all be drawn by the mercy and the love that is on offer from You.
34.	Ascribe power to God, whose majesty is over Israel, and whose power is in the	**34.**	I ask for grace and strength to continue spreading the good news of Jesus Christ to all I come into contact with.
35.	Awesome is God from	**35.**	Let Your glory continue

His sanctuary; the God of Israel—He is the one who gives power and strength to His people. Blessed be God!	to stir the hearts of men into Your presence. Let Your presence give strength to Your children. Let us all experience Your power in Jesus name.

Psalm 69 NASB

The Psalm is a deep call for deliverance by God and joy at God's answer to prayer.

For the choir director; according to Shoshannim.
A Psalm of David.

BIBLE	**PRAYER**
1. Save me, O God, for the waters have threatened my life.	**1.** I am deeply troubled. You are the only one who can come to my rescue. Save me O God.
2. I have sunk in deep mire, and there is no foothold; I have come into deep waters, and a flood overflows me.	**2.** Help me for I am sinking under the weight of the troubles afflicting me.
3. I am weary with my crying; my throat is parched; Myeyes fail while I wait for my God.	**3.** Help me stand firm not giving up. Give me the strength to pray through till You answer me.
4. Those who hate me without a cause are more than the hairs of my head; Those who would destroy me are powerful, being wrongfully my enemies; What I did not steal, I then have	**4.** I am surrounded by people who hate me for no reason. Make me conscious of my actions so I will not do wrong to my neighbours.

to restore.

5. O God, it is You who knows my folly, and my wrongs are not hidden from You.

6. May those who wait for You not be ashamed through me, O Lord God of hosts; May those who seek You not be disoured through me, O God of Israel,

7. Because for Your sake I have borne reproach; Dishonour has covered my face.

8. I have become estranged from my brothers and an alien to my mother's sons.

9. For zeal for Your house has consumed me, and the reproaches of those who reproach You have fallen on me.

10. When I wept in my soul with fasting, It became my reproach.

11. When I made sackcloth my clothing, I became a byword to them.

12. Those who sit in the gate talk about me, and I am the song of the drunkards.

13. But as for me, my prayer

5. I confess every sin before You, for there is nothing I can hide from You.

6. Lord I ask that You answer me so that I will not be put to shame. Do not let anyone be discouraged as we wait on You.

7. I ask that You roll away every reproach that I am suffering at this present time.

8. Friends and family are ashamed of me. May I never be ashamed of my relationship with Jesus Christ our saviour.

9. I pray I am consumed by zeal for everything that relates to things of God.

10-11. Give me a heart that will delight in fasting and praying. As I do so, let my actions encourage people rather than attract those who will despise me.

12. I plead the blood of Jesus Christ against every gang up and discussion against me.

13. Let the spirit of prayer

is to You, O Lord, at an acceptable time; O God, in the greatness of Your lovingkindness, answer me with Your saving truth.

14. Deliver me from the mire and do not let me sink; May I be delivered from my foes and from the deep waters.

15. May the flood of water not overflow me nor the deep swallow me up, nor the pit shut its mouth on me.

16. Answer me, O Lord, for Your lovingkindness is good; According to the greatness of Your compassion, turn to me,

17. And do not hide Your face from Your servant, for I am in distress; answer me quickly.

18. Oh draw near to my soul and redeem it; Ransom me because of my enemies!

19. You know my reproach and my shame and my dishonour; All my adversaries are before You.

20. Reproach has broken my heart and I am so sick. And I looked for sympathy, but there was

rest upon me. In Your mercy answer me speedily.

14. Deliver me from the hands of my enemies. Do not let my situation get worse before You deliver me my Lord.

15. Have mercy on me; do not let me drown in my sorrows. Rescue me from the depths that I find myself in today.

16. From my heart I appeal to You; answer me out of Your lovingkindness.

17-18. Show up Lord for I am in trouble. Do not turn away from me now, for my case is very urgent.

19. Lord of all, You are everywhere and You know everything. That is why I ask that You intervene now I pray.

20. Men have disappointed as they always do. You are my comforter and helper of the helpless.

none, and for comforters, but I found none.	Show me compassion I pray.
21. They also gave me gall for my food and for my thirst they gave me vinegar to drink.	**21.** My enemies continue trying to worsen my situation. Let all their efforts come to nothing in Jesus name.
22. May their table before them become a snare; And when they are in peace, may it become a trap.	**22.** Let every snare laid for me trap whosoever laid them. As my enemies have tried to take away my peace, I pray that whatever they have planned for enjoyment should turn into misery.
23. May their eyes grow dim so that they cannot see, and make their loins shake continually.	**23.** Let blindness fall on them such that they see me no more. Let them tremble in fear from this moment until judgement comes upon them.
24. Pour out Your indigination on them, and may Your burning anger overtake them.	**24.** Let Your anger swallow them so they do not escape Your judgement here and now O Lord.
25. May their camp be desolate; May none dwell in their tents.	**25.** Let their homes become wasteland and become uninhabitable. Let ruin come upon them.
26. For they have persecuted him whom You yourself have smitten, and they tell of the pain of those whom You have wounded.	**26-27.** As they are enemies of the gospel of Jesus Christ, add punishment to their punishment. They have chosen the way of unrighteousness, let righteousness be far away from them in Jesus name.
27. Add iniquity to their iniquity, and may they not come into Your	

	righteousness.		
28.	May they be blotted out of the book of life and may they not be recorded with the righteous.	**28.**	As their continued existence damages Your children and the gospel, let them all be wiped out.
29.	But I am afflicted and in pain; May Your salvation, O God, set me securely on high.	**29.**	I pray that You will lift me on high far above where principalities and powers can touch me in Jesus name.
30.	I will praise the name of God with song and magnify Him with thanksgiving.	**30.**	Thank You for answered prayers. I will praise You in word and song. Help me as I magnify Your name here on earth.
31.	And it will please the Lord better than an ox or a young bull with horns and hoofs.	**31.**	Let my sacrifice of praise be acceptable to You in Jesus name.
32.	The humble have seen it and are glad; You who seek God, let your heart revive.	**32.**	Help me testify of Your lovingkindness and faithfulness to all I come into contact with. Let my testimony cause men to seek You with all their heart in Jesus name.
33.	For the Lord hears the needy and does not despise His who are prisoners.	**33.**	Thank You Father for You are the defender of the defenceless.
34.	Let heaven and earth praise Him, the seas and everything that moves in them.	**34.**	Let the earth be filled with praise of who You are. Let my praise join with the hosts of heaven in adoration always.
35.	For God will save Zion and build the cities of Judah, that they may	**35.**	I pray that You will keep the church away from the clutches of the evil

dwell there and possess it.	one and every promise You have given in Jesus will come to pass.
36. The descendants of His servants will inherit it, and those who love His name will dwell in it.	**36.** Help me love You with all my soul, spirit and body. Let me enjoy all the benefits of being a joint heir with Jesus Christ.

Psalm 70 NKJV

The Psalm is a desperate cry for help and a request that God should shame the enemy.

To the Chief Musician.

A Psalm of David. To bring to remembrance.

BIBLE	**PRAYER**
1. Make haste, O God, to deliver me! Make haste to help me, O Lord!	**1.** I need Your help urgently Lord. Do not tarry; deliver me now I ask with a contrite heart. I have no other help but You.
2. Let them be ashamed and confounded who seek my life; Let them be turned back and confused who desire my hurt.	**2.** I ask that You deliver me now so all who seek my failure are put to shame. Let my deliverance put confusion in their midst as they ask where is my God?
3. Let them be turned back because of their shame, who say, "Aha, aha!"	**3.** Let all who rejoice at my situation be put to shame.
4. Let all those who seek You rejoice and be glad in You; And let those who love Your salvation say	**4.** Reward all who diligently seek You. Let all who appreciate what You have done for them

continually, "Let God be magnified!"

5. But I am poor and needy; Make haste to me, O God! You are my help and my deliverer; O Lord, do not delay.

worship You.

5. I need You my Father. Thank You for hastening unto me, for helping me and delivering me.

Psalm 71 ESV

The Psalm is a prayer of the faithful for help against enemies and a request for blessings and protection from the righteous God.

BIBLE

1. In You, O Lord, do I take refuge; let me never be put to shame!

2. In Your righteousness deliver me and rescue me; incline Your ear to me, and save me!

3. Be to me a rock of refuge, to which I may continually come; You have given the comm-

PRAYER

1. Lord I put my trust in You, and as I do so give me a greater understanding of You as the all sufficient God. Let me never be put to shame or confused as I trust You O God.

2. Be true to Your word for You are righteous. Make a way of escape for me out of the dangers that I am facing. Attend to my prayers speedily. I ask that You save me from the afflictions from the wicked that surround me.

3. Let me find rest in You. Let the doors be open to me so I can be protected from my enemies. Let

	and to save me, for You are my rock and my fortress.		the hosts of heaven be alert to save me from every evil plan of the enemy. Thank You for You are my rock and my fortress. In You Lord my security is complete.
4.	Rescue me, O my God, from the hand of the wicked, from the grasp of the unjust and cruel man.	**4.**	Deliver me out of the hands of the wicked. Do not allow them to defeat me.
5.	For You, O Lord, are my hope, my trust, O Lord, from my youth.	**5.**	I have trusted You from the beginning and my hopes have never been dashed.
6.	Upon You I have leaned from before my birth; You are He who took me from my mother's womb. My praise is continually of You.	**6.**	I will praise You forever because You have been responsible for me from my mother's womb.
7.	I have been as a portent to many, but You are my strong refuge.	**7.**	Let me continue to be a wonder. Lord let me succeed where others are failing. Lord give me victory against all the wiles of the devil. Thank You for You continue to shield and protect me.
8.	My mouth is filled with Your praise, and with Your glory all the day.	**8.**	Give me a grateful heart. Let my mouth be filled with praise at all times.
9.	Do not cast me off in the time of old age; forsake me not when my strength is spent.	**9.**	Lord I pray that You will never leave me nor forsake me as long as I live in Jesus name.
10.	For my enemies speak	**10.**	Let all who gang up to

concerning me; those who watch for my life consult together	speak against me be scattered by fire in Jesus name.
11. And say, "God has forsaken him; pursue and seize him, for there is none to deliver him."	**11.** I nullify every falsehood peddled against me with the blood of Jesus.
12. O God, be not far from me; O my God, make haste to help me!	**12.** Your presence at all times is my security. I ask in the name of Jesus Christ that You should not be far away from me.
13. May my accusers be put to shame and consumed; with scorn and disgrace may they be covered who seek my hurt.	**13.** Let all who do not wish me well be destroyed by the fire of the Holy Ghost. Let shame and dishonour follow them for the rest of their lives.
14. But I will hope continually and will praise You yet more and more.	**14.** Let me continue to hope that You will come good as You have always done all the days of my life.
15. My mouth will tell of Your righteous acts, of Your deeds of salvation all the day, for their number is past my knowledge.	**15.** Help me testify to all of Your righteousness. Let the price Jesus Christ paid for my salvation not be in vain.
16. With the mighty deeds of the Lord God I will come; I will remind them of Your righteousness, Yours alone.	**16.** Grant me the strength to complete every assignment that You give me.
17. O God, from my youth You have taught me, and I still proclaim Your wondrous deeds.	**17.** I thank You for using every opportunity to teach me Your precepts. Help me so I do not depart from Your teach-

18. So even to old age and grey hairs, O God, do not forsake me, until I proclaim Your might to another generation, Your power to all those to come.

19. Your righteousness, O God, reaches the high heavens. You who have done great things, O God, who is like You?

20. You who have made me see many troubles and calamities will revive me again; from the depths of the earth You will bring me up again.

21. You will increase my greatness and comfort me again.

22. I will also praise You with the harp for Your faithfulness, O my God; I will sing praises to You with the lyre, O Holy One of Israel.

23. My lips will shout for joy, when I sing praises to

ings. Let declaring Your wonders in my life become part and parcel of my life.

18. Help me pass on my knowledge to the younger generation for Your name to be glorified.

19. My Lord, You define what righteousness is. From the beginning of time You have done great and mighty things. I give You praise.

20. Father You have promised me that You will not allow me to be tempted with what I cannot bear. I ask that You deliver me from every affliction that confronts me.

21. I ask that You increase me on every side. Let me manifest Your power and bring glory to You. I pray You will envelope me with comfort at all times.

22-23. Let my heart be filled with praise of Your goodness and loving kindness to me.

You; my soul also, which You have redeemed.

24. And my tongue will talk of Your righteous help all the day long, for they have been put to shame and disappointed who sought to do me hurt.

24. All who seek my hurt; I pray will be put to shame permanently in Jesus name.

Psalm 72 ESV

The Psalm acknowledges the coming reign of the Messiah and all shall bow before Him.
Of Solomon.

BIBLE

1. Give the king Your justice, O God, and Your righteousness to the royal son!

2. May he judge Your people with righteousness, and Your poor with justice!

3. Let the mountains bear prosperity for the people, and the hills, in righteousness!

4. May he defend the cause of the poor of the people, give deliverance to the children of the needy, and crush the oppressor!

PRAYER

1. ALMIGHTY GOD I ask that You grant all who are In authority the grace and wisdom to be godly rulers.

2. I pray that all rulers rule with a sense of justice and righteousness.

3. I pray for peace and prosperity for all people of God all over the world.

4. I ask that You give the rulers hearts that make decisions that will help the poor and needy. I ask that You make heads of government stand on the side of the people, while breaking and dest-

5. May they fear You while the sun endures, and as long as the moon, throughout all generaations!
6. May he be like rain that falls on the mown grass, like showers that water the earth!
7. In his days may the righteous flourish, and peace abound, till the moon be no more!
8. May He have dominion from sea to sea, and from the River to the ends of the earth!
9. May desert tribes bow down before Him, and His enemies lick the dust!
10. May the kings of Tarshish and of the coastlands render Him tribute; may the kings of Sheba and Seba bring gifts!
11. May all kings fall down before Him, all nations serve Him!
12. For He delivers the needy when he calls, the poor and him who has no helper.

roying all who oppress the people.

5. The fear of God shall rule the hearts of rulers for ever I pray in Jesus name.
6. I pray that my country shall enjoy unending fruitfulness in Jesus name.
7. Let the righteous flourish; do not let the wicked ask where their God is? Let Your peace reign in all the earth I pray.
8. Lord I pray that Jesus shall rule over all the earth.
9. As the Lordship of Jesus Christ is established all over the world the kingdom of satan shall be completely subugated in Jesus name.

10-11. All nations shall worship and adore the Messiah in Jesus name.

12. The Messiah shall answer when the poor and the needy call on Him, for He is a refuge

for all who run to Him.

13. He has pity on the weak and the needy, and saves the lives of the needy.

13. Out of Your compassion have mercy on all poor and needy. I pray that Your free gift of salvation will be accepted by all who are not yet saved.

14. From oppression and violence He redeems their life, and precious is their blood in His sight.

14. Thank You Lord for You have already paid the supreme price for all mankind. I know that You continue to go the extra mile for the soul of everyone who is in danger from the plans of the enemy.

15. Long may He live; may gold of Sheba be given to Him! May prayer be made for Him continually, and blessings invoked for Him all the day!

15. I pray that the gospel of Jesus Christ shall extend to the ends of the earth speedily.

16. May there be abundance of grain in the land; on the tops of the mountains may it wave; may its fruit be like Lebanon; and may people blossom in the cities like the grass of the field!

16. As we enjoy the reign of the Messiah, we shall live in plenty and we shall be satisfied. The church of God shall experience growth in Jesus name.

17. May His name endure forever, His fame continue as long as the sun! May people be blessed in Him, all nations call Him blessed!

17. In Jesus shall all nations of the earth be blessed. Let it be so, as You have spoken O God.

18. Blessed be the Lord, the God of Israel, who alone

18. Thank You God for the great and mighty things

does wondrous things.

19. Blessed be His glorious name forever; may the whole earth be filled with His glory! Amen and Amen!

20. The prayers of David, the son of Jesse, are ended.

You have done and all that You will continue to do.

19-20. Lord I pray that the whole earth will behold Your glory and dwell in it in Jesus name.

BOOK 3

Psalm 73 NASB

The Psalm shows how to deal with the inner conflict we sometimes have; the prosperity of the ungodly compared to the seeming suffering of the righteous.

A Psalm of Asaph.

BIBLE	PRAYER
1. Surely God is good to Israel, to those who are pure in heart!	**1.** Thank You God for You are good to me. Let Your blood purify my heart so that I will see You at all times.
2. But as for me, my feet came close to stumbling, my steps had almost slipped.	**2.** I have nearly given up on my faith. I ask that You uphold me so that I do not fall.
3. For I was envious of the arrogant as I saw the prosperity of the wicked.	**3.** Take the spirit of envy away from me. Help me continue to trust Your faithfulness even when doubt tries to seep into me.
4. For there are no pains in their death, and their body is fat. **5.** They are not in trouble as other men, nor are they plagued like mankind.	**4-5.** The unbeliever looks healthy even in old age. Life rolls on for them without any obvious challenges. I pray that Your promise of abundant life in Christ Jesus will come to pass in my life in Jesus name.
6. Therefore pride is their necklace; The garment of violence covers them.	**6.** I pray Father that the spirit of pride dies completely in me in Jesus

	name. I pray for a heart that will love my neighbour rather than violence of any kind towards them in Jesus name.
7. Their eye bulges from fatness; The imaginations of their heart run riot.	**7.** Let lust and desire for things of the world not overwhelm me.
8. They mock and wickedly speak of oppression; They speak from on high.	**8.** Let every malicious word spoken against me fall to the ground in Jesus name.
9. They have set their mouth against the heavens, and their tongue parades through the earth.	**9.** Let all who deny that You are Almighty feel the brunt of Your name. I condemn every tongue that rises against me in Jesus name.
10. Therefore His people return to this place, and waters of abundance are drunk by them.	**10.** With Your help I will not turn away from You because of the prosperity of the wicked.
11. They say, "How does God know? And is there knowledge with the Most High?"	**11.** It is foolishness to think anything can be hidden from You. Let the spirit of the fear of God dwell in me.
12. Behold, these are the wicked; And always at ease, they have increased in wealth. **13.** Surely in vain I have kept my heart pure and washed my hands in innocence;	**12-13.** Despite the prosperity of the wicked, help me maintain purity and righteousness in Jesus name. I ask for forgiveness of my sins and I pray You'll help me turn away completely from them all.

	Psalm		Prayer
14.	For I have been stricken all day long and chastened every morning.	**14.**	Grant me the grace to receive Your rebuke with joy knowing it is out of Your love for me.
15.	If I had said, "I will speak thus," Behold, I would have betrayed the generation of Your children.	**15.**	Help me think of the impact of what I want to say before I open my mouth.
16.	When I pondered to understand this, It was troublesome in my sight	**16.**	Help me understand how the wicked can prosper and the righteous struggle considering that You are the God of heaven and the earth.
17.	Until I came into the sanctuary of God; Then I perceived their end.	**17.**	Let my heart seek You every time I need answers to the questions that trouble me. Open my heart to know that the wicked are assured of an evil end.
18.	Surely You set them in slippery places; You cast them down to destruction.	**18.**	Let all the wicked fall to their ruin speedily in Jesus name.
19.	How they are destroyed in a moment! They are utterly swept away by sudden terrors!	**19.**	Let the wicked and all that concerns them be destroyed suddenly. Let them be enveloped by the terror they have previously unleashed on Your children.
20.	Like a dream when one awakes, O Lord, when aroused, You will despise their form.	**20.**	Arise O Lord, let all who despise You and Your works be scattered and forgotten.
21.	When my heart was	**21.**	It is foolishness of me to

	embittered and I was pierced within,		be bitter and angry with You. I pray my heart will be right with You in Jesus name.
22.	Then I was senseless and ignorant; I was like a beast before You.	**22.**	Help me spend time developing my relationship with You so I no longer live in ignorance.
23.	Nevertheless I am continually with You; You have taken hold of my right hand.	**23.**	Thank You because You have promised You will not leave me nor forsake me. You are the great shepherd; I ask that You lead me all the days of my life to my destiny in Jesus name.
24.	With Your counsel You will guide me, and afterward receive me to glory.	**24.**	As I commit my life into Your mighty hands, I ask for guidance in every area of my life. My aim in life is to make heaven. Let it be so in Jesus name.
25.	Whom have I in heaven but You? And besides You, I desire nothing on earth.	**25.**	I thank You because You have made me realise that I have no reason to envy anyone. Thank You again for being my all in all.
26.	My flesh and my heart may fail, but God is the strength of my heart and my portion forever.	**26.**	As I am human, I know that I might fail You sometimes; I ask that You uphold me for I have no power of my own. Lord You are my rock forever.
27.	For, behold, those who are far from You will	**27.**	Lord I ask that You draw me close to You for

perish; You have destroyed all those who are unfaithful to You.	distance from You leads to death. Help me to be faithful to You for I do not want to fall into the punishment reserved for the wicked.
28. But as for me, the nearness of God is my good; I have made the Lord God my refuge, That I may tell of all Your works.	**28.** Let Your grace draw me near to You. I want You to be my shield and my resting place. Help me testify of Your works for Your name to be glorified. Halleluiah

Psalm 74 ESV

This is an instructional Psalm for how to respond to God in times of trouble.
A Maskil of Asaph.

BIBLE	PRAYER
1. O God, why do You cast us off forever? Why does Your anger smoke against the sheep of Your pasture?	**1.** Lord have mercy on me. Let Your anger against me subside. Do not cast me out of Your presence.
2. Remember Your congregation, which You have purchased of old, which You have redeemed to be the tribe of Your heritage! Remember Mount Zion, where You have dwelt.	**2.** Thank You for purchasing me with the life of Your Son, Jesus Christ.
3. Direct Your steps to the perpetual ruins; the enemy has destroyed	**3.** The wicked continue to trample on the church. Arise quickly to the

Scripture	Prayer
everything in the sanctuary!	defence of the church worldwide.
4. Your foes have roared in the midst of Your meeting place; they set up their own signs for signs.	**4.** Help me identify quickly every enemy within my environment. Let every evil banner from the enemy be burned in Jesus name.
5. They were like those who swing axes in a forest of trees. **6.** And all its carved wood they broke down with hatchets and hammers	**5-6.** Let every builder turned destroyer, every supporter turned enemy be frustrated by Your mighty hand in Jesus name.
7. They set Your sanctuary on fire; they profaned the dwelling place of Your name, bringing it down to the ground. **8.** They said to themselves, "We will utterly subdue them"; they burned all the meeting places of God in the land.	**7-8.** Help Your church survive every fire from the agents of darkness meant to stop saints gathering together to worship You. Let their plans come to nothing in Jesus name. We return every arrow of fire back to where it has come from in Jesus name.
9. We do not see our signs; there is no longer any prophet, and there is none among us who knows how long.	**9.** Open my inner eyes and eyes to see and hear You. Let there be a connection between me and You and between ordained men of God and You. Let there be a hunger and fire inside me to seek and find You.
10. How long, O God, is the foe to scoff? Is the enemy to revile Your name forever?	**10.** Let every form of reproach and blasphemy from the enemy come to an end. Let shame be

poured upon the enemy and his agents. My Lord, let Your name be exalted in all the earth in Jesus name.

11. Why do you hold back Your hand, Your right hand? Take it from the fold of Your garment and destroy them!

11. Dear Lord do not withdraw Your mighty hand any longer. Show Your power and con- sume all Your enemies.

12. Yet God my King is from of old, working salvation in the midst of the earth.

12. From the beginning of time You have been God and You do not change. In times past You have delivered Your people including me from many adversaries.

13. You divided the sea by Your might; You broke the heads of the sea monsters on the waters.

13. As You divided the Red sea by Your power, let every barrier before me give way now in Jesus name. Let all who chase after me perish as Pharaoh and his armies perished by Your power.

14. You crushed the heads of Leviathan; You gave him as food for the creatures of the wilderness.

14. Just as You crushed the heads of Leviathan, let the heads of every enemy be crushed. Let them be food for one another in their wilder- ness.

15. You split open springs and brooks; You dried up ever-flowing streams.

15. Thank You for the miracles of the past, for they increased our faith. You are more than able to deliver Your people from oppression in Jesus name.

16. Yours is the day, Yours also the night; You have established the heavenly lights and the sun.

17. You have fixed all the boundaries of the earth; You have made summer and winter.

18. Remember this, O Lord, how the enemy scoffs, and a foolish people reviles Your name.

19. Do not deliver the soul of Your dove to the wild beasts; do not forget the life of Your poor forever.

20. Have regard for the covenant, for the dark places of the land are full of the habitations of violence.

21. Let not the downtrodden turn back in shame; let the poor and needy praise Your name.

22. Arise, O God, defend Your cause; remember how the foolish scoff at You all the day!

23. Do not forget the clamour of Your foes, the uproar of those who rise against You, which goes up continually!

16-17. We praise You for Your works of creation. All You did is still evident today. Glory be to Your name.

18. Remember how the foolish continue to despise Your holy name. Arise speedily for Your name to be glorified.

19. Do not let the life of Your children be snuffed out by the wicked. Deliver us all from the evil one for we can't help ourselves.

20. You are the covenant keeping God. I ask that You do not allow the w wickedness of the wicked to destroy Your children.

21. By Your power I know I will not be ashamed. In my deliverance let Your praise continually fill my mouth in Jesus name.

22-23. Arise O God and let Your enemy be scattered. Let their voices be silenced forever.

Psalm 75 AMP

This is a Psalm of judgement.

To the Chief Musician; [set to the tune of] "Do Not Destroy."

A Psalm of Asaph. A song.

BIBLE

1. We give praise and thanks to You, O God, we praise and give thanks; Your wondrous works declare that Your Name is near and they who invoke Your Name rehearse Your wonders.
2. When the proper time has come [for executing My judgments], I will judge uprightly [says the Lord].
3. When the earth totters, and all the inhabitants of it, it is I Who will poise and keep steady its pillars. Selah [pause, and calmly think of that]!
4. I said to the arrogant and boastful, Deal not arrogantly [do not boast]; and to the wicked, Lift not up the horn [of personal aggrandizement].
5. Lift not up your [aggressive] horn on high, speak not with a stiff

PRAYER

1. Thank You for the great and mighty things You have done for me. Thank You because the things You have done indicate to me and the whole world that You are indeed Almighty.
2. Whenever I have to pass judgement help me judge uprightly, give me the amount of wisdom that will do me well.
3. Lord I ask that You uphold the world, do not let the earth disintegrate, we have no powers of our own.
4. All You have put in my hands, I ask that You help me administer effectively in Jesus name. Give me the wisdom to correct people when they do wrong.
5. I ask that You take away every form of pride and arrogance from my life

neck and insolent arrogance.

helping me to understand that all power belongs to You. No man can lift me up.

6. For not from the east nor from the west nor from the south come promotion and lifting up.

6. Lord I ask that You favour me and set me on high in Jesus name.

7. But God is the Judge! He puts down one and lifts up another.

7. Help me so I will not do anything that will attract Your wrath.

8. For in the hand of the Lord there is a cup [of His wrath], and the wine foams and is red, well mixed; and He pours out from it, and all the wicked of the earth must drain it and drink its dregs.

8. By Your grace I will not partake of the drink of the wicked.

9. But I will declare and rejoice forever; I will sing praises to the God of Jacob.

9. Help me praise You forever.

10. All the horns of the ungodly also will I cut off [says the Lord], but the horns of the [uncompromisingly] righteous shall be exalted.

10. Let every symbol of the wicked be destroyed totally in the name of Jesus even as You exalt the strength of Your children in Jesus name.

Psalm 76 NASB

This Psalm shows us who God is, what He can do and how He can deliver us.

For the choir director; on stringed instruments.

A Psalm of Asaph, a Song.

BIBLE	**PRAYER**
1. God is known in Judah; His name is great in Israel.	**1.** You are great in my life and in the whole world. I know You Lord, but I want to know You more.
2. His tabernacle is in Salem; His dwelling place also is in Zion.	**2.** I invite You to come and dwell in my heart.
3. There He broke the flaming arrows, the shield and the sword and the weapons of war. Selah.	**3.** Lord destroy the defences of my enemies; take away the weapons they use against me.
4. You are resplendent, more majestic than the mountains of prey.	**4.** Let Your light overshadow and destroy the defences of my enemies
5. The stout hearted were plundered, they sank into sleep; And none of the warriors could use his hands.	**5.** Release the hosts of heaven to fight on my behalf. Let my attackers sleep the sleep of death. Let all they have plundered be restored unto me in Jesus name.
6. At Your rebuke, O God of Jacob, both rider and horse were cast into a dead sleep.	**6.** Render the weapons being used against me dead on arrival O God.
7. You, even You, are to be feared; And who may stand in Your presence when once You are angry?	**7.** Let me have a reverential fear of You. I ask that You show Your power, put fear in the heart of all my enemies.

8. You caused judgment to be heard from heaven; The earth feared and was still	**8.** Let my enemies hear Your voice from heaven, stop them in their tracks, bring judgement on them all, I ask in Jesus name.
9. When God arose to judgment, to save all the humble of the earth. Selah.	**9.** Arise O Lord, save me from my enemies.
10. For the wrath of man shall praise You; With a remnant of wrath You will gird Yourself.	**10.** The destruction of my enemies shall bring praise to Your name.
11. Make vows to the Lord your God and fulfil them; Let all who are around Him bring gifts to Him who is to be feared.	**11.** Help me meet all my vows to You. I pray that all who worship You will have it in their hearts to bring good gifts to You.
12. He will cut off the spirit of princes; He is feared by the kings of the earth	**12.** Thank You for cutting off the wicked and bringing all their plans to nothing

Psalm 77 ESV

The Psalmist is in trouble which causes him to doubt God. His spirit causes him to remember the numerous wonders God has done in the past. This leads him to question – has God forgotten me?

To the choirmaster: according to Jeduthun. A Psalm of Asaph.

BIBLE	PRAYER
1. I cry aloud to God, aloud to God, and He will hear me.	**1.** I cry to You my God with all my heart, hear me, and send Your angels to deliver me.
2. In the day of my trouble I	**2.** The troubles are unend-

seek the Lord; in the night my hand is stretched out without wearying; my soul refuses to be comforted.

ding. Come to my rescue, help me my Lord. Different thoughts fill my mind. You are the God of peace. Give me peace.

3. When I remember God, I moan; when I meditate, my spirit faints. Selah

3. Help me for I have been ungrateful. Have mercy on me. I have allowed the troubles of the day to cloud my mind.

4. You hold my eyelids open; I am so troubled that I cannot speak.

4. Thank You for keeping me awake to pray even though I am finding it difficult to say anything. I need help Lord.

5. I consider the days of old, the years long ago.

5. Help me remember who You are and what You have done, Ancient of days.

6. I said, "Let me remember my song in the night; let me meditate in my heart." Then my spirit made a diligent search:

6. Put songs of praise and worship in my heart so I can use them during the nights and day too.

7. "Will the Lord spurn forever, and never again be favourable?

7. Help me put away doubts from my mind. I ask that You show me favour O Lord.

8. Has His steadfast love forever ceased? Are His promises at an end for all time?

8. Lord Your mercies have never failed and Your promises are forever. Let all Your promises to me come to pass.

9. Has God forgotten to be gracious? Has He in anger shut up His compassion?" Selah

9. Do not be angry with me. I ask that You be gracious and merciful unto me.

10.	Then I said, "I will appeal to this, to the years of the right hand of the Most High."	**10.**	Have mercy on me. I have sinned because I doubted You. Let my heart remember the great and mighty things You have done in the past.
11.	I will remember the deeds of the Lord; yes, I will remember Your wonders of old.	**11.**	Help me focus on You. Let me remember all You have done from time immemorial.
12.	I will ponder all Your work, and meditate on Your mighty deeds.	**12.**	Teach me how to meditate on Your words. Help me obey You by talking to people about You and Your Son Jesus Christ.
13.	Your way, O God, is holy. What god is great like our God?	**13.**	Teach me how to know Your ways so I will not be far from You. There is none that can be compared to You. Let Your name be glorified.
14.	You are the God who works wonders; You have made known Your might among the peoples.	**14.**	You are wonderful and powerful. I ask that You do wonders in my life. Let there be a manifestation of Your power in my life.
15.	You with Your arm redeemed Your people, the children of Jacob and Joseph. Selah	**15.**	Thank You for redeeming me from the law of sin and death. I also ask that You deliver me from everything that is holding me down.
16.	When the waters saw You, O God, when the waters saw You, they	**16-18.**	Let every barrier before me give way in Jesus name. Speak into my life

were afraid; indeed, the deep trembled.

17. The clouds poured out water; the skies gave forth thunder; Your arrows flashed on every side.

18. The crash of Your thunder was in the whirlwind; Your lightnings lighted up the world; the earth trembled and shook.

19. Your way was through the sea, Your path through the great waters; yet Your footprints were unseen.

20. You led Your people like a flock by the hand of Moses and Aaron.

O God and as You do so, let Your voice sound like thunder in the ears of the agents of the enemy. Let my enemy shake and tremble in Jesus name. Let all Your creation work for my good, the waters, the cloud, the skies and everything on the earth in Jesus name.

19-20. As You heard the cry of the people of Israel, hear my cry; lead me out of bondage for You are the way, the truth and the life.

Psalm 78 NIV

This Psalm shows how the sins of men provoked God but in His mercy there is forgiveness. It should encourage us to pass adequate instruction and guidance to the next generation.

A maskil of Asaph.

BIBLE

1. My people, hear my teaching; listen to the words of my mouth.

2. I will open my mouth with a parable; I will utter hidden things, things from of old—

PRAYER

1. Teach me to hear Your words. Let me have a desire for Your words.

2-3. Help me understand all You want to tell me and help me retain all I hear in Jesus name.

3. Things we have heard and known, things our ancestors have told us.

4. We will not hide them from their descendants; we will tell the next generation the praiseworthy deeds of the Lord, His power, and the wonders he has done.

5. He decreed statutes for Jacob and established the law in Israel, which He commanded our ancestors to teach their children,

6. So the next generation would know them, even the children yet to be born, and they in turn would tell their children.

4-6. Help me teach my children all I know about You and how to praise You. Help my children pass all they learn to their own children.

7. Then they would put their trust in God and would not forget His deeds but would keep His commands.

7. Let my hope be in You and I pray that my children will depend on You alone. Help them to be obedient to You.

8. They would not be like their ancestors— a stubborn and rebellious generation, whose hearts were not loyal to God, whose spirits were not faithful to Him.

8. I pray that my children will not become stubborn or disobedient. Let them not be consumed by the spirit of the world.

9. The men of Ephraim, though armed with bows, turned back on the day of battle;

9. Help me stand by my brothers and sisters in their time of need.

10. They did not keep God's

10. Give me a good under-

	covenant and refused to live by His law.		standing of my covenant relationship with You. Help me keep to the terms of Your covenant with me.
11.	They forgot what He had done, the wonders He had shown them.	**11-12.**	Help me Lord so I do not forget the wonderful things You have done in my life and all the things You have done from the beginning of time.
12.	He did miracles in the sight of their ancestors in the land of Egypt, in the region of Zoan.		
13.	He divided the sea and led them through; He made the water stand up like a wall.	**13.**	I pray that every obstacle before me will split into two for me to pass through just as the Israelites passed through the Red sea in Jesus name.
14.	He guided them with the cloud by day and with light from the fire all night.	**14.**	I pray that at all times Your presence will be with me; I pray Your presence in my life will be evident and will determine how much progress I make day by day in Jesus name.
15.	He split the rocks in the wilderness and gave them water as abundant as the seas;	**15-16.**	Everything You have created will be of benefit to me. All things that are meant to supply my needs will do so in Jesus name.
16.	He brought streams out of a rocky crag and made water flow down like rivers.		
17.	But they continued to sin against Him, rebelling in the wilderness against	**17.**	Have mercy on me as I confess my sins before You. Help me turn away

the Most High.

18. They wilfully put God to the test by demanding the food they craved.

19. They spoke against God; they said, "Can God really spread a table in the wilderness?

20. True, He struck the rock, and water gushed out, streams flowed abundantly, but can He also give us bread? Can He supply meat for His people?"

21. When the Lord heard them, He was furious; His fire broke out against Jacob, and His wrath rose against Israel,

22. For they did not believe in God or trust in His deliverance.

23. Yet He gave a command to the skies above and opened the doors of the heavens;

24. He rained down manna for the people to eat, He gave them the grain of heaven.

25. Human beings ate the bread of angels; He sent

from sin.

18. Take away wickedness from my heart. Help me so that I do not do things that will test Your patience.

19. Lord, the thoughts of my heart are before You and my words too. Have mercy on me.

20. You are my provider. Thank You for providing for me even before I was born.

21. Do not send fire against me. Remember the blood of Your Son shed for the remission of my sins.

22. Help me, teach me to believe and trust in all situations that You are my God and there is nothing too hard for You to do.

23-25 Lord, command the skies, let the doors of heaven be opened unto me. Thank you for past provisions, You have always met me at the point of my need. Thank you for all the spiritual and physical food that You have sent in

them all the food they could eat.

26. He let loose the east wind from the heavens and by His power made the south wind blow.

27. He rained meat down on them like dust, birds like sand on the seashore.

28. He made them come down inside their camp, all around their tents.

29. They ate till they were gorged— He had given them what they craved.

30. But before they turned from what they craved, even while the food was still in their mouths,

31. God's anger rose against them; He put to death the sturdiest among them, cutting down the young men of Israel.

32. In spite of all this, they kept on sinning; in spite of His wonders, they did not believe.

33. So he ended their days in futility and their years in terror.

34. Whenever God slew them, they would seek Him; they eagerly turned to Him again.

abundance.

26. I ask that You cause the east wind to blow away every impediment before me in Jesus name.

27-28. Let there be a rain of divine provision upon me to meet all my needs in Jesus name. Let nothing stand between me and the provisions in Jesus name.

29-30. Thank you Father for You will give me all I need and I will be satisfied.

31-32. I pray for a heart that believes all Your wonderful works. Help me in fulfilling my desire to stop living a life of sin. Have mercy on me Father. Spare me Your wrath.

33. Let me make headway in life. Let troubles cease in my life.

34. Do not slay me in Your wrath. Give me a heart that will seek after You at all times even when things do not seem to be going well.

35. They remembered that God was their Rock, that God Most High was their Redeemer.

36. But then they would flatter Him with their mouths, lying to Him with their tongues;

37. Their hearts were not loyal to Him, they were not faithful to His covenant.

38. Yet He was merciful; He forgave their iniquities and did not destroy them. Time after time He restrained His anger and did not stir up his full wrath.

39. He remembered that they were but flesh, a passing breeze that does not return.

40. How often they rebelled against Him in the wilderness and grieved Him in the wasteland!

41. Again and again they put God to the test; they vexed the Holy One of Israel.

42. They did not remember His power—the day He redeemed them from the oppressor,

35. Help me remember that You are my rock and my redeemer. You paid a high price for saving me.

36-37. Give me a heart that will be right with You. Help me for I do not want to lie to You or to anybody. Help me keep my promises, fulfilling my own part of Your covenant with me.

38-39. I thank You for showing me compassion. Thank You for forgiving me all of my sins and not withholding Your wrath from me.

40. Help me Lord, I do not want to do anything that will provoke or grieve You.

41. Help me Lord for I do not want to ever go back to my old self. Give me the grace never to doubt You, let my faith be built up day by day.

42-43. Help me never to forget the things that You have done, the deliverance from the clutches of the enemy, the signs and wonders You have shown me.

43. The day He displayed His signs in Egypt, His wonders in the region of Zoan.

44. He turned their river into blood; they could not drink from their streams.

45. He sent swarms of flies that devoured them, and frogs that devastated them.

46. He gave their crops to the grasshopper, their produce to the locust.

47. He destroyed their vines with hail and their sycamore-figs with sleet.

48. He gave over their cattle to the hail, their livestock to bolts of lightning.

44-48. Take away their provision, turn their rivers into blood, devour and destroy every agent of the enemy. Let all their labours come to nothing.

49. He unleashed against them His hot anger, His wrath, indignation and hostility—a band of destroying angels.

50. He prepared a path for His anger; He did not spare them from death but gave them over to the plague.

51. He struck down all the firstborn of Egypt, the firstfruits of manhood in the tents of Ham.

52. But He brought His people out like a flock;

49. I ask that You show the devil and his agents Your anger. Send the hosts of heaven to fight for me O God.

50. Do not spare the agents of my enemy. Send pestilence into their camp to destroy them.

51. Strike at the source of strength of my enemy. Let there be weeping in their camp.

52. Deliver me with Your mighty hand out of the

He led them like sheep through the wilderness.

53. He guided them safely, so they were unafraid; but the sea engulfed their enemies.

54. And so He brought them to the border of His holy land, to the hill country His right hand had taken.

55. He drove out nations before them and allotted their lands to them as an inheritance; He settled the tribes of Israel in their homes.

56. But they put God to the test and rebelled against the Most High; they did not keep His statutes.

57. Like their ancestors they were disloyal and faithless, as unreliable as a faulty bow.

58. They angered Him with their high places; they aroused His jealousy with their idols.

59. When God heard them, He was furious; He rejected Israel completely.

60. He abandoned the tabernacle of Shiloh, the tent He had set up among humans.

territory of my enemy. I ask that You protect me from all evil.

53. Thank You for leading me into safety. Thank You for causing the seas to swallow all my enemies.

54. Thank You for the blood of Jesus that was shed on the cross for my redemption.

55. Thank You Lord for restoring unto me all that has been stolen by the kingdom of darkness.

56-57. Help me Lord so that I do not go back to my past life. Help me keep Your word. With Your help I must run away from every form of unfaithfulness.

58-59. Do not be angry with me at any time. Let my worship of You be true. By Your grace I will worship none but You.

60. You have promised, You will never leave me nor forsake me. I am nothing without You.

61. He sent the ark of His might into captivity, His splendour into the hands of the enemy.

62. He gave His people over to the sword; He was furious with His inheritance.

63. Fire consumed their young men, and their young women had no wedding songs;

64. Their priests were put to the sword, and their widows could not weep.

65. Then the Lord awoke as from sleep, as a warrior wakes from the stupor of wine.

66. He beat back His enemies; He put them to everlasting shame.

67. Then He rejected the tents of Joseph, He did not choose the tribe of Ephraim;

68. But He chose the tribe of Judah, Mount Zion, which He loved.

69. He built His sanctuary like the heights, like the earth that He established forever.

70. He chose David His servant and took Him

61. By Your grace I will not do anything that will cause Your glory to be withdrawn from my presence.

62. Help me, do not give me over to the devil and his agents, rather I ask that You be my shield against all the fiery darts from the enemy.

63-64. With Your help I will fulfil my purpose and all You have said concerning me will come to pass.

65. Remember me O Lord and fight for me. Grant me victory on every side.

66. Smite my enemies, such that it will be impossible for them to rise again.

67. Help me so that I will do nothing that will cause You to reject me and my offspring.

68. Thank You for loving me, giving up Your Son Jesus for my sake.

69-72. Thank You for Your Son Jesus, who though equal to You gave up heaven to come to the earth. He knew no sin, but took upon himself

from the sheep pens;
71. From tending the sheep He brought him to be the shepherd of His people Jacob, of Israel His inheritance.
72. And David shepherded them with integrity of heart; with skillful hands he led them.

the sins of the world. He completed his assignment on earth and is now with You in heaven.

Psalm 79 NASB

The Psalm shows the bad condition of God's people and the resultant cry for the mercy of God.

A Psalm of Asaph.

BIBLE

1. O God, the nations have invaded Your inheritance; They have defiled Your holy temple; They have laid Jerusalem in ruins.
2. They have given the dead bodies of Your servants for food to the birds of the heavens, The flesh of Your godly ones to the beasts of the earth.
3. They have poured out their blood like water round about Jerusalem; And there was no one to

PRAYER

1. O God the enemy has come into the church. The church is defiled in many ways by the enemy. In certain areas the reputation of some people of God is in tatters.
2. Do not let us as a church be meat in the mouth of the enemy to be consumed as the enemy pleases.
3. Help us Lord, for so much damage has been done. We have found it difficult to come together

bury them.

4. We have become a reproach to our neighbours, a scoffing and derision to those around us.
5. How long, O Lord? Will You be angry forever? Will Your jealousy burn like fire?
6. Pour out Your wrath upon the nations which do not know You, and upon the kingdoms which do not call upon Your name.
7. For they have devoured Jacob and laid waste his habitation.
8. Do not remember the iniquities of our forefathers against us; Let Your compassion come quickly to meet us, for we are brought very low.
9. Help us, O God of our salvation, for the glory of Your name; And deliver us and forgive our sins for Your name's sake.
10. Why should the nations say, "Where is their

so that the shame can be covered.

4. We are held in scorn by people. I ask that You remove every reproach in our lives in the name of Jesus.
5. Have mercy on us O God. Do not allow Your anger to bring disgrace on Your children.
6. I ask that You pour Your wrath on all who do not acknowledge that You are God.
7. Do not allow the enemy to devour Your children and all that we have been able to gather.
8. I ask for Your tender mercies over all Your children. Do not allow our sins and those of our Fathers to continue to bring us down.
9. You alone can save us from hell and deliver us from our enemies. Help us repent of our sins and we also ask that You forgive us all our sins and our unrighteousness. Let Your name alone be glorified.
10. We cry to You, do not let the heathen ask us

God?" Let there be known among the nations in our sight, vengeance for the blood of Your servants which has been shed.

where our God is.

11. Let the groaning of the prisoner come before You; According to the greatness of Your power preserve those who are doomed to die.

11. Let my cry come unto You today. Deliver all who are already in the clutches of the enemy.

12. And return to our neighbours sevenfold into their bosom the reproach with which they have reproached You, O Lord.

12. I ask that You heap upon all who have laid a reproach on us, seven times what they have put upon us.

13. So we Your people and the sheep of Your pasture will give thanks to You forever; To all generations we will tell of Your praise.

13. Help me give thanks to You at all times. Give me a heart that will continually praise You.

Psalm 80 NASB

The Psalm is a prayer to God to restore His people.
For the choir director; set to El Shoshannim; Eduth.
A Psalm of Asaph.

BIBLE

1. Oh, give ear, Shepherd of Israel, You who lead Joseph like a flock; You who are enthroned above the cherubim, shine forth!

PRAYER

1. As I call on You, who seats between the Cherubim answer me speedily. You are my Shepherd, I ask that You protect me and lead me

			to where my blessings are located. Let Your light shine on me, displacing darkness and showing me the paths to follow.
2.	Before Ephraim and Benjamin and Manasseh, stir up Your power and come to save us!	**2.**	Arise my Father and save me from my enemies. Save my children and future generations from shame.
3.	O God, restore us and cause Your face to shine upon us, and we will be saved.	**3.**	Turn my heart to repentance and let the blood of Jesus wash away my sins so that Your face can shine on me again. Let me find favour with You my Lord. Save me and let Your name be glorified.
4.	O Lord God of hosts, how long will You be angry with the prayer of Your people?	**4.**	Have mercy on me O LORD God of hosts. Do not be angry with me any longer. Do not be angry at my prayers. I ask that You cleanse my heart so that my prayers are inspired by the Holy Spirit.
5.	You have fed them with the bread of tears, and You have made them to drink tears in large measure.	**5.**	Intervene O God and turn my tears of sorrow into tears of joy.
6.	You make us an object of contention to our neighbours, and our enemies laugh among themselves.	**6.**	Have mercy on me. Do not allow my enemies to laugh over my predicament.

7.	O God of hosts, restore us and cause Your face to shine upon us, and we will be saved.	**7.**	Restore me to my place in You, O God of hosts. Let me experience a change in Your countenance towards me. Save me O God.
8.	You removed a vine from Egypt; You drove out the nations and planted it.	**8.**	Lord I ask that you take me out of the grasp of oppression and plant me where You have ordained me to be. Plant me in my home, in my ministry, on my job, in my business and in my community in Jesus name.
9.	You cleared the ground before it, and it took deep root and filled the land.	**9.**	I ask that You cause all who occupy my place to give it up in defeat in Jesus name. Establish me in the land You have given me in Jesus name.
10.	The mountains were covered with its shadow, and the cedars of God with its boughs.	**10-11.**	Enlarge my coast O God. I also pray that the influence of the churches will be felt in every community in which they are planted in Jesus name
11.	It was sending out its branches to the sea and its shoots to the River.		
12.	Why have You broken down its hedges, so that all who pass that way pick its fruit?	**12.**	I pray that You will continue to be a hedge of protection round my household, my community and Your church. Do not give up on me for the enemy will rush in like a flood.
13.	A boar from the forest	**13.**	The devourer is always

eats it away and whatever moves in the field feeds on it.

14. O God of hosts, turn again now, we beseech You; Look down from heaven and see, and take care of this vine,

15. Even the shoot which Your right hand has planted, and on the Son whom You have strengthened for Yourself.

16. It is burned with fire, it is cut down; They perish at the rebuke of Your countenance.

17. Let Your hand be upon the man of Your right hand, upon the Son of Man whom You made strong for Yourself.

18. Then we shall not turn back from You; Revive us, and we will call upon Your name.

19. O Lord God of hosts, restore us; Cause Your

seeking for prey. I ask that You do not let me become mincemeat for the devil to destroy. Have mercy on me and protect me my Father.

14. Show me compassion and return to me again O God of hosts. Open Your eyes and look down from heaven. Out of Your mercy I plead that You visit me again.

15-16. I do not want to lose what You have blessed me with. Do not be angry with me anymore for Your rebuke causes me distress. Do not let the work of Jesus Christ on the cross be in vain concerning me and concerning my community.

17. Let the hand of Your Son Jesus Christ be upon me. Let Your hand protect me and strengthen me, let Your hand lead me and guide me to success.

18. I have no hope if You do not revive me. Help me revive my prayer life so I do not sink deeper into the mire.

19. As I call on You, because of Your infinite mercy I

face to shine upon us, and we will be saved.

pray You will restore me and cause Your face to shine upon me in Jesus name.

Psalm 81 ESV

The Psalm is a call to praise God. The Psalmist recalls what God has done in the past and the ingratitude of His people.

To the choirmaster: according to The Gittith. Of Asaph.

BIBLE	PRAYER
1. Sing aloud to God our strength; shout for joy to the God of Jacob!	**1.** Thank You God for being my strength. You have fought for me and You have made a way for me. Give me a voice that will continue to sing praises and make joyful noises unto You in Jesus name.
2. Raise a song; sound the tambourine, the sweet lyre with the harp.	**2.** Help me praise You with all I can lay my hands on. Give me the ability to play instruments that will make a joyful noise to You I pray.
3. Blow the trumpet at the new moon, at the full moon, on our feast day. **4.** For it is a statute for Israel, a rule of the God of Jacob.	**3-4.** I want to be able to praise You at all times for I know You are always ready to receive praise. Help me Lord to attend church programs at the appointed times without excuses. I pray my heart must start accepting that praise is a duty that I

must perform without been nudged.

5. He made it a decree in Joseph when he went out over the land of Egypt. I hear a language I had not known:

5. Dear Lord I ask that You take me out of every situation that is contrary to my destiny.

6. "I relieved your shoulder of the burden; your hands were freed from the basket.

6. I ask that You remove every evil hand holding me down. Deliver me from every form of bondage. Let the power of satan and his agents over me be broken completely in Jesus name.

7. In distress you called, and I delivered you; I answered you in the secret place of thunder; I tested you at the waters of Meribah. Selah

7. Thank You Father for You are a prayer answering God. In times of trouble You have delivered me. Miraculously You have showed up and bailed me out of testy situations. My prayer is that You continue to do so in Jesus name.

8. Hear, O My people, while I admonish you! O Israel, if you would but listen to Me!

8. Help me listen to You and do as You instruct me.

9. There shall be no strange god among you; you shall not bow down to a foreign god.

9. Let Your Spirit separate my heart from every idol or every material in the form of an idol in Jesus name.

10. I am the Lord your God, who brought you up out of the land of Egypt.

10. Thank You for by Your grace I will always remember what You

Open your mouth wide, and I will fill it.

have done for me. As I open my mouth wide in expectation, You will fill it with blessings. As I open my mouth wide You will fill it with words of wisdom which will edify the people I come into contact with in Jesus name.

11. "But My people did not listen to My voice; Israel would not submit to Me.

11. I not only want to hear You. I want to obey, so help me make the right choices at all times.

12. So I gave them over to their stubborn hearts, to follow their own counsels.

13. Oh, that My people would listen to me, that Israel would walk in My ways!

12-13. Do not give up on me my Lord, for if You do so I am finished. Please continue to be patient with me. I promise that I would listen and turn a new leaf by walking with You.

14. I would soon subdue their enemies and turn My hand against their foes.

14. I ask that You subdue my enemies. Give me victory over them in Jesus name.

15. Those who hate the Lord would cringe toward Him, and their fate would last forever.

15. Let my behaviour cause Your enemies to surrender to Your sovereignty. I ask that You establish me in prosperity for Your name to be glorified.

16. But He would feed you with the finest of the wheat, and with honey from the rock I would satisfy you."

16. As I walk with You I am assured You will provide me with abundance of food to feed my family in Jesus name.

Psalm 82 ESV

The Psalm gives instruction to rulers of the nations on how to rule justly.

A Psalm of Asaph.

BIBLE

1. God has taken His place in the divine council; in the midst of the gods He holds judgment:
2. "How long will you judge unjustly and show partiality to the wicked? Selah
3. Give justice to the weak and the fatherless; maintain the right of the afflicted and the destitu te.
4. Rescue the weak and the needy; deliver them from the hand of the wicked."
5. They have neither knowledge nor understanding, they walk about in darkness; all the foundations of the earth are shaken.

PRAYER

1. I pray that the rulers of this nation at all levels will realise that they are accountable to You.
2. Touch their hearts so they will rule justly, teach them to follow Your example in dispensing justice.
3. I pray that all in authority will defend the rights of the oppressed and the weak. Lord I ask for a heart that will speak up for the poor and the weak.
4. I ask Lord that You stop all who use the law or their access to the law to intimidate the less privileged.
5. All who continue to do as they please will be cove covered by darkness and their lack of understanding will lead to failure. I pray in Your mercy You will bring deliverance to such lands in Jesus name.

6.	I said, "You are gods, sons of the Most High, all of you;	6.	Give me understanding of the fact that I am a god unto the heathen with responsibility to take the word to them at all times.
7.	Nevertheless, like men you shall die, and fall like any prince."	7.	I pray all in government who misrule the people will be judged by You. Let them realise that it is appointed that all men will die.
8.	Arise, O God, judge the earth; for You shall inherit all the nations!	8.	Thank You Lord because a day will come when You will come and inherit all the earth again.

Psalm 83 NASB

The Psalm is a request that God should destroy the enemies of His children.

A Song, a Psalm of Asaph.

BIBLE		PRAYER	
1.	O God, do not remain quiet; Do not be silent and, O God, do not be still.	1.	Father I ask that You intervene in my situation, for Your silence indicates to my enemies that I am alone and You are not with me.
2.	For behold, Your enemies make an uproar, and those who hate You have exalted themselves.	2.	Do not keep silent as the enemies are making so much noise. They act as if You are non-existent.
3.	They make shrewd plans against Your people, and conspire toge-	3.	My enemies have ganged up, I am asking that You respond to my pray-

ther against Your treasured ones.

4. They have said, "Come, and let us wipe them out as a nation, that the name of Israel be remembered no more."

5. For they have conspired together with one mind; Against You they make a covenant:

6. The tents of Edom and the Ishmaelites, Moab and the Hagrites;

7. Gebal and Ammon and Amalek, Philistia with the inhabitants of Tyre;

8. Assyria also has joined with them; They have become a help to the children of Lot. Selah.

9. Deal with them as with Midian, as with Sisera and Jabin at the torrent of Kishon,

10. Who were destroyed at En-dor, who became as dung for the ground.

11. Make their nobles like Oreb and Zeeb and all their princes like Zebah and Zalmunna,

ers by fighting against my enemies.

4. The enemies want to wipe my name and that of my children off the face of the earth.

5. They have ganged up against You too. Help me O God; do not hold Your peace any longer.

6-8. I am surrounded by enemies; even members of my extended family have joined the camp of my enemies. Remember me and fight for me O God.

9. Let fear grip their hearts; As the enemies of Your children were destroyed in the times of old, I ask that You do the same to these ones.

10. I ask that You do unto them as they are doing unto me. Just as they want me to perish, let them perish one after another.

11. In times past, the leaders of conspiracies against Your people met their end in different ways; show that You are

			Almighty by destroying them in ways that will surprise them.
12.	Who said, "Let us possess for ourselves the pastures of God."	**12.**	The enemies want to strip me of my blessings, let their wealth be turned over to Your children for use in Your house in Jesus name.
13.	O my God, make them like the whirling dust, like chaff before the wind.	**13.**	Let them start turning like a wheel. Let them know no peace from this moment; and as stubble is blown into the wind, let them be blown off by a mighty wind in Jesus name.
14.	Like fire that burns the forest and like a flame that sets the mountains on fire.	**14.**	Let them all be consumed by fire.
15.	So pursue them with Your tempest and terrify them with Your storm.	**15.**	Let the destruction unleashed on my enemies put fear and terror into their hearts. Let the rain of Godly blows be like a storm from heaven.
16.	Fill their faces with dishonour, that they may seek Your name, O Lord.	**16.**	After the onslaught on the enemies, fill their hearts with shame. Let them realise the error of their ways. Touch their hearts and draw them to Yourself.
17.	Let them be ashamed and dismayed forever, and let them be humilated and perish,	**17.**	Let those who do not give up and surrender to You be confounded and destroyed forever.
18.	That they may know that	**18.**	Let the whole world see

You alone, whose name is the Lord, are the Most High over all the earth.	and hear what You have done. Let them know that You are JEHOVAH, the Most High God. Halleluiah

Psalm 84 ESV

The Psalm teaches that men should desire God's presence. It shows the blessings that accrue to those who yearn to live in His presence.

To the choirmaster: according to The Gittith.

A Psalm of the Sons of Korah.

BIBLE	PRAYER
1. How lovely is Your dwelling place, O Lord of hosts!	**1.** Thank You Lord for giving me a heart that enjoys being in Your presence, whether it is in church or when I am alone with You.
2. My soul longs, yes, faints for the courts of the Lord; my heart and flesh sing for joy to the living God.	**2.** All I want is to be in Your presence. Show up my Lord and God.
3. Even the sparrow finds a home, and the swallow a nest for herself, where she may lay her young, at Your altars, O Lord of hosts, my King and my God.	**3.** Help me do all I can to find a place in Your temple. As I do so I pray my children will follow my footsteps and find a place in Your house too.
4. Blessed are those who dwell in Your house, ever singing Your praise! Selah	**4.** I pray You will bless me as You bless all who live and work in Your house. I also do not want to be an occasional visitor, I want

to start dwelling in Your house. Give me a heart of praise O God.

5.	Blessed are those whose strength is in You, in whose heart are the highways to Zion.	5.	I pray for strength to continue to come into Your presence. Help me as I do things the way You would want me to do them.
6.	As they go through the Valley of Baca they make it a place of springs; the early rain also covers it with pools.	6.	Give me the grace to continue to worship You no matter the situation I am in. Help me go the extra mile in my desire to worship You.
7.	They go from strength to strength; each one appears before God in Zion.	7.	I pray I will never go weary because You will renew my strength at all times.
8.	O Lord God of hosts, hear my prayer; give ear, O God of Jacob! Selah	8.	I pray Lord that whenever I call on You, You will hear me. I ask that You cause the hosts of heaven to work on my behalf.
9.	Behold our shield, O God; look on the face of Your anointed!	9.	I pray You will be my shield and You will protect me from the evil darts of the enemy.
10.	For a day in Your courts is better than a thousand elsewhere. I would rather be a doorkeeper in the house of my God than dwell in the tents of wickedness.	10.	Help me; keep me from every form of wickedness.
11.	For the Lord God is a sun and shield; the Lord	11.	Thank You Lord for bringing light into my life

bestows favour and honour. No good thing does He withhold from those who walk uprightly.	and keeping me from darkness. I pray that Your grace will abound towards me. I will become what You have ordained for me. I pray that Your glory will rest upon me causing Your favour to surround me. Help me live uprightly so that all You have promised I will receive in Jesus name.
12. O Lord of hosts, blessed is the one who trusts in You!	**12.** Help me walk by faith. Hold me by the hand as You show me how to trust You.

Psalm 85 ESV

The Psalmist asks God to revive His people and shows the righteousness and mercies of God.

To the choirmaster. A Psalm of the Sons of Korah.

BIBLE	**PRAYER**
1. Lord, You were favourable to Your land; You restored the fortunes of Jacob.	**1.** Thank You Lord for divine favour in every area of my life and for delivering me from the captivity of the enemy.
2. You forgave the iniquity of Your people; You covered all their sin. Selah	**2.** Thank You for forgiving me of all my sins through the blood of Your Son Jesus Christ. You have made me righteous

	through Jesus Christ.
3. You withdrew all Your wrath; You turned from Your hot anger.	**3.** Thank You Lord for withdrawing Your wrath and anger against me.
4. Restore us again, O God of our salvation, and put away Your indignation toward us!	**4.** Help me turn away from sin so You will turn to me. Help me as I determine to stop doing anything that will make You angry.
5. Will You be angry with us forever? Will You prolong Your anger to all generations?	**5.** In Your mercy do not let Your anger continue to future generations.
6. Will You not revive us again, that Your people may rejoice in You?	**6.** Let me live again that I may rejoice in You. Pour Your spirit upon me I pray.
7. Show us Your steadfast love, O Lord, and grant us Your salvation.	**7.** Father demonstrate your steadfast love to us; let us enjoy your saving and enabling grace in every situation.
8. Let me hear what God the Lord will speak, for He will speak peace to His people, to His saints; but let them not turn back to folly.	**8.** Help me pay attention to what You say. Let Your words bring peace to my heart. I pray I will not go back to my past errors in Jesus name.
9. Surely His salvation is near to those who fear Him, that glory may dwell in our land.	**9.** Give me a heart that would develop a reverential fear of You. Let Your glory rest upon me; let it rest upon this land too in Jesus name.
10. Steadfast love and faithfulness meet; righteouseousness and peace kiss each other.	**10-11.** You are the only one who can be merciful and truthful to me at the same time. Let me

11. Faithfulness springs up from the ground, and righteousness looks down from the sky.

experience both in Jesus name. Let the work of Christ on the cross give me the peace that You desire for me I pray.

12. Yes, the Lord will give what is good, and our land will yield its increase.

12. Thank You Lord for You shall give me every good thing that I need. As You have spoken I will be fruitful in every area of my life.

13. Righteousness will go before Him and make His footsteps a way.

13. As You are coming back soon, I pray that the world turns away from sin and righteousness shall fill the land.

Psalm 86 ESV

The Psalm is both a prayer asking the merciful God for help and also praises God for His love.

A Prayer of David.

BIBLE

1 . Incline Your ear, O Lord, and answer me, for I am poor and needy.

2. Preserve my life, for I am godly; save Your servant, who trusts in You—You are my God.

PRAYER

1. I humble myself before You. I have no one to turn to but You. I need Your help Lord. I ask that You bow Your ears to me.

2. Protect me from satan and his agents; I ask that You preserve me so I can be of use to Your Kingdom here on earth. Help me remain holy. I

3. Be gracious to me, O Lord, for to You do I cry all the day.
4. Gladden the soul of Your servant, for to You, O Lord, do I lift up my soul.
5. For You, O Lord, are good and forgiving, abounding in steadfast love to all who call upon You.
6. Give ear, O Lord, to my prayer; listen to my plea for grace.
7. In the day of my trouble I call upon You, for You answer me.
8. There is none like You among the gods, O Lord, nor are there any works like Yours.
9. All the nations You have made shall come and worship before You, O Lord, and shall glorify Your name.

ask that You save me because all my trust is in You.

3. Your mercy is all I need in life. Help me as I cry unto You day by day.
4. Make me rejoice for it is within Your power. Help me lift up my soul to You in prayer at all times.
5. Thank you Lord for You are good and forgiving. You are merciful to all who call on You. I bless Your holy name.
6. Attend to me O Lord. Grant me the grace to tarry in the place of prayer.
7. I pray that when trouble comes my way, You are my only port of call. As I pray my expectation is that You will answer me speedily in Jesus name.
8. You can't be compared to gods made by hands. Your works can't be compared to any works as these idols themselves are works of men. You are the Almighty God.
9. The grip of the devil on nations will be removed in Jesus name. I pray that nations would bow down and worship You

			and Your name will be glorified from one end of the earth to the other.
10.	For You are great and do wondrous things; You alone are God.	**10.**	The wonders You have performed from creation testify of Your greatness. You are the One and Only God.
11.	Teach me Your way, O Lord, that I may walk in Your truth; unite my heart to fear Your name.	**11.**	Teach me Your way, open my eyes to the truth in Your word. Let me be a hearer and a doer of Your word. Let my heart be focused on You alone. Let me live in awe of You.
12.	I give thanks to You, O Lord my God, with my whole heart, and I will glorify Your name forever.	**12.**	I want to praise You forever. Give me a heart of praise. I will glorify Your name forever.
13.	For great is Your steadfast love toward me; You have delivered my soul from the depths of Sheol.	**13.**	I shout for the world to hear that Your mercy towards me is great. I bless and magnify Your holy name. Thank You for delivering my soul from hell. Jesus Christ has given me eternal life.
14.	O God, insolent men have risen up against me; a band of ruthless men seeks my life, and they do not set You before them.	**14.**	My God, the proud and arrogant have ganged up against me. They are ready to destroy me but I thank You for with You on my side, their wickedness will come to nothing in Jesus name.
15.	But You, O Lord, are a	**15.**	I worship You for Your

God merciful and gracious, slow to anger and abounding in steadfast love and faithfulness.

compassion to the high, the low, and to the weak. We would be nowhere without Your grace towards us. I sometimes provoke You by my actions and omissions but You show long suffering towards me. I am grateful for without Your mercy I would be dead and buried. You have not given up on me in Your faithfulness and righteousness. Blessed be Your holy name.

16. Turn to me and be gracious to me; give Your strength to Your servant, and save the son of Your maidservant.

16. Turn Your face unto me and have mercy upon me. Give me the strength that will see me through all trials that will come my way. My Lord I am happy to be Your bondservant forever. Help me my Father.

17. Show me a sign of Your favour, that those who hate me may see and be put to shame because You, Lord, have helped me and comforted me.

17. I ask that You do something miraculous in my life that can be attributed to You alone. Let it be obvious to the wicked, let them see it and be put to shame forever. Let it be known that You are my helper and my comforter. Halleluiah

Psalm 87 ESV

The Psalm speaks about God's love of His church and the joy that is in the heart of citizens of God's Kingdom.

A Psalm of the Sons of Korah. A Song.

BIBLE	PRAYER
1. On the holy mount stands the city He founded;	**1.** Thank You Lord for being the foundation of the church. You are also my foundation; I remain unshakeable and firm in You.
2. The Lord loves the gates of Zion more than all the dwelling places of Jacob.	**2.** Thank You Lord for loving the gates of the church, giving confidence that all who seek You will find You there and receive favour from You.
3. Glorious things of you are spoken, O city of God. Selah	**3.** Thank You Father for the beautiful things You have done for the church.
4. Among those who know me I mention Rahab and Babylon; behold, Philistia and Tyre, with Cush— "This one was born there," they say.	**4.** I pray that as the gospel is proclaimed throughout the world, many will be drawn to You and we all will stand together glorifying You.
5. And of Zion it shall be said, "This one and that one were born in her"; for the Most High himself will establish her.	**5.** Thank You for giving me the privilege of being accepted into Your family after You found me.Thank You for establishing me in the family of God.
6. The Lord records as He	**6.** Thank You Father for

registers the peoples, "This one was born there." Selah

7. Singers and dancers alike say, "All my springs are in You."

counting me worthy of honour.

7. Help me to be part of every procession praising and worshiping You.

Psalm 88 NASB

The Psalm describes the sorrows of the writer and subsequent call to God for help and deliverance.
A Song. A Psalm of the sons of Korah. For the choir director; according to Mahalath Leannoth.
A Maskil of Heman the Ezrahite.

BIBLE

1. O Lord, the God of my salvation, I have cried out by day and in the night before You.
2. Let my prayer come before You; Incline Your ear to my cry!
3. For my soul has had enough troubles, and my life has drawn near to Sheol.
4. I am reckoned among those who go down to

PRAYER

1. I thank You for You are the only One who can save me. You are the God of my salvation. You have instructed that I should pray without ceasing. Give me the spirit of prayer and as I pray let my cry come unto You.
2. Let all barriers to my prayers catch fire and be removed now in Jesus name. Incline Your ear to my cry.
3. The troubles I have are suffocating life out of me. In times like this send Your spirit to comfort me.
4. I refuse to die before my appointed time. Grant

the pit; I have become like a man without strength,

5. Forsaken among the dead, like the slain who lie in the grave, whom You remember no more, and they are cut off from Your hand.

6. You have put me in the lowest pit, in dark places, in the depths.

7. Your wrath has rested upon me, and You have afflicted me with all Your waves. Selah.

8. You have removed my acquaintances far from me; You have made me an object of loathing to them; I am shut up and cannot go out.

9. My eye has wasted away because of affliction; I have called upon You every day, O Lord; I have spread out my hands to You.

10. Will You perform wonders for the dead? Will the departed spirits rise

me the strength that will see me through this season.

5. You have said You will not leave me or forsake me. I ask that You remember me and draw me away from the valley of death in Jesus name.

6. The devil bombards me with thoughts of giving up. Grant me the strength to resist dark thoughts when they come in Jesus name.

7. In Your mercy You will not afflict me with wrath any longer because whenever You see me, it is the blood of Your son Jesus Christ that will speak on my behalf.

8. With all honesty, help me depend on You alone. Whenever I call on You, please answer me.

9. Help me pray fervently at all times. Let my tears matter to You too. As I sow tears in prayer, let me reap answered prayer in joy in Jesus name.

10. The dead here on earth cannot sing praises. Do not let me die before my

and praise You? Selah.

time. Let me live and praise You until the time appointed to join the saints triumphant.

11. Will Your lovingkindness be declared in the grave, Your faithfulness in Abaddon?

12. Will Your wonders be made known in the darkness? And Your righteousness in the land of forgetfulness?

11-12. Let me live to declare Your faithfulness and lovingkindness for the world to know. I can't share a testimony in death. Let me live to declare Your glory.

13. But I, O Lord, have cried out to You for help, and in the morning my prayer comes before You.

13. By Your grace I will not give up praying and I know in Your time my answers will manifest in Jesus name.

14. O Lord, why do You reject my soul? Why do You hide Your face from me?

14. I pray with all humility that You will never turn Your face away from me; I pray You will never be angry with me and cast me out of Your presence.

15. I was afflicted and about to die from my youth on; I suffer Your terrors; I am overcome.

15. Every long standing issue in my life must come to an end in Jesus name. Affliction that You have dealt with will not arise again. No affliction will kill me because I will not die but I will live to declare the glory of God.

16. Your burning anger has passed over me; Your terrors have destroyed me.

16. Rather than wrath, Father pour your manifest and enduring blessings over my household, my loved ones, my helpers and my community in Jesus' name. I am a joint heir with Christ so I will not be cut off in Jesus name.

17. They have surrounded me like water all day long; They have encompassed me altogether.

17. My prayer is that the hosts of heaven will surround me at all times bringing answers to me and protecting me from my enemies. I will not be compassed with terror and evil in Jesus name.

18. You have removed lover and friend far from me; My acquaintances are in darkness.

18. I pray that I will be surrounded by light and not darkness from this moment in Jesus name. Halleluiah.

Psalm 89 NIV

The Psalm teaches us about a faithful God's covenant with His children.

A maskil of Ethan the Ezrahite.

BIBLE

1. I will sing of the Lord's great love forever; with my mouth I will make Your faithfulness known through all generations.

PRAYER

1. Thank You Father for Your unending, permanent and abundant mercies over me. After I am long gone, let what I leave behind speak of Your mercies towards me. You have been faithful to me in all ways. Help me broadcast Your faithfulness all over the

2. I will declare that Your love stands firm forever, that You have established Your faithfulness in heaven itself.

3. You said, "I have made a covenant with My chosen one, I have sworn to David My servant,

4. 'I will establish your line forever and make your throne firm through all generations.'"

5. The heavens praise Your wonders, Lord, Your faithfulness too, in the assembly of the holy ones.

6. For who in the skies above can compare with the Lord? Who is like the Lord among the heavenly beings?

7. In the council of the holy ones God is greatly feared; He is more awesome than all who surround Him.

8. Who is like You, Lord God Almighty? You, Lord, are mighty, and Your faithfulness surrounds You.

world.

2. Let Your mercy towards me continue to grow day by day. Thank You Lord for Your essence is faithfulness.

3-4. Thank You for I am a party to Your covenant through Jesus Christ.

5. I join the heavens in praising You for the great and mighty wonders that You have done. Your faithfulness is forevermore.

6. There is none that can be compared to You either in the heavens or on earth. You are Almighty.

7. Let there be a holy fear in my heart. Teach me to revere You at all times. You told Moses to remove his shoes in Your presence. Let all of my being be in awe of You O God.

8. Thank you LORD for You are stronger than the strongest. I am secure in You. Your faithfulness is evident all around.

9. You rule over the surging sea; when its waves mount up, You still them.	**9.** The waters and the waves obey You; there is indeed none like You.
10. You crushed Rahab like one of the slain; with Your strong arm You scattered Your enemies.	**10.** You are victorious over all Your enemies. As You scattered every enemy, let all agents of the devil be scattered in the name of Jesus. Let confusion reign in their midst.
11. The heavens are Yours, and Yours also the earth; You founded the world and all that is in it. **12.** You created the north and the south; Tabor and Hermon sing for joy at Your name.	**11-12.** All things belong to You, for You created them. The heavens, the earth, the mountains, the seas and all resources that You put in them give glory to You.
13. Your arm is endowed with power; Your hand is strong, Your right hand exalted.	**13.** Thank You for Your mighty hand which You have used to save me. You have also used Your hand to destroy Your enemy and mine too. There is none that can hide from You. You are the all-powerful God.
14. Righteousness and justice are the foundation of Your throne; love and faithfulness go before You.	**14.** Your throne is founded on the basis of righteousness and justice. I thank You because You have continually shown me mercy. Help me live according to the truth of Your word.
15. Blessed are those who have learned to acclaim You, who walk in the light	**15.** Thank You for the gospel of Christ, His atonement for my sins and victory

	of Your presence, Lord.		over the enemy. Help me to continue participating in the gospel. Thank You for enabling me to walk in Your presence and also to enjoy Your love.
16.	They rejoice in Your name all day long; they celebrate Your righteousness.	**16.**	I will find reason to rejoice in Your name at all times. Your righteousness has lifted me out of the pits of sin. I bless You my Lord.
17.	For You are their glory and strength, and by Your favour You exalt our horn.	**17.**	Thank You for giving me strength. I look good because of my strength in You. Thank you for favouring me. I have done nothing to deserve it.
18.	Indeed, our shield belongs to the Lord, our king to the Holy One of Israel.	**18.**	Thank You Lord for protecting me from my enemy. Holy one of Israel, You are my King and the King of kings.
19.	Once You spoke in a vision, to Your faithful people You said: "I have bestowed strength on a warrior; I have raised up a young man from among the people.	**19.**	I ask that You speak to me in visions. Help me become who You have endowed me to be. I thank You for choosing me despite my humble beginnings.
20.	I have found David My servant; with My sacred oil I have anointed him.	**20.**	Thank You for finding me, revealing Yourself to me. I ask that You continue to anoint me for greatness.
21.	My hand will sustain him; surely My arm will	**21.**	Lord, I rely on You. Let Your mighty hand

	strengthen him.		strengthen me and defend me from all who attack me.
22.	The enemy will not get the better of him; the wicked will not oppress him.	**22.**	As the enemy has nothing in me, he will have nothing to extract from me in Jesus name. I will not fall into the hands of the wicked in Jesus name.
23.	I will crush his foes before him and strike down his adversaries.	**23.**	Show Your power and destroy all who attempt to destroy me.
24.	My faithful love will be with him, and through My name his horn will be exalted.	**24.**	Thank You Lord for Your faithfulness and mercy will be with me forever and ever. By Your grace I will glory in Your name at all times.
25.	I will set his hand over the sea, his right hand over the rivers.	**25.**	According to Your word wherever I go I will prosper in Jesus name.
26.	He will call out to Me, 'You are My Father, My God, the Rock My Saviour.'	**26.**	As I cry unto You my Father and my God answer me speedily in Jesus name.
27.	And I will appoint him to be my firstborn, the most exalted of the kings of the earth.	**27.**	As I humble myself before You, lift me up in ways only You can do.
28.	I will maintain My love to him forever, and My covenant with him will never fail.	**28.**	Covenant keeping God, be true to Your word and have mercy on me.
29.	I will establish his line forever, his throne as long as the heavens	**29.**	I pray as a joint heir with Jesus my seed will endure forever.

endure.

30. If his sons forsake My law and do not follow My statutes,

31. If they violate My decrees and fail to keep My commands,

32. I will punish their sin with the rod, their iniquity with flogging;

33. But I will not take My love from him, nor will I ever betray My faithfulness.

34. I will not violate My covenant or alter what My lips have uttered.

35. Once for all, I have sworn by My holiness —and I will not lie to David—

36. That his line will continue forever and his throne endure before Me like the sun;

37. It will be established forever like the moon, the faithful witness in the sky."

38. But You have rejected, You have spurned, You have been very angry

30. I pray my children will not forsake You; rather they will serve You until the very end.

31-32. Incline my heart to obey You always. I ask that You show me mercy when I do wrong. Let my heart take Your correction with meekness and humility.

33. Thank You Father, for despite my sins You will continue to show me lovingkindness. You are truly faithful.

34-35. Your words are yea and amen. Thank You Father because every word You have spoken concerning me will surely come to pass.

36-37. As You have promised that the seed of David will endure let me continually stand before You. As the moon is evidence of Your faithfulness, I pray You will cause my descendants and I to partake of Your faithfulness every day in Jesus name.

38-39. Do not be angry with me, do not treat me with contempt. Have mercy

Psalm	Prayer
with Your anointed one.	on me my LORD.
39. You have renounced the covenant with Your servant and have defiled his crown in the dust.	
40. You have broken through all his walls and reduced his strongholds to ruins.	**40.** Do not treat me like You do not have a covenant with me through Your son Jesus. Do show me mercy. I pray You do not remove the protection around me. Let me not come to ruin before Your eyes O God.
41. All who pass by have plundered him; he has become the scorn of his neighbours. **42.** You have exalted the right hand of his foes; You have made all his enemies rejoice.	**41-42.** Do not let me become an object of ridicule. Every agent of the enemy wants to win against me. That will not be so in Jesus name.
43. Indeed, You have turned back the edge of his sword and have not supported him in battle.	**43.** I will not give up in battle. I pray that rather than becoming ineffective, I pray that my sword which is the word of God will not depart from my mouth in Jesus name.
44. You have put an end to his splendour and cast his throne to the ground.	**44.** Do not let Your glory depart from my life. Let Your light continue to shine all over me.
45. You have cut short the days of his youth; You have covered him with a mantle of shame.	**45.** I pray sorrow or disgrace will not cause me to age prematurely. I reject every garment of shame in Jesus' name. I thank

46. How long, Lord? Will You hide Yourself forever? How long will Your wrath burn like fire?

47. Remember how fleeting is my life. For what futility You have created all humanity!

48. Who can live and not see death, or who can escape the power of the grave?

49. Lord, where is Your former great love, which in Your faithfulness You swore to David?

50. Remember, Lord, how Your servant has been mocked, how I bear in my heart the taunts of all the nations,

51. The taunts with which Your enemies, Lord, have mocked, with which they have mocked every step of Your anointed one.

52. Praise be to the Lord forever! Amen and Amen.

Jesus Christ for taking my shame to the cross.

46. Do not hide from me any longer O Lord. My present situation must come to an end. Let Your anger be tempered by Your mercy.

47. Let the blessings You have promised me be released speedily Lord. Remember me Father for I am not getting any younger.

48. I pray that I do not die before the time appointed by You. Help me fulfil my time on earth faithfully.

49. Let me experience Your lovingkindness; let me continuously enjoy all spiritual blessings that are in Jesus Christ

50-51. I ask that You cast away every reproach intended for me both by the mighty and the not so mighty in Jesus name. Let every reproach placed upon me because of my faith in Your son come to nothing.

52. I bless You my Father and I thank You for who You are. Amen

BOOK 4

Psalm 90 ESV

The Psalm written by Moses shows how we should pray to God who is eternal compared to man whose days on earth are numbered.

A Prayer of Moses, the man of God.

BIBLE	PRAYER
1. Lord, You have been our dwelling place in all generations.	**1.** Thank You Lord for being my dwelling place. In times of oppression and torment by the enemy, You protected and sustained me.
2. Before the mountains were brought forth, or ever You had formed the earth and the world, from everlasting to everlasting You are God.	**2.** You have been God before the beginning of time. All glory and honour to You.
3. You return man to dust and say, "Return, O children of man!"	**3.** The power of life and death is in Your hands. I am but a mere mortal.
4. For a thousand years in Your sight are but as yesterday when it is past, or as a watch in the night.	**4.** None can be compared with You. You are the eternal God. I exalt Your holy name.
5. You sweep them away as with a flood; they are like a dream, like grass that is renewed in the morning: **6.** In the morning it flourish-	**5-6.** Men are alive today and dead tomorrow. Men flourish and suddenly they are as grass cut down and withered. Lord do not let me die before

	es and is re- newed; in the evening it fades and withers.		my time.
7.	For we are brought to an end by Your anger; by Your wrath we are dismayed.	**7.**	Do not be angry with me for I do not want to be consumed.
8.	You have set our iniquities before You, our secret sins in the light of Your presence.	**8.**	There is nothing that is hid from Your light. I ask that the blood of Jesus Christ wash away my sins.
9.	For all our days pass away under Your wrath; we bring our years to an end like a sigh.	**9.**	Not a day do I want to spend in Your wrath. I pray that I experience Your goodness all the days of my life.
10.	The years of our life are seventy, or even by reason of strength eighty; yet their span is but toil and trouble; they are soon gone, and we fly away.	**10.**	I ask that I live long O God, not dying in my youth. I pray I do not live a life of labour and sorrow, rather let me eat in plenty and be satisfied.
11.	Who considers the power of Your anger, and Your wrath according to the fear of You?	**11.**	Help me so that I never experience the power of Your anger.
12.	So teach us to number our days that we may get a heart of wisdom.	**12.**	Lord teach me to utilise every day I am alive wisely.
13.	Return, O Lord! How long? Have pity on Your servants!	**13.**	Have mercy upon me. Let me enjoy Your presence and Your blessings again.
14.	Satisfy us in the morning with Your steadfast love, that we may rejoice and be glad all our days.	**14.**	Show me Your mercy quickly so that I can start rejoicing again.

15. Make us glad for as many days as You have afflicted us, and for as many years as we have seen evil.	**15.** In Your goodness let my days be filled with gladness replacing the days of suffering and affliction.
16. Let Your work be shown to Your servants, and Your glorious power to their children.	**16.** Let Your glory rest upon me and my children forever.
17. Let the favour of the Lord our God be upon us, and establish the work of our hands upon us; yes, establish the work of our hands!	**17.** Beautify my life and let Your countenance be my countenance. I ask that You prosper the work of my hands. Let my work outlive me in Jesus mighty name. Amen

Psalm 91 NKJV

The Psalm teaches relationship and dependence on God through trust.

BIBLE	PRAYER
1. He who dwells in the secret place of the Most High shall abide under the shadow of the Almighty.	**1.** I want to live in Your inner sanctuary. I want Your presence to be my home. Let me enjoy being alone with You. Let Your shadow shield and protect me from all evil.
2. I will say of the Lord, "He is my refuge and my fortress; My God, in Him I will trust."	**2.** I choose You to be my refuge and fortress. Help me trust You genuinely with all my heart at all times.
3. Surely He shall deliver you from the snare of the	**3.** Thank You for the guarantee of deliverance

fowler and from the perilous pestilence.	from every trap laid by the devil and his agents. Thank You for protection from arrows of sickness and disease unleashed by the evil one.
4. He shall cover you with His feathers, and under His wings you shall take refuge; His truth shall be your shield and buckler.	**4.** Thank You for the special love and care You have bestowed upon me. Help me trust in the protection You have offered me, never turning away from it in Jesus name. Thank You Father for making Your Son Jesus available to be my shield and buckler.
5. You shall not be afraid of the terror by night, nor of the arrow that flies by day, **6.** Nor of the pestilence that walks in darkness, nor of the destruction that lays waste at noonday.	**5-6.** With You being my shield, I will not be afraid. The terror of the night, the arrow that flies during the day, the pestilence that walks in darkness and destruct-ion that wastes at noon will not cause me fear in Jesus name.
7. A thousand may fall at your side, and ten thousand at your right hand; but it shall not come near you.	**7.** People dying in their thousands around me will have no impact on me. Father please help me have complete trust in You.
8. Only with your eyes shall you look, and see the reward of the wicked.	**8.** I pray I will be alive to see the wicked punished for their evil deeds.
9. Because you have made	**9-10.** There are too many

the Lord, who is my refuge, even the Most High, your dwelling place,

10. No evil shall befall you, nor shall any plague come near your dwelling;

11. For He shall give His angels charge over you, to keep you in all your ways.

12. In their hands they shall bear you up, lest you dash your foot against a stone.

13. You shall tread upon the lion and the cobra, the young lion and the serpent you shall trample underfoot.

14. "Because he has set his love upon Me, therefore I will deliver him; I will set him on high, because he has known My name.

15. He shall call upon Me, and I will answer him; I will be with him in

benefits to the one who trusts You Lord. Let the grace to trust You rest on me so I make You my habitation. In You evil cannot befall me neither can any plague come near me.

11. Lord of the hosts of heaven, I thank You for giving Your angels charge over me at all times, both night and day.

12. Thank You Father for I am sure of victory through Jesus Christ. The angels are to ensure that I will not dash my feet against any stone.

13. I am grateful Father because I will tread upon every lion, adder and dragon for You have put them all under my feet.

14. Let me have a desire to love You with all my soul, spirit and body. I ask that You set me on high above every danger and plan of the enemy. Let there be a craving in me to know You and all Your attributes in Jesus name.

15. I ask for the spirit of prayer, a spirit that wants to communicate with

trouble; I will deliver him and honour him.

You at all times. Let all my prayers be answered in Jesus name. Deliver me from every trouble, remove every reproach and instead I ask that You put me in a place of honour in Jesus name.

16. With long life I will satisfy him, and show him My salvation."

16. Thank You Father for long life and a big thank You for the gift of salvation. Halleluiah

Psalm 92 ESV

The Psalm is a song of praise of God especially His work of creation.

A Psalm. A Song for the Sabbath.

BIBLE

1. It is good to give thanks to the Lord, to sing praises to Your name, O Most High;

2. To declare Your steadfast love in the morning, and Your faithfulness by night,

3. To the music of the lute and the harp, to the

PRAYER

1. It is a privilege to be alive and I want to give thanks to You O Lord. I praise You the Almighty Father who is higher than the highest and bigger than the biggest.

2. As I wake up in the morning, let my heart burst forth into singing of Your lovingkindness. Before I sleep help me give thanks for Your faithfulness to me all through the day.

3. With or without instruments let my praise and

	melody of the lyre.		worship of You be a sweet smelling aroma in Your nostrils.
4.	For You, O Lord, have made me glad by Your work; at the works of Your hands I sing for joy.	4.	When I think of what You have done, joy and gladness fills my soul. Thank you because I am certain that Your works will give me victory on every side.
5.	How great are Your works, O Lord! Your thoughts are very deep!	5.	Your works are great and are greatly to be praised. I ask that You bless me with the depth of counsel and thought that exists in You.
6.	The stupid man cannot know; the fool cannot understand this:	6-7.	Open the hearts of the fools so that they come to surrender to You and accept the depths of Your works. Let them know that their initial prosperity cannot save them and that without You they are lined up for complete destruction.
7.	That though the wicked sprout like grass and all evildoers flourish, they are doomed to destruction forever;		
8.	But You, O Lord, are on high forever.	8.	The wicked come and the wicked go, but You O Lord are on high for ever and ever.
9.	For behold, Your enemies, O Lord, for behold, Your enemies shall perish; all evildoers shall be scattered.	9.	All who continue to reject You as God are assured of destruction. I will not partake of such in Jesus name.
10.	But You have exalted my horn like that of the wild ox; You have poured	10.	Thank You Lord for as my enemies perish and scatter, You will exalt

over me fresh oil.

me. I pray for the fresh oil which will strengthen and cause me to fulfil my purpose.

11. My eyes have seen the downfall of my enemies; my ears have heard the doom of my evil assailants.

11. I pray I will not die in defeat; rather I will be alive to see the downfall of my enemies. I pray I will hear of the doom that has befallen all enemies in Jesus name.

12. The righteous flourish like the palm tree and grow like a cedar in Lebanon.

12. I ask that You cause me to flourish in every area of my life. Let me live under Your grace growing stronger in You daily.

13. They are planted in the house of the Lord; they flourish in the courts of our God.

13. Plant me in Your house O Lord and help me flourish as well. Help me so that I never become a waste of space in Jesus name.

14. They still bear fruit in old age; they are ever full of sap and green,

14. As You have promised I will be fruitful, I pray Lord that in my old age I will be fruitful in all areas and on all sides.

15. To declare that the Lord is upright; He is my rock, and there is no unrighteousness in Him.

15. As long as I live with Your help my life will testify that You are a covenant keeping God. I will declare that You are my rock and there is no unrighteousness in You

Psalm 93 ESV

The Psalm starts with the declaration of the majesty and power of God and ends with the holiness of God.

BIBLE

1. The Lord reigns; He is robed in majesty; the Lord is robed; He has put on strength as His belt. Yes, the world is established; it shall never be moved.
2. Your throne is established from of old; You are from everlasting.
3. The floods have lifted up, O Lord, the floods have lifted up their voice; the floods lift up their roaring.
4. Mightier than the thunders of many waters, mightier than the waves of the sea, the Lord on high is mighty!
5. Your decrees are very trustworthy; holiness befits Your house, O Lord, forevermore.

PRAYER

1. You reign in the heavens, You reign on earth. You are clothed in majesty and strength. Your power established the earth and there is no one who can change what You have done.
2. Lord You have reigned from the beginning of time till now, none can contest with You.
3. The enemies have ganged up ready to pounce, the storms are raging but storms bow before You.Halleluiah
4. You are stronger than all the enemy can put together, indeed You are Almighty, Jehovah El Gibbor
5. I thank You Father because Your word is settled forever. You are holy, everything about You is holy. Help me to be holy.

Psalm 94 NASB

The Psalm is a call on God to avenge the wickedness unleashed on His people. The Psalmist shows us that there is an assurance that the wicked will suffer for their deeds and the righteous will enter into the rest of God.

The Lord Implored to Avenge His People.

BIBLE		PRAYER	
1.	O Lord, God of vengeance, God of vengeance, shine forth!	1.	Lord You have said I should not avenge myself for vengeance belongs to You. I ask that You show up with all Your power and let Your name be glorified.
2.	Rise up, O Judge of the earth, render recompense to the proud.	2.	Arise O God, do not allow the wicked to think they can get away with their wickedness. I ask that You reward them immediately for their dastardly acts.
3.	How long shall the wicked, O Lord, how long shall the wicked exult?	3.	How long shall the wicked continue to triumph over me? Have mercy on me O God.
4.	They pour forth words, they speak arrogantly; All who do wickedness vaunt themselves.	4-6.	The wicked continue to damage with their speech. Their words are calculated to destroy my character. Widows and fatherless children are not out of their reach. I ask that You silence them O God. Do not let them trample on me like I am
5.	They crush Your people, O Lord, and afflict Your heritage.		
6.	They slay the widow and the stranger and murder the orphans.		

			defenceless.
7.	They have said, "The Lord does not see, nor does the God of Jacob pay heed."	**7.**	Thank You Lord for I know that You can see all that is happening to Your children, for You do not sleep or slumber.
8.	Pay heed, You senseless among the people; And when will You understand, stupid ones?	**8.**	The wicked have refused wisdom, let them all start to pay for their stupidity.
9.	He who planted the ear, does He not hear? He who formed the eye, does He not see?	**9.**	You who gave me eyes and ears; You who made me in Your image and after Your likeness will certainly see and hear all that is being done to me.
10.	He who chastens the nations, will He not rebuke, even He who teaches man knowledge?	**10.**	Lord You punish the unbelievers when they do wrong. Therefore You will punish those who say they are Your children and are behaving like unbelievers too. You know everything, that is why You are God. I am asking for Your intervention in these matters my Lord.
11.	The Lord knows the thoughts of man, that they are a mere breath.	**11.**	Help me watch over my thoughts, because they are not hidden from You.
12.	Blessed is the man whom You chasten, O Lord, and whom You teach out of Your law.	**12.**	It is a blessing to be corrected by You because all You do is out of love. I ask that You teach me with Your word, my Lord and my God.
13.	That You may grant him	**13.**	Give me rest from every

relief from the days of adversity, until a pit is dug for the wicked.

14. For the Lord will not abandon His people, nor will He forsake His inheritance.

15. For judgment will again be righteous, and all the upright in heart will follow it.

16. Who will stand up for me against evildoers? Who will take his stand for me against those who do wickedness?

17. If the Lord had not been my help, my soul would soon have dwelt in the abode of silence.

18. If I should say, "My foot has slipped," Your lovingkindness, O Lord, will hold me up.

19. When my anxious thoughts multiply within me, Your consolations delight my soul.

20. Can a throne of destruction be allied with You, one which devises mischief by decree?

21. They band themselves

adversity confronting me. Let the pit of destruction consume the wicked now I pray.

14. You are a loving God. Please do not cast me out of Your covenant promise.

15. You are the righteous judge. It is guaranteed that righteous judgement shall be meted out on the wicked.

16-17. There is none who can stand up for me. I depend on You Lord as my helper. My Father, without Your help I would have been silenced forever.

18. Thank You Lord for when I am in danger of slipping, Your mercy holds me up. Halleluiah

19. When my mind is filled with many thoughts, help me lean on You. Show me how to delight in the comfort that is on offer from You.

20. You are a holy and righteous God. Therefore You will not support or give any backup to workers of iniquity.

21. Let every gathering and

together against the life of the righteous and condemn the innocent to death.

gang up against my household, my community and Your Church come to nothing. I apply the blood of Jesus against every evil decision taken against us in Jesus name.

22. But the Lord has been my stronghold, and my God the rock of my refuge.

22. Thank You because You are my first and last defence. The Alpha and Omega. Thank You for being my shield and for allowing me to take shelter in You.

23. He has brought back their wickedness upon them and will destroy them in their evil; The Lord our God will destroy them..

23. You will visit the wicked with a dose of their medicine. I ask that the hosts of heaven cut them off forever.

Psalm 95 NASB

The Psalm is a call to worship God.

BIBLE

1. O come, let us sing for joy to the Lord, let us shout joyfully to the rock of our salvation.

2. Let us come before His presence with thanksgiving, let us shout joyfully to Him with

PRAYER

1. I praise You with joy and gladness in my heart. Thank You Lord for being the rock and foundation of my salvation.

2. Help me as I desire to come into Your presence with thanksgiving. Let my heart be filled with

Psalms.

3. For the Lord is a great God and a great King above all gods,

4. In whose hand are the depths of the earth, the peaks of the mountains are His also.

5. The sea is His, for it was He who made it, and His hands formed the dry land.

6. Come, let us worship and bow down, let us kneel before the Lord our Maker.

7. For He is our God, and we are the people of His pasture and the sheep of His hand. Today, if You would hear His voice,

8. Do not harden Your hearts, as at Meribah, as in the day of Massah in the wilderness,

9. "When Your fathers tested Me, they tried Me, though they had seen My work.

10. "For forty years I loathed that generation, and said they are a people who err in their heart, and they do not know My ways.

11. "Therefore I swore in My

songs of praise to You.

3. I praise You for You are great, the King of kings and the Lord of Lords. There is none like You.

4. You created the things seen and unseen, everything is within Your control.

5. You set the boundaries of the sea and the land, You own everything inside them.

6. I bow before You my Maker, in worship and adoration.

7. Thank You for being my God and providing for me. Help me obey You at all times.

8. Give me a heart that is trusting, a heart that will be convicted when I hear the truth.

9. I have done wrong so many times; have mercy on me, for in Your righteousness You sit in judgement.

10. Teach me Your ways and incline my heart to walk according to Your ways.

11. I do not want to come

anger, truly they shall not enter into My rest."

under Your wrath, rather I ask for Your peace to come all over me in Jesus name

Psalm 96 NASB

The Psalm is a persistent call to worship God because He reigns.

A Call to Worship the Lord the Righteous Judge.

BIBLE	PRAYER
1. Sing to the Lord a new song; Sing to the Lord, all the earth.	**1.** I praise You with new understanding in my heart. I sing a new song to You O God and I call on the world to join me in worshipping You.
2. Sing to the Lord, bless His name; Proclaim good tidings of His salvation from day to day.	**2.** My soul sings to You Lord, I bless Your wonderful name, You who delivered me from the clutches of death.
3. Tell of His glory among the nations, His wonderful deeds among all the peoples.	**3.** I give glory to You: Your love, majesty and power are clear to the world at large. You are seated at the right hand of God.
4. For great is the Lord and greatly to be praised; He is to be feared above all gods.	**4.** I bear witness to what You have done and I give You praise. Help me O God to walk in fear of You.
5. For all the gods of the peoples are idols, but the Lord made the heavens.	**5.** You created the heavens and the earth; You cannot be compared to gods made by the hands

of men.

6.	Splendour and majesty are before Him, strength and beauty are in His sanctuary.	**6.**	Let me be endowed with Your strength and furnished with Your beauty every time I come into Your sanctuary.
7.	Ascribe to the Lord, O families of the peoples, ascribe to the Lord glory and strength.	**7.**	Help me Lord as I give glory and honour to Your name, for You deserve all the glory.
8.	Ascribe to the Lord the glory of His name; Bring an offering and come into His courts.	**8.**	Do not let me be far from Your presence and as I come, incline my heart to bring an offering so I do not come into Your presence empty handed.
9.	Worship the Lord in holy attire; Tremble before Him, all the earth.	**9.**	Give me a heart that will worship You at all times.
10.	Say among the nations, "The Lord reigns; indeed, the world is firmly established, it will not be moved; He will judge the peoples with equity."	**10.**	Help me declare that You reign everywhere I go. I want to be a carrier of the good news.
11.	Let the heavens be glad, and let the earth rejoice; Let the sea roar, and all it contains;	**11-12.**	As the people receive the gospel and accept You as Saviour, let there be rejoicing in the heavens and on earth below.
12.	Let the field exult, and all that is in it. Then all the trees of the forest will sing for joy		
13.	Before the Lord, for He is coming, for He is coming to judge the earth. He	**13.**	Thank You Lord for sending Your son Jesus Christ to the world, as we

will judge the world in righteousness and the peoples in His faithfulness.	await the second coming we pray Your perfect will, will be done here on earth.

Psalm 97 NASB

The Psalm proclaims the sovereignty of God.

BIBLE	PRAYER
1. The Lord reigns, let the earth rejoice; Let the many islands be glad.	**1.** I worship the Lord of all the earth who has reigned from the beginning and who will reign forever. I call on the world to join me in worshipping the Almighty.
2. Clouds and thick darkness surround Him; Righteousness and justice are the foundation of His throne.	**2.** Lord You rule in righteousness and justice, may Your name be praised.
3. Fire goes before Him and burns up His adversaries round about.	**3.** May Your wrath come down on every enemy of the gospel.
4. His lightnings lit up the world; The earth saw and trembled.	4. I thank You for Your presence brings light into every situation. As the supernatural continues, I pray that the world would come to accept You as Lord and Saviour.
5. The mountains melted like wax at the presence of the Lord, at the presence of the Lord of the whole earth.	**5.** Every opposition to the gospel will melt before You in Jesus name.

	Scripture		Prayer
6.	The heavens declare His righteousness, and all the peoples have seen His glory.	**6.**	Open the hearts of the people so they can join in declaring Your glory.
7.	Let all those be ashamed who serve graven images, who boast themselves of idols; Worship Him, all You gods.	**7.**	Help me educate those who worship gods made of wood or stone which are lifeless and of no benefit to those who worship such items.
8.	Zion heard this and was glad, and the daughters of Judah have rejoiced because of Your judgments, O Lord.	8.	I pray that as more people will hear the gospel and with rejoicing they will accept You into their lives.
9.	For You are the Lord Most High over all the earth; You are exalted far above all gods.	**9.**	Give me a heart that will lift You up for You are higher than all things. Jehovah El Elyon
10.	Hate evil, You who love the Lord, who preserves the souls of His godly ones; He delivers them from the hand of the wicked.	**10.**	Teach me to love You and hate evil of any kind. I ask that You deliver me from the hands of the evil one.
11.	Light is sown like seed for the righteous and gladness for the upright in heart.	**11.**	Thank You for the joy and gladness that fills my heart.
12.	Be glad in the Lord, You righteous ones, and give thanks to His holy name.	**12.**	I pray I will never stop rejoicing in Jesus name. Halleluiah

Psalm 98 NKJV

The Psalm is a prophesy of the coming of the Messiah.
A Psalm.

BIBLE

1. Oh, sing to the Lord a new song! For He has done marvellous things; His right hand and His holy arm have gained Him the victory.
2. The Lord has made known His salvation; His righteousness He has revealed in the sight of the nations.
3. He has remembered His mercy and His faithfulness to the house of Israel; All the ends of the earth have seen the salvation of our God.
4. Shout joyfully to the Lord, all the earth; Break forth in song, rejoice, and sing praises.
5. Sing to the Lord with the harp, with the harp and the sound of a Psalm,
6. With trumpets and the sound of a horn; Shout joyfully before the Lord, the King.
7. Let the sea roar, and all

PRAYER

1. Thank You Lord for giving me a new song to sing to You. It is marvellous in my eyes. You have personally delivered me from the hands of the enemy. Your right hand gave me the victory.
2. Thank You for giving up Your Son Jesus Christ for the salvation of mankind. You have shown You are a good God and You are just.
3. Thank You for remembering Your mercy by sending Jesus to die for the salvation of both the Jew and the gentile.

4-6. Thank You Father for the opportunity to sing praises unto You with our voices and instruments. Let our praise be acceptable unto You.

7-8. Lord let the elements join

its fullness, The world and those who dwell in it;

8. Let the rivers clap their hands; Let the hills be joyful together before the Lord,

9. For He is coming to judge the earth. With righteousness He shall judge the world, and the peoples with equity.

in Your praises and all who inhabit the earth praise You. I ask that You open their hearts to behold the great things You have done for them.

9. Come Lord to judge the world with justice and righteousness.

Psalm 99 NKJV

The Psalm focuses on the holiness of God and teaches that we should exalt Him.

BIBLE

1. The Lord reigns; Let the peoples tremble! He dwells between the cherubim; Let the earth be moved!

2. The Lord is great in Zion, and He is high above all the peoples.

PRAYER

1. Lord You have reigned from the beginning, You reign now and You will reign forevermore. I stand in awe of You. The wicked tremble in fear of You, but I glorify Your holy name. As You sit in glory between the Cherubim let the people be stirred up to worship You.

2. You are great, and I magnify Your holy name. You are higher than the highest, Jehovah El Elyon. You are seated in the heaven and the earth is Your footstool.

3.	Let them praise Your great and awesome name—He is holy.	**3.**	I praise Your holy name, You who are pure and without sin.
4.	The King's strength also loves justice; You have established equity; You have executed justice and righteousness in Jacob.	**4.**	Thank You Lord for You are a King that is powerful and just, Your righteousness is seen in Your judgement.
5.	Exalt the LORD our God, And worship at His footstool—He is holy.	**5.**	Help me worship You with all my heart. I exalt You LORD as I humble myself before You; I bow at Your feet and honour You.
6.	Moses and Aaron were among His priests, and Samuel was among those who called upon His name; They called upon the Lord, and He answered them.	**6.**	Whenever Moses, Aaron and Samuel called, You answered them; I pray that You will be my first port of call whenever I need solutions. As I call, answer me speedily I pray.
7.	He spoke to them in the cloudy pillar; They kept His testimonies and the ordinance He gave them.	**7.**	You did not hide Yourself from them; do not hide Yourself from me. Help me keep all ordinances You have given me.
8.	You answered them, O LORD our God; You were to them God-Who-Forgives, though You took vengeance on their deeds.	**8.**	Thank You LORD for forgiving me of all my sins.
9.	Exalt the LORD our God, and worship at His holy hill; For the LORD our God is holy.	**9.**	I worship You LORD.

Psalm 100 NKJV

A Psalm of thanksgiving.

BIBLE	PRAYER
1. Make a joyful shout to the Lord, all You lands!	**1.** I join the people in making a joyful noise to You, my Lord.
2. Serve the Lord with gladness; Come before His presence with singing.	**2.** Let me appreciate it is an honour to serve You. Help me serve You with gladness in my heart. Help me come into Your presence with songs.
3. Know that the Lord, He is God; It is He who has made us, and not we ourselves; We are His people and the sheep of His pasture.	**3.** You are God. Help me understand this truth and what it entails. You created me, I did not create myself. Help me behave like sheep that is dependent on the shepherd.
4. Enter into His gates with thanksgiving, and into His courts with praise. Be thankful to Him, and bless His name.	**4.** I come to You today with thanksgiving in my heart. I give thanks to You for all the benefits You have bestowed upon me. I am happy that You created me in Your likeness and after Your own image. I bless Your holy name.
5. For the Lord is good; His mercy is everlasting, And His truth endures to all generations.	5. You are good, You are merciful and kind. Your truths are forever sure. All glory and honour to Your name.

Psalm 101 NASB

The Psalm is a call to holy living in all areas of our lives.

A Psalm of David.

BIBLE		PRAYER	
1.	I will sing of loving-kindness and justice, to You, O Lord, I will sing praises.	**1.**	Lord I have experienced Your mercies, kindness, faithfulness and judgement. Help me sing of all these attributes of Yours.
2.	I will give heed to the blameless way. When will You come to me? I will walk within my house in the integrity of my heart.	**2.**	Help me behave wisely, help me walk with integrity; help me strive for a perfect heart towards You and all around me. I ask that You take up residence in my house and in my heart O Lord.
3.	I will set no worthless thing before my eyes; I hate the work of those who fall away; It shall not fasten its grip on me.	**3.**	Help me to be careful about the places I go and the things that I watch. Help me reject the acts of evil people. Help me so I do not retain evil in my heart.
4.	A perverse heart shall depart from me; I will know no evil.	4.	Help me have a heart that will not entertain evil in me or in other people.
5.	Whoever secretly slanders his neighbour, him I will destroy; No one who has a haughty look and an arrogant heart will I endure.	**5.**	Lord keep me away from slander or those who partake in it, take pride and arrogance away from me.
6.	My eyes shall be upon	**6.**	Steer my heart towards

the faithful of the land, that they may dwell with me; He who walks in a blameless way is the one who will minister to me.

7. He who practices deceit shall not dwell within my house; He who speaks falsehood shall not maintain his position before me.

8. Every morning I will destroy all the wicked of the land, so as to cut off from the city of the Lord all those who do iniquity.

faithfulness to You; I want to dwell in Your house never departing from Your presence. Just as You are perfect, help me to be perfect.

7. Let Your eyes be upon me forever O Lord. I want to forever be in Your presence, I do not want to ever leave Your sight. I ask that You take away from me every spirit of deceit and lying in Jesus name.

8. Do not spare the wicked; destroy them now in Jesus name.

Psalm 102 ESV

As the first verse reads the Psalm is a prayer of one who is distressed about his personal condition and that of his nation.

BIBLE

1. Hear my prayer, O Lord; let my cry come to You!

2. Do not hide Your face from me in the day of my distress! Incline Your ear to me; answer me speedily in the day when

PRAYER

1. I call on You in my distress; my prayer has become a cry, let it come unto You.

2. My situation requires haste, so I ask for speedy answer.

	I call.		
3.	For my days pass away like smoke, and my bones burn like a furnace.	**3.**	The days come and go and life seems to be a waste; I need You O Lord.
4.	My heart is struck down like grass and has withered; I forget to eat my bread.	**4.**	I am in anguish and pain has overtaken my soul.
5.	Because of my loud groaning my bones cling to my flesh.	**5.**	I have lost weight as a result of my situation, help me O Lord.
6.	I am like a desert owl of the wilderness, like an owl of the waste places;	**6-7.**	I am alone without any help. Help me to depend on You.
7.	I lie awake; I am like a lonely sparrow on the housetop.		
8.	All the day my enemies taunt me; those who deride me use my name for a curse.	**8.**	Many have ganged up against me. Let their coming together come to nothing in Jesus name.
9.	For I eat ashes like bread and mingle tears with my drink, and mingle tears with my drink,	**9.**	I have found it difficult even to eat. Sadness seems to have overwhelmed me. Have mercy on me.
10.	Because of Your indignation and anger; for You have taken me up and thrown me down.	**10.**	Spare me Your wrath O Lord. In Your mercy lift me up, do not cast me down.
11.	My days are like an evening shadow; I wither away like grass.	**11.**	Do not let my life ebb away before my eyes.
12.	But You, O Lord, are enthroned forever; You are remembered throughout all generations.	**12.**	You are the same yesterday, today and forever. Glory to You O Lord.

13. You will arise and have pity on Zion; it is the time to favour her; the appointed time has come.	**13.** Arise my Lord in Your mighty power. Breathe a breath of favour over me. Do not let this season pass me by.
14. For Your servants hold her stones dear and have pity on her dust.	**14.** Give me a heart that will delight in everything You created. Help me have compassion on the weak in the society.
15. Nations will fear the name of the Lord, and all the kings of the earth will fear Your glory.	**15.** Let Your name be glorified such that the unbeliever will be drawn to You.
16. For the Lord builds up Zion; He appears in His glory;	**16.** Build me up and build Your church up too. Let Your name be glorified.
17. He regards the prayer of the destitute and does not despise their prayer.	**17.** In Your mercy hear my prayer whenever I call on You.
18. Let this be recorded for a generation to come, so that a people yet to be created may praise the Lord:	**18.** Help me record and testify of Your deeds to future generations in Jesus name.
19. That He looked down from His holy height; from heaven the Lord looked at the earth.	**19-20.** Look down from heaven, move now and deliver me from the clutches of death.
20. To hear the groans of the prisoners, to set free those who were doomed to die,	
21. That they may declare in Zion the name of the Lord, and in Jerusalem His praise,	**21.** Help me declare Your goodness in my life at every opportunity, in Jesus name.
22. When peoples gather	**22.** I pray that the time will

together, and kingdoms, to worship the Lord.

come soon when the nations will have godly leaders leading the people to serve You my Lord.

23. He has broken my strength in midcourse; he has shortened my days.

24. "O my God," I say, "take me not away in the midst of my days—You whose years endure throughout all generations!

23-24. Grant me the grace that will see me through every trial that comes my way O Lord. Let me fulfil the number of my days.

25. Of old You laid the foundation of the earth, and the heavens are the work of Your hands.

26. They will perish, but You will remain; they will all wear out like a garment. You will change them like a robe, and they will pass away,

25-26. In Your wisdom You created the heavens and the earth. You are the unchanging changer; heaven and earth shall pass away but You shall remain forever.

27. But You are the same, and Your years have no end.

27. Unlike men, You are dependable for You are the same One. You are worthy to be praised.

28. The children of Your servants shall dwell secure; their offspring shall be established before You.

28. I pray that my children will follow and serve You. I pray they will be established in Your house and nothing will move them away in Jesus name.

Psalm 103 ESV

The Psalm is about the mercy, God has extended to us and His attributes. It is a call to praise God with every fibre of our being.

A Psalm Of David.

BIBLE	PRAYER
1. Bless the Lord, O my soul, and all that is within me, bless His holy name!	1. I recognise that You are the Almighty, the All in All. I bless You with all that I am and all that I have.
2. Bless the Lord, O my soul, and forget not all His benefits,	2. Give me the ability to recall and never forget all the benefits that have come my way.
3. Who forgives all Your iniquity, who heals all Your diseases,	3. Thank You for forgiving me my sins and healing me of every disease.
4. Who redeems Your life from the pit, who crowns You with steadfast love and mercy,	4. I thank You that rather than destruction appointed for sins, You have showered me Your lovingKindness and tender mercies. Your Son Jesus Christ has paid the price of redempion for me.
5. Who satisfies You with good so that Your Youth is renewed like the eagle's.	5. Thank Ytou for all the good things that You have given me which provide sustenance for me.
6. The Lord works righteousness and justice for all who are oppressed.	6. Judge all who oppress me and deliver me from their hands I pray.
7. He made known His	7. Teach me Your ways so

	Psalm		Prayer
	ways to Moses, His acts to the people of Israel.		that as Your child I would be the better for it. As I see Your acts, help me so my faith in You will grow more every day.
8.	The Lord is merciful and gracious, slow to anger and abounding in steadfast love.	**8.**	Thank You for the mercies extended to me despite my short comings. I appreciate You for the abundant grace that is upon me.
9.	He will not always chide, nor will He keep His anger forever.	**9.**	Thank You Lord for never holding grudges against me; You deal with me in love at all times.
10.	He does not deal with us according to our sins, nor repay us according to our iniquities.	**10-11.**	You do not give me what I deserve. You continue to temper justice with mercy. I praise You with all my heart. My sins deserve death, but You have given me eternal life.
11.	For as high as the heavens are above the earth, so great is His steadfast love toward those who fear Him;		
12.	As far as the east is from the west, so far does He remove our transgressions from us.	**12.**	Thank You because You do not remember my sins anymore.
13.	As a father shows compassion to His children, so the Lord shows compassion to those who fear Him.	**13.**	Thank You for adopting me as Your child, thank You for Your compassion towards me. Help me as I pray for godly fear to envelope my heart.
14.	For He knows our frame; He remembers that we are dust.	**14.**	Thank You for taking me as I am; an ordinary human being.

15. As for man, his days are like grass; he flourishes like a flower of the field; **16.** For the wind passes over it, and it is gone, and its place knows it no more.	**15-16.** I could be here today and gone tomorrow; the wind blows and perils could follow, I am in total surrender to You.
17. But the steadfast love of the Lord is from everlasting to everlasting on those who fear Him, and His righteousness to children's children,	**17.** You do not change, my Father. Thank You for continuing to have mercy on me. You are the faithful God.
18. To those who keep His covenant and remember to do His commandments.	**18.** You have put Your law in my heart. Help me keep my part of the covenant by remembering what You said and obeying Your word.
19. The Lord has established His throne in the heavens, and His kingdom rules over all.	**19.** As You reign in heaven, You reign and rule the universe, all glory and honour to You.
20. Bless the Lord, O You His angels, You mighty ones who do His word, obeying the voice of His word!	**20.** Lord I ask that You command Your angels to perform all that You have said concerning me and my destiny.
21. Bless the Lord, all His hosts, His ministers, who do His will!	**21.** Let the hosts of heaven join the ministers of God on earth to give continuous praise to the Almighty God.
22. Bless the Lord, all His works, in all places of His dominion. Bless the Lord, O my soul!	**22.** Let everything inside of me bless You forever more.

Psalm 104 ESV

The Psalm is a song of praise. It allows us to appreciate creation and the Creator.

BIBLE	PRAYER
1. Bless the Lord, O my soul! O Lord my God, You are very great! You are clothed with splendour and majesty,	**1.** I bless You with all my heart O Lord. Your glory is seen in the works of Your hands.
2. Covering Yourself with light as with a garment, stretching out the heavens like a tent.	**2.** You are light and You dwell inside the light You created. The heavens You created at the beginning are still in existence today.
3. He lays the beams of His chambers on the waters; He makes the clouds His chariot; he rides on the wings of the wind;	**3.** Help my little mind to understand that heaven hangs on water; help me understand that You move in and on the clouds; help me understand that the winds are a means of transport for You. Glory to You O God.
4. He makes His messengers winds, His ministers a flaming fire.	**4.** I ask that You send Your angels to minister to my needs by fire now in Jesus name.
5. He set the earth on its foundations, so that it should never be moved. **6.** You covered it with the deep as with a garment; the waters stood above the mountains.	**5-6.** Help me appreciate what You did at creation. Those structures are still in place today working without a need for You to maintain them. Indeed You are greater than the greatest and better than

7. At Your rebuke they fled; at the sound of Your thunder they took to flight.

8. The mountains rose, the valleys sank down to the place that You appointed for them.

9. You set a boundary that they may not pass, so that they might not again cover the earth.

10. You make springs gush forth in the valleys; they flow between the hills;

11. They give drink to every beast of the field; the wild donkeys quench their thirst.

12. Beside them the birds of the heavens dwell; they sing among the branches.

13. From Your lofty abode You water the mountains; the earth is satisfied with the fruit of Your work.

14. You cause the grass to grow for the livestock and plants for man to cultivate, that he may bring forth food from the earth

15. And wine to gladden the heart of man, oil to make his face shine and bread

the best.

7-8. Just as You spoke at creation let Your words cause every formlessness in my life to disappear. Let me be renewed now in Jesus name.

9-10. I pray that every poundary against the enemy remains so in Jesus name. Everything You have directed for my good must come to pass in Jesus name.

11-13. Thank You Father for I am indeed satisfied with all You have created. Your creation continues to work for me in every area of life.

14. Thank You for divine provision. There is a variety of food available for me to eat. Glory be to God.

15. In Your wisdom, there are luxuries available to me too. Help me as I do to strengthen man's heart.

16. The trees of the Lord are watered abundantly, the cedars of Lebanon that he planted.

17. In them the birds build their nests; the stork has her home in the fir trees.

18. The high mountains are for the wild goats; the rocks are a refuge for the rock badgers.

19. He made the moon to mark the seasons; the sun knows it's time for setting.

20. You make darkness, and it is night, when all the beasts of the forest creep about.

21. The Young lions roar for their prey, seeking their food from God.

22. When the sun rises, they steal away and lie down in their dens.

23. Man goes out to his work and to his labour until the evening.

24. O Lord, how manifold are Your works! In wisdom have You made them all; the earth is full of Your creatures.

not want to abuse them.

16-18. Everything You made has a purpose. Trees grow on their own accord, they serve birds and hills serve goats. You are indeed Almighty.

19-20. The moon and the sun do as You directed them. Day has followed night from the beginning. Glory be to Your name.

21. You made animals too, and You are faithful in providing food for them too.

22. At each new day the animals retreat and men move around. I thank You for Your thoight-fulness.

23. Thank You for providing a means of income for me. I am grateful.

24. Help me appreciate Your works of creation as I continue to enjoy them all. I desire Your wisdom too my Lord and my

God.

25. Here is the sea, great and wide, which teems with creatures innumerable, living things both small and great.

26. There go the ships, and Leviathan, which You formed to play in it.

25-26. The seas have their own purpose. The animals that live therein are well provided for. You are an awesome God.

27. These all look to You, to give them their food in due season.

28. When You give it to them, they gather it up; when You open Your hand, they are filled with good things.

27-28. You are the great provider. Help me wait on You at all times. Thank You for every good and perfect gift comes from You.

29. When You hide Your face, they are dismayed; when You take away their breath, they die and return to their dust.

29. Do not hide Your face away from me, for without You I am nothing.

30. When You send forth Your Spirit, they are created, and You renew the face of the ground.

30. In Your almighty power, there is continued renewal on the face of the earth. Up until now, the earth has not run out of anything. You are a great God.

31. May the glory of the Lord endure forever; may the Lord rejoice in His works,

31. Your glory has no end. Your works are perfect and You will continue to delight in all that You do.

32. Who looks on the earth and it trembles, who touches the mountains and they smoke!

32. Let Your awe fill my heart. Let the spirit of the fear of the Lord fill my heart.

33. I will sing to the Lord as

33. As long as I live let Your

long as I live; I will sing praise to my God while I have being.

34. May my meditation be pleasing to Him, for I rejoice in the Lord.

35. Let sinners be consumed from the earth, and let the wicked be no more! Bless the Lord, O my soul! Praise the Lord!

praises fill my heart.

34. Meditation requires patience. Teach me how to meditate. Let Your joy fill my soul.

35. Let all who refuse to accept Jesus Christ as Your Son and as Saviour be consumed.

Psalm 105 NIV

The Psalm is a Psalm of thanksgiving enumerating God's faithfulness from the beginning of time.

BIBLE

1. Give praise to the Lord, proclaim His name; make known among the nations what He has done.

2. Sing to Him, sing praise to Him; tell of all His wonderful acts.

3. Glory in His holy name; let the hearts of those

PRAYER

1. I thank You Lord, for You have given me the enablement to appreciate You. I call upon Your name that is above every other name. Help me testify of all You have done so that those who have not accepted You as Lord will be drawn towards You.

2. Help me turn my thoughts into song unto You. Let my praise be like a sweet smelling fragrance unto You.

3. Help me glory in Your name. Help me identify

	who seek the Lord rejoice.		with You and all You stand for at all times in Jesus name. As long as I live help me seek You and as I do so let rejoicing fill my heart continually.
4.	Look to the Lord and His strength; seek His face always.	**4.**	Help me seek You for strength and protection. Help me seek Your face for I want to live in Your presence at all times.
5.	Remember the wonders He has done, His miracles, and the judgments He pronounced,	**5.**	Help me remember the great things You have done. I pray that as Your works remain in my thoughts, my faith in You will increase daily.
6.	You His servants, the descendants of Abraham, His chosen ones, the children of Jacob.	**6.**	Thank You Father for through Your Son Jesus Christ, I am of the lineage of Abraham and I am part of the chosen ones.
7.	He is the Lord our God; His judgments are in all the earth.	**7.**	You are indeed the Almighty; my Lord and my God. Your justice which is infallible is known and seen by all the earth.
8.	He remembers His covenant forever, the promise He made, for a thousand generations,	**8.**	Thank You Father for You are a covenant keeping God. Your promises are yea and amen.
9.	The covenant He made with Abraham, the oath He swore to Isaac.	**9-10**.	Thank You for reaffirm-reaffirming this covenant with the descendants of

10. He confirmed it to Jacob as a decree, to Israel as an everlasting covenant:
11. To You I will give the land of Canaan as the portion You will inherit."
12. When they were but few in number, few indeed, and strangers in it,
13. They wandered from nation to nation, from one kingdom to another.
14. He allowed no one to oppress them; for their sake he rebuked kings:

15. "Do not touch My anointed ones; do My prophets no harm."

16. He called down famine on the land and destroyed all their supplies of food;
17. And He sent a man before them— Joseph, sold as a slave.
18. They bruised his feet with shackles, his neck was put in irons,
19. Till what he foretold came to pass, till the word of the Lord proved him true.
20. The king sent and

Abraham.

11-12. I praise You because every promise to me will surely come to pass. By Your grace my faith will not be dependent on what I see.
13-14. I pray that as You protected the Israelites, so will You protect my household and my community in Jesus name. Let Your fire fall on all who try to oppress me in Jesus name.
15. I praise You Lord for You have made me the apple of Your eyes. Let Your angels continue to keep me from harm in Jesus name.
16. I pray that whatever the situation that I am in, You will use it to bless me in Jesus name.
17-18. I pray that as I go through challenges, my faith will hold up and I will not give in to doubt in Jesus name.

19-20. Let the helper of my destiny whom You have ordained from the beginning of time locate me now in Jesus name.

	Scripture		Prayer
	released him, the ruler of peoples set him free.		
21.	He made him master of his household, ruler over all he possessed,	**21.**	As You have said, I will be head and not the tail. I will be in charge ruling and reigning here on earth in Jesus name.
22.	To instruct his princes as he pleased and teach his elders wisdom.	**22.**	Endow me with the wisdom of Jesus Christ. Let me be in the position to teach people how to live using the wisdom of God.
23.	Then Israel entered Egypt; Jacob resided as a foreigner in the land of Ham.	**23-24.**	I pray that wherever You lead me to, You will bless me; You will protect me and You will increase me on all sides.
24.	The Lord made his people very fruitful; He made them too numerous for their foes,		
25.	Whose hearts He turned to hate His people, to conspire against His servants.	**25.**	I ask that You harden the hearts of satanic agents so that they may be destroyed immediately.
26.	He sent Moses His servant, and Aaron, whom He had chosen.	**26.**	Send my deliverer now O Lord; the one whom You have chosen from the beginning of time.
27.	They performed His signs among them, His wonders in the land of Ham.	**27.**	Let my enemies see Your power through the wonders that You will perform in their midst.
28.	He sent darkness and made the land dark— for had they not rebelled against His words?	**28.**	Let darkness which they can do nothing about, envelope them physically and spiritually in Jesus name.

29. He turned their waters into blood, causing their fish to die.

30. Their land teemed with frogs, which went up into the bedrooms of their rulers.

31. He spoke, and there came swarms of flies, and gnats throughout their country.

32. He turned their rain into hail, with lightning throughout their land;

33. He struck down their vines and fig trees and shattered the trees of their country.

34. He spoke, and the locusts came, grass-hoppers without number;

35. They ate up every green thing in their land, ate up the produce of their soil.

36. Then He struck down all the firstborn in their land, the firstfruits of all their manhood.

37. He brought out Israel, laden with silver and gold, and from among their tribes no one faltered.

38. Egypt was glad when they left, because dread of Israel had fallen on

29. I ask that You take away the source of sustenance of my enemy.

30-31. Let my enemy know disgrace on every side. Wherever my enemies turn to, let them meet with torment and failure.

32. Let hailstones and fire from heaven fall on them in Jesus name.

33. As the enemy continues to work against me, torch their sources of income.

34-35. Let there be a release of locusts to lick and destroy their vegetation.

36. Let the chief of their strength be taken away from them; let anguish and tribulation be heard in their cities.

37. Thank You for taking care of me; Thank You for blessing me with good health, strength and wealth.

38. Let my story change such that the enemy will be happy to see me go.

	them.		
39.	He spread out a cloud as a covering, and a fire to give light at night.	**39.**	You are my shield, buckler and light. I pray that when my enemies are covered in darkness, Your light will lead me to my destiny in Jesus name.
40.	They asked, and He brought them quail; He fed them well with the bread of heaven.	**40.**	Thank You for whenever I ask from You I receive. Thank You for the unending divine provision.
41.	He opened the rock, and water gushed out; it flowed like a river in the desert.	**41.**	I pray for unending provision from You in Jesus name. Wherever I turn to, blessings will gush out towards me in Jesus name.
42.	For He remembered His holy promise given to His servant Abraham.	**42.**	In times past as You remembered Your promises to the people of Israel, I am certain You will remember Your promises to me in Christ Jesus.
43.	He brought out His people with rejoicing, His chosen ones with shouts of joy;	**43.**	Help me never to depart from Your presence, so that I can continue to live in joy and pleasure forevermore.
44.	He gave them the lands of the nations, and they fell heir to what others had toiled for—	**44.**	Lord I know that when Your grace is in action, I will not have to fight to inherit Your promises. Let it be so in Jesus name.
45.	That they might keep His precepts and observe	**45.**	Help me to do as You please. Let my desire be

His laws. Praise the Lord.	to obey You. Help me to praise You forever.

Psalm 106 NIV

The Psalm lists the sins of Israel and the consequences thereafter. The Psalm ends with God showing His grace towards His people despite their sins.

BIBLE	PRAYER
1. Praise the Lord. Give thanks to the Lord, for He is good; His love endures forever.	**1.** I thank You LORD for being good to me. I thank You that despite my sins You have always shown me mercy.
2. Who can proclaim the mighty acts of the Lord or fully declare His praise?	**2.** There is no man who can fully comprehend all You have done. Give me voice to be able to appreciate Your mighty works.
3. Blessed are those who act justly, who always do what is right.	**3.** Help me to do what is right at all times. Help me resist temptation.
4. Remember me, Lord, when You show favour to Your people, come to my aid when You save them,	**4.** You are my God and my Father. I ask that You remember me for good. Let Your favour locate me now in Jesus name. Let Your salvation come upon my soul.
5. That I may enjoy the prosperity of Your chosen ones, that I may share in the joy of Your nation and join Your inheritance in giving	**5.** Let me enjoy the benefits available to me through Jesus Christ. Let me have cause to glory in the salvation of Your people.

praise.

6. We have sinned, even as our ancestors did; we have done wrong and acted wickedly.

7. When our ancestors were in Egypt, they gave no thought to Your miracles; they did not remember Your many kindnesses, and they rebelled by the sea, the Red Sea.

8. Yet He saved them for His name's sake, to make His mighty power known.

9. He rebuked the Red Sea, and it dried up; He led them through the depths as through a desert.

10. He saved them from the hand of the foe; from the hand of the enemy He redeemed them.

11. The waters covered their adversaries; not one of them survived.

12. Then they believed His promises and sang His praise.

13. But they soon forgot what He had done and did not wait for His plan to unfold.

6. I have sinned; I inherited the sin nature from my Fathers. I ask that You continue to have mercy on me.

7. Help me so that I never forget the wonders that You have done from the beginning of time. I do not want to ever provoke You to wrath.

8. Do not look at my worth. I ask that You save me for Your name alone to be glorified.

9. Let every red sea before me dry up now in Jesus name. Lead me through every barrier before me now in Jesus name.

10. Save me from the hands of my enemy. Let the power of God move on my behalf.

11. Let my enemies and all enemies of Jesus Christ be completely destroyed in Jesus name.

12. I pray my faith is based on my belief in You not on what I see.

13. Help me remember who You are, what You have done in the past and what You can do. Let my heart direct me to You at all times when I am in need of counsel.

14. In the desert they gave in to their craving; in the wilderness they put God to the test.

14. Give me a heart that will always be contented with what You have blessed me with. Help me as I never doubt Your power in my life.

15. So He gave them what they asked for, but sent a wasting disease among them.

15. I pray You will never answer my prayers out of anger. May all You bless me with come out of Your love for me in Jesus name.

16. In the camp they grew envious of Moses and of Aaron, who was consecrated to the Lord.

16. Help me bury the spirit of envy and all that is associated with it. Give unto me a spirit that will appreciate and support the people You have given spiritual authority over me.

17. The earth opened up and swallowed Dathan; it buried the company of Abiram.

18. Fire blazed among their followers; a flame consumed the wicked.

17. Help me such that I am never in a place where You have lost patience with me.

18. Let every trace of the wicked and their wickedness be burned up in Jesus name.

19. At Horeb they made a calf and worshiped an idol cast from metal.

20. They exchanged their glorious God for an image of a bull, which eats grass.

19-20. Let every desire for idolatry in me die in Jesus name. I pray for a heart that will desire to worship You and You only in Jesus name.

21. They forgot the God who saved them, who had done great things in Egypt, **22.** Miracles in the land of Ham and awesome deeds by the Red Sea.	**21-22.** I pray that nothing will make me forget You considering all that You've done for me.
23. So He said he would destroy them—had not Moses, His chosen one, stood in the breach before Him to keep his wrath from destroying them.	**23.** I call on Jesus Christ who is seated on Your right hand side in heaven to intercede on my behalf. Do not destroy me Father.
24. Then they despised the pleasant land; they did not believe His promise.	**24.** I pray that I will never despise Your blessings. Let my heart believe every word You say to me.
25. They grumbled in their tents and did not obey the Lord.	**25.** Murmuring will not allow me to hear You. Let the desire to murmur end in me in Jesus name.
26. So He swore to them with uplifted hand that He would make them fall in the wilderness,	**26.** Do not lift Your hand against me. Have mercy on me my Lord.
27. Make their descendants fall among the nations and scatter them throughout the lands.	**27.** Do not allow my enemies ever to defeat me.
28. They yoked themselves to the Baal of Peor and ate sacrifices offered to lifeless gods;	**28.** Help me keep away from false gods and every form of idolatry. I also pray that I do not knowingly or unknowingly partake of eating any-

thing sacrificed to idols.

29. They aroused the Lord's anger by their wicked deeds, and a plague broke out among them.

29. I pray that my heart will not conceive anything that will bring You to anger. I pray that You will be merciful towards me at all times.

30. But Phinehas stood up and intervened, and the plague was checked.

30. I pray that the zeal of the Lord will move in me to do whatever I can do to stop unrighteousness in Jesus name.

31. This was credited to him as righteousness for endless generations to come.

31. My prayer is that all I do will not be for personal gain but to bring glory to Your holy name.

32. By the waters of Meribah they angered the Lord, and trouble came to Moses because of them;

32. Help me never to do or think or say anything that will cause You to be angry with me.

33. For they rebelled against the Spirit of God, and rash words came from Moses' lips.

33. t is easy to be provoked; help me focus on You alone so that I do not give in to provocation.

34. They did not destroy the peoples as the Lord had commanded them,

34. Complete obedience comes out of loving You with all my heart. Give me a new heart I pray.

35. But they mingled with the nations and adopted their customs.

35. Help me to be mindful of the company I keep. Help me to be the one influencing people not the other way round in Jesus name.

36. They worshiped their idols, which became a snare to them.

36. Help me so that I do not do anything that will become a snare unto me. I do not want to look back and regret my actions.

37. They sacrificed their sons and their daughters to false gods.

38. They shed innocent blood, the blood of their sons and daughters, whom they sacrificed to the idols of Canaan, and the land was desecrated by their blood.

37-38. I refuse to sacrifice my children who are blessings from God to the devil. I refuse to hear or listen to any demonic request in Jesus name.

39. They defiled themselves by what they did; by their deeds they prostituted themselves.

39. I pray that nothing I have will become an idol in my life. No other god apart from the most High God, Jehovah El Elyon will have a place in my life in Jesus name.

40. Therefore the Lord was angry with His people and abhorred His inheritance.

40. Have mercy on me O God. Let nothing I do cause You to break Your covenant with me. I pray the blood of Your Son Jesus Christ will always work on my behalf.

41. He gave them into the hands of the nations, and their foes ruled over them.

41. Do not give me up to my enemy; do not let my enemy rule over me in Jesus name.

42. Their enemies oppressed them and subjected them to their power.

42. Let every power of my enemy in every form be broken now by fire in Jesus name.

43. Many times He delivered them, but they were bent on rebellion and they wasted away in their sin.

43. Give me a heart that will seek counsel from You alone. Help me so I do not return to my old ways. I ask that You deliver me totally from my enemy in Jesus mighty name.

44. Yet He took note of their distress when He heard their cry;

44. Hear my cry this day, and attend to my prayer.

45 For their sake He remembered His covenant and out of His great love He relented.

45. I have sinned; in Your mercy I ask that You remember Your covenant with me through Your Son, Jesus.

46. He caused all who held them captive to show them mercy.

46. The heart of men is in Your hands. I ask that You cause my enemies to become my helpers in Jesus name.

47. Save us, Lord our God, and gather us from the nations, that we may give thanks to Your holy name and glory in Your praise.

47. Save me from the wicked, give me cause to come and give praise to You.

48. Praise be to the Lord, the God of Israel, from everlasting to everlasting. Let all the people say, “Amen!” Praise the Lord.

48. I bless the LORD God Almighty. Thank You for Your goodness and lovingKindness.

BOOK 5

Psalm 107 NIV

The Psalm is a Psalm of thanksgiving after deliverance.

BIBLE	PRAYER
1. Give thanks to the Lord, for He is good; His love endures forever.	**1.** I thank You Lord for You are good. Everything about You is good and You are worthy to be praised. You have been merciful from the beginning of time and You continue to be so.
2. Let the redeemed of the Lord tell their story—those He redeemed from the hand of the foe,	**2.** Help me as I shout to the world that You delivered me from the hands of my enemies.
3. Those He gathered from the lands, from east and west, from north and south.	**3.** I thank You for I am a proud member of the body of Christ.
4. Some wandered in desert wastelands, finding no way to a city where they could settle. **5.** They were hungry and thirsty, and their lives ebbed away.	**4-5.** I wandered away from You, flirting with lesser gods. I was empty and I needed help. Thank You Lord for opening my eyes to my emptiness.
6. Then they cried out to the Lord in their trouble, and He delivered them from their distress.	**6.** Give me a heart that will always cry to You. Thank You for delivering me fro-m every trouble afflicting me.
7. He led them by a straight	**7.** Thank You for leading

	way to a city where they could settle.		me the right way; the way of salvation and freedom from sin.
8.	Let them give thanks to the Lord for His unfailing love and His wonderful deeds for mankind,	8.	Help me continue praising You all the days of my life. Thank You for Your daily miracles which are out of Your goodness and loving-kindness.
9.	For He satisfies the thirsty and fills the hungry with good things.	9.	Thank You for satisfying my longing for You. Thank You for filling me with Your presence.
10.	Some sat in darkness, in utter darkness, prisoners suffering in iron chains,	10-11	Thank You for the freedom and liberty You have given me. Help me not to rebel against Your word. Let my heart seek after Your counsel alone.
11.	Because they rebelled against God's commands and despised the plans of the Most High.		
12.	So He subjected them to bitter labour; they stumbled, and there was no one to help.	12.	Father help me to be humble as I have nowhere to turn. I know my help comes from You alone.
13.	Then they cried to the Lord in their trouble, and He saved them from their distress.	13.	I am hopeless without You. Hear my cry and save me from my distress.
14.	He brought them out of darkness, the utter darkness, and broke away their chains.	14.	Thank You for rescuing me from certain death; thank You for complete deliverance, sin has no hold over me anymore.
15.	Let them give thanks to the Lord for His unfailing	15.	Thank You for Your goodness to me, thank

	Scripture		Prayer
	love and His wonderful deeds for mankind,		You for having mercy on me. Thank You for the great and mighty things You have done in my life.
16.	For He breaks down gates of bronze and cuts through bars of iron.	**16.**	You broke down the prison doors. The gates of hell will never prevail against me in Jesus name.
17.	Some became fools through their rebellious ways and suffered affliction because of their iniquities.	**17.**	I pray I will not be foolish. I will not do things that will open the door to affliction in Jesus name.
18.	They loathed all food and drew near the gates of death.	**18.**	No type of illness whatsoever will lead to my death in Jesus name.
19.	Then they cried to the Lord in their trouble, and He saved them from their distress.	**19.**	Have mercy on me as I cry to You. Thank You for hearing me. Thank You for saving me.
20.	He sent out His word and healed them; He rescued them from the grave.	**20.**	The power behind every word You have spoken gives life. Thank You for healing and deliverance.
21.	Let them give thanks to the Lord for His unfailing love and His wonderful deeds for mankind.	**21.**	I thank You for restoration and healing. I thank You for all that You have done for me.
22.	Let them sacrifice thank offerings and tell of His works with songs of joy.	**22.**	Let my sacrifice of praise be acceptable to You in Jesus name.
23.	Some went out on the sea in ships; they were merchants on the mighty waters.	**23-24**	Thank You for protecting all who sail on the oceans of the world. They come across the wonders of Your mighty hands arising from the
24.	They saw the works of the Lord, His wonderful		

deeds in the deep.	depths of many seas.
25. For He spoke and stirred up a tempest that lifted high the waves. **26.** They mounted up to the heavens and went down to the depths; in their peril their courag me melted away. **27.** They reeled and staggered like drunkards; they were at their wits' end.	**25-27.** When You speak, the winds and the waves have to respond. Sometimes fear grips the hearts of the sailors and panic sets in. Indeed You are the all-powerful God.
28. Then they cried out to the Lord in their trouble, and He brought them out of their distress.	**28.** I praise You for at all times You have always attended to the prayers of all who cried to You.
29. He stilled the storm to a whisper; the waves of the sea were hushed.	**29.** You are the All in All. All creation obeys the voice of the Maker. Glory to You alone.
30. They were glad when it grew calm, and he guided them to their desired haven.	**30.** I bless Your name for Your children will always arrive at their destination.
31. Let them give thanks to the Lord for His unfailing love and His wonderful deeds for mankind.	**31.** Thank You for deliverance and protection at all times. Thank You for the unending wonders that You continue to perform.
32. Let them exalt Him in the assembly of the people and praise Him in the council of the elders.	**32.** Help me exalt You in the city and in the countryside. Let my praises bring honour to You at all times.
33. He turned rivers into a desert, flowing springs into thirsty ground,	**33.** I pray that all resources You have made available to me will work for

34. And fruitful land into a salt waste, because of the wickedness of those who lived there.

35. He turned the desert into pools of water and the parched ground into flowing springs;

36. There He brought the hungry to live, and they founded a city where they could settle.

37. They sowed fields and planted vineyards that yielded a fruitful harvest;

38. He blessed them, and their numbers greatly increased, and He did not let their herds diminish.

39. Then their numbers decreased, and they were humbled by oppression, calamity and sorrow;

40. He who pours contempt on nobles made them wander in a trackless waste.

41. But He lifted the needy out of their affliction and increased their families

me. I know that there is nothing You can't do.

34. I pray that my fruitfulness will not be cut short. Let Your mercy prevail despite the wickedness of the people, O Lord.

35. Let every wilderness experience be turned into a fruitful one in Jesus name.

36-37. Thank You for providing all my needs, You have blessed me with a suitable dwelling place, jobs, businesses, food and many more. Thank You for blessing the work of my hands. I appreciate You for the increase in every area of my life.

38. Lord Your blessing is all I need. Thank You for the many blessings. Thank You for protecting me from decrease and failure.

39. Help me keep away from everything that will open the door to oppression, affliction and sorrow.

40. Help me stay humble so that I do not end up lost in the wilderness, where I was before meeting Jesus Christ.

41. I ask that You lift me far above my enemies. I pray that You also

like flocks.

42. The upright see and rejoice, but all the wicked shut their mouths.

43. Let the one who is wise heed these things and ponder the loving deeds of the Lord.

surround me with my family so that I will not be alone.

42. Let joy fill my heart as I see and appreciate Your mighty hand in all that concerns me. Let the mouth of the wicked be shut permanently in Jesus name.

43. Grant me wisdom to see and understand Your lovingkindness.

Psalm 108 NIV

The Psalm is a Psalm of thanksgiving to God for His mercies and promises.

A song. A Psalm of David.

BIBLE

1. My heart, O God, is steadfast; I will sing and make music with all my soul.
2. Awake, harp and lyre! I will awaken the dawn.
3. I will praise You, Lord, among the nations; I will sing of You among the peoples.
4. For great is Your love,

PRAYER

1. Let every doubt in my mind come to an end O God. Help me give praise to You from the depths of my heart.
2. Help me praise You at all times and with anything I can lay my hands upon.
3. Give me a heart that will praise You when I am alone. I must be bold enough to praise You in the presence of people too.
4. Thank You Father for

higher than the heavens; Your faithfulness reaches to the skies.

5. Be exalted, O God, above the heavens; let Your glory be over all the earth.

6. Save us and help us with Your right hand, that those You love may be delivered.

7. God has spoken from His sanctuary: "In triumph I will parcel out Shechem and measure off the Valley of Sukkoth.

8. Gilead is mine, Manasseh is mine; Ephraim is My helmet, Judah is My sceptre.

9. Moab is My washbasin, on Edom I toss My sandal; over Philistia I shout in triumph."

10. Who will bring me to the fortified city? Who will lead me to Edom?

11. Is it not You, God, You who have rejected us and no longer go out with our armies?

12. Give us aid against the enemy, for human help is worthless.

13. With God we will gain the victory, and He will

Your mercy and truth do not have any limits.

5. Help me give You praise forever just as Your mercy has no limit. Let me behold Your glory.

6. Lord in Your glory deliver all Your children with Your righteous right hand. Answer me speedily too O Lord.

7-9. Thank You Lord for Your promise which states that I will rejoice. Rejoicing will not cease in my life in Jesus name. My blessings will not pass me by. Thank You for the gifts I have already received, thank You for those that are on the way too.

10-11. Thank You Lord for Your faithfulness. You are more than able to see me through every barrier that stands in my way. I ask that You make a way for me.

12. I have none to turn to but You. Give me victory in every area and on every side.

13. Thank You Lord for with You my victory is

trample down our enemies.

assured. Thank You for fighting for me, thank You for the ministering spirits assigned to me.

Psalm 109 NIV

The Psalm is both a call to God for deliverance and judgement for the wicked for He is the only one who can provide justice.

For the director of music. Of David. A Psalm.

BIBLE		PRAYER	
1.	My God, whom I praise, do not remain silent,	**1.**	My Lord, do not be silent any longer concerning me. Help me to continue praising You at all times.
2.	For people who are wicked and deceitful have opened their mouths against me; they have spoken against me with lying tongues.	**2.**	The wicked have risen against me in deceit and lies; Let the heavens respond on my behalf O Lord.
3.	With words of hatred they surround me; they attack me without cause.	**3.**	I have not done anything to warrant the hatred. I ask for Your intervention my Father.
4.	In return for my friendship they accuse me, but I am a man of prayer.	**4.**	Help me to show the love of Christ despite adversity. Grant me the spirit of prayer so that I never give up praying.
5.	They repay me evil for good, and hatred for my friendship.	**5.**	The wicked have rewar ded my good with evil. Intervene O Lord.
6.	Appoint someone evil to oppose my enemy; let	**6.**	Let the wicked experien-ce greater wickedness

an accuser stand at his right hand.

7. When he is tried, let him be found guilty, and may his prayers condemn him.
8. May his days be few; may another take his place of leadership.
9. May his children be fatherless and his wife a widow.
10. May his children be wandering beggars; may they be driven from their ruined homes.
11. May a creditor seize all he has; may strangers plunder the fruits of his labour.
12. May no one extend kindness to him or take pity on his fatherless children.
13. May his descendants be cut off, their names blotted out from the next generation.
14. May the iniquity of his fathers be remembered before the Lord; may the sin of his mother never be blotted out.

from his own camp.

7. Let the wicked receive judgement and condemnation. Let his attempt to pray be very unfruitful.
8. Let the life of the wicked be cut short immediately.
9. Have no pity on his wife and children. Let them all experience the loss of their Father or husband as his life is cut short.
10. As the wicked have sought my ruin, let the children of the wicked have no roof over their heads. Let desolation and poverty follow them all their lives.
11. Let the wealth of the wicked be confiscated. Let strangers enjoy what he has gained in wickedness.
12. As the wicked show no mercy, may his children not find mercy or favour.
13. Let there be no remembrance for the family of the wicked. Let them all be wiped out.
14. Just as the wicked suffer for their wickedness, let them partake of the suffering too as an example to other wicked people.

15. May their sins always remain before the Lord, that he may blot out their name from the earth.

16. For he never thought of doing a kindness, but hounded to death the poor and the needy and the brokenhearted.

17. He loved to pronounce a curse—may it come back on him. He found no pleasure in blessing —may it be far from him

18. He wore cursing as his garment; it entered into his body like water, into his bones like oil.

19. May it be like a cloak wrapped about him, like a belt tied forever around him.

20. May this be the Lord's payment to my accusers, to those who speak evil of me.

21. But You, Sovereign Lord, help me for Your name's sake; out of the goodness of Your love, deliver me.

22. For I am poor and needy, and my heart I wounded within me.

23. I fade away like an evening shadow; I am shaken off like a locust.

15. Do not let them out of Your sight so they can continue to eat of the works of their hands.

16. The wicked have oppressed the poor and shown no mercy; may they never find mercy too.

17-18. Let every curse from the wicked fall upon their heads. I pray I will always delight in all blessing from You in Jesus name.

19. Let his curses follow him wherever he goes all the days of his life.

20. Let all my adversaries receive vengeance from You.

21. Let Your name be glorified. Have mercy upon me and deliver me

22. Help me for my heart is troubled. I have no one to turn to but You.

23. I am powerless and confused because of what I am going through. Help me O Lord.

24. My knees give way from fasting; my body is thin and gaunt

25. I am an object of scorn to my accusers; when they see me, they shake their heads.

26. Help me, Lord My God; save me according to Your unfailing love.

27. Let them know that it is Your hand, that You, Lord, have done it

28. While they curse, may You bless; may those who attack me be put to shame, but may Your servant rejoice.

29. May my accusers be clothed with disgrace and wrapped in shame as in a cloak.

30. With my mouth I will greatly extol the Lord; in the great throng of worshipers I will praise Him.

31. For He stands at the right hand of the needy, to save their lives from those who would condemn them.

24. Help me fast as often as I should. Let my fasting not be in vain. Answer me speedily O God.

25. I cry to You, take away every reproach in my life. Let the story of my life be rewritten so that the wicked would not have their way.

26. Save me from every trouble and torment before me. You are my shield and protection.

27. Deliver me in such a way that it will be known You are in charge of my life.

28. I ask that You pour me a blessing that will make their cursing irrelevant. Let me rejoice in You and let my enemies be put to shame.

29. Send confusion into their camp and let them be enveloped in shame.

30. Fill my mouth wit praises for You, the Most High God. Help me praise You with all my heart and with boldness at all times.

31. Thank You for being my ever present help in times of trouble.

Psalm 110 ESV

The Psalm speaks about the Messiah, His ascension, priesthood and final victory.

A Psalm of David.

BIBLE

1. The Lord says to my Lord: "Sit at my right hand, until I make Your enemies Your footstool."
2. The Lord sends forth from Zion Your mighty sceptre. Rule in the midst of Your enemies!
3. Your people will offer themselves freely on the day of Your power, in holy garments; from the womb of the morning, the dew of Your Youth will be Yours.
4. The Lord has sworn and will not change His mind, "You are a priest forever after the order of Melchizedek."
5. The Lord is at Your right hand; He will shatter

PRAYER

1. Thank You Lord for inviting Your Son Jesus to sit at Your right hand. He is in heaven partaking of Your majesty and Your glory.
2. Thank You Father because as He sits, He is interceding on my behalf. All enemies are His footstool in Jesus name.
3. The power of God shall drive the gospel forward on earth. God's will, will be done on earth no matter the opposition from the enemies of the Kingdom.
4. Help me start serving in Your Kingdom with a holy heart. I pray that converts will make a decision to serve in Your Kingdom sooner rather than later in life. I thank You for giving me Jesus who serves as High Priest.
5. Thank You Father because every enemy shall

kings on the day of His wrath.

be struck down and utterly destroyed in Jesus name. Let that day of wrath continue to happen in Jesus name.

6. He will execute judgment among the nations, filling them with corpses; He will shatter chiefs over the wide earth.

6. Let the Lord judge the wicked, cutting off the heads of every agent of the enemy wherever they exist in Jesus name.

7. He will drink from the brook by the way; therefore He will lift up his head.

7. The Messiah shall prevail against all His enemies.

Psalm 111 NASB

The Psalm tells of the greatness of the works of God.

BIBLE

1. Praise the Lord! I will give thanks to the Lord with all my heart, in the company of the upright and in the assembly.
2. Great are the works of the Lord; They are studied by all who delight in them.
3. Splendid and majestic is His work, and His righteousness endures forever.

PRAYER

1. I give thanks to You with my whole heart. Help me as I do not want to forsake the assembly of the brethren.
2. Help me appreciate all Your works from the beginning of time up until now.
3. Your works show how great You are, they display Your glory. You are a righteous God and this has continued to benefit mankind.

4. He has made His wonders to be remembered; The Lord is gracious and compassionate.

5. He has given food to those who fear Him; He will remember His covenant forever.

6. He has made known to His people the power of His works, in giving them the heritage of the nations.

7. The works of His hands are truth and justice; all His precepts are sure.

8. They are upheld forever and ever; They are performed in truth and uprightness.

9. He has sent redemption to His people; He has ordained His covenant forever; Holy and awesome is His name.

10. The fear of the Lord is the beginning of wisdom; A good understanding have all those who do His commandments; His praise endures forever.

4. Thank You for Your grace and compassion towards me. I have received Your grace through Your works.

5. Teach me to fear You, help me remember Your covenant, thank You for every provision You have supplied unto me.

6. Thank You Father for the battles known and unknown that You have fought and won for me.

7. Thank You for Your righteous judgement. Thank You for Your commandments which have passed from generation to generation.

8. Thank You for Your commandments which are borne out of Your righteousness.

9. Thank You for sending Jesus Christ to redeem me from the curse of the law.

10. Teach me how to fear You for I need wisdom to live here on earth. I pray for a heart that wants to obey Your commandments at all times. Help me praise You forever and ever.

Psalm 112 NASB

The Psalm teaches the works of the righteous man.

BIBLE	PRAYER
1. Praise the Lord! How blessed is the man who fears the Lord, who greatly delights in His commandments.	1. I praise You my Lord. Teach me how to fear You. Incline my heart to delight in Your comman-dments, reading and putting them in my heart and doing them.
2. His descendants will be mighty on earth; The generation of the upright will be blessed.	2. As I fear You, I pray You will make my descend-ants mighty and You bless all of them in Jesus name.
3. Wealth and riches are in his house, and his righteousness endures forever.	3. Thank You for the wealth and different types of riches given to me. Thank You also for my righteousness through Jesus Christ, I have not worked for it, but You deemed me fit to receive the gift.
4. Light arises in the dark-ness for the upright; He is gracious and com-passionate and right-eous.	4. Let Your light shine all over me, causing dark-ness to be displa- ced in Jesus name. Give me a heart just like Yours so I'll show compassion to all who come my way.
5. It is well with the man who is gracious and lends; He will maintain his cause in judgment.	5. I sincerely want to be a good man. Give me a heart that is helpful to the needy. Help me to be di-

screet about my affairs, speaking out only when necessary.

6. For he will never be shaken; The righteous will be remembered forever.

6. Thank You Father for nothing can move me out of Your protection. Thank You Lord as You will not forget me.

7. He will not fear evil tidings; His heart is steadfast, trusting in the Lord.

7. Thank You for establishing my faith in You. My confidence is in You, therefore it is impossible for me to be afraid.

8. His heart is upheld, he will not fear, until he looks with satisfaction on his adversaries.

8. Thank You for taking away fear. My victory over my enemies is settled in Jesus name.

9. He has given freely to the poor, his righteousness endures forever; His horn will be exalted in honour.

9. Give me a heart that would serve the needy in the society with everything You have blessed me with.

10. The wicked will see it and be vexed, he will gnash his teeth and melt away; The desire of the wicked will perish.

10. Thank You for exalting me far above my enemies, as they see me above them, let their hearts melt away.

Psalm 113 NASB

The Psalm shows that God should be praised

BIBLE

1. Praise the Lord! Praise, O servants of the Lord, Praise the name of the Lord.

PRAYER

1. I praise You Lord and I praise Your Holy name. I want to enjoy praising You, teach me to praise

You at all times.

2. Blessed be the name of the Lord from this time forth and forever.

2. Blessed be the name of the Lord. I pray that Your praises would never cease, future generations will forever be praising You.

3. From the rising of the sun to its setting the name of the Lord is to be praised.

3. Let all creation who experience the rising of the sun and its setting see reason why they must praise You.

4. The Lord is high above all nations; His glory is above the heavens.

4. You are higher than the highest whether on the earth or in the heavens. None can be compared to You. Your glory is above the heavens, it is so bright that it is seen on the earth.

5. Who is like the Lord our God, who is enthroned on high,

5. There is none like You, the all-knowing, all powerful, ever present, righteous, just and merciful God.

6. Who humbles Himself to behold the things that are in heaven and in the earth?

6. You who allow the hosts of heaven to come into Your presence, You instruct them and they report back to You. You allow the petitions of Your children on earth, You guide them, You watch out for them. Indeed You are gracious unto us. Thank You for caring for all Your children.

7. He raises the poor from the dust and lifts the needy from the ash heap,

7. Thank You for promoting me and whomsoever You wish to promote.

8. To make them sit with princes, with the princes of His people.

8. Thank You Father for giving me a seat in heaven and also for ensuring that I am in the band of the peculiar people.

9. He makes the barren woman abide in the house as a joyful mother of children. Praise the Lord!

9. Thank You Father for taking away shame, giving me a wife/ husband and children too.

Psalm 114 ESV

The Psalm is an acknowledgement of God's power in the deliverance of the people of Israel. It shows that only the power of God can save us from satan.

BIBLE

1. When Israel went out from Egypt, the house of Jacob from a people of strange language

2. Judah became His sanctuary, Israel His dominion.

3. The sea looked and fled; Jordan turned back.

PRAYER

1. You delivered Your people after showing Pharaoh that all power belongs to You.

2. Thank You for providing a sanctuary where You can be worshipped. I also thank You for being accessible to me now. It's great that You dwell in the midst of Your people.

3-6. Just as Your creation, the seas, rivers, moun-

	tains and hills fled and were driven back before the children of Israel, let every obstacle before me be driven back in Jesus name.
4. The mountains skipped like rams, the hills like lambs.	
5. What ails You, O sea, that You flee? O Jordan, that You turn back?	
6. O mountains, that You skip like rams? O hills, like lambs?	
7. Tremble, O earth, at the presence of the Lord, at the presence of the God of Jacob,	**7.** Let me know Your presence, let me feel Your presence O God of Jacob. I pray let every sea that wants to drown me or every physical or spiritual obstacle flees at the presence of God in my life in Jesus name.
8. Who turns the rock into a pool of water, the flint into a spring of water.	**8.** Thank You for miraculous provision for all Your children.

Psalm 115 NASB

The Psalm shows the folly of those who do not believe in God. It also calls on the children of God to trust God and continue to praise Him.

BIBLE	**PRAYER**
1. Not to us, O Lord, not to us, but to Your name give glory because of Your lovingkindness, because of Your truth.	**1.** I ask that You forgive me because I have not given You all the glory for my successes in the past. I now give You all the glory. I thank You for without You I am nothing. I thank You for being

merciful unto me.

2. Why should the nations say, "Where, now, is their God?"	**2.** I sincerely pray that the church will not be in a situation where the heathen would ask us where our God is. Do not allow them to sneer at Your name any longer O God.
3. But our God is in the heavens; He does whatever He pleases.	**3.** Thank You Father for You are in heaven and You do as You please for You are the King. You are directing the affairs of men and answering prayers.
4. Their idols are silver and gold, the work of man's hands.	**4.** I bow down and worship You for You are God. You are not a product of any man as You are Spirit. It is impossible for an idol to be equated with You for it is made by men.
5. They have mouths, but they cannot speak; They have eyes, but they cannot see;	**5.** I worship and adore You for making it possible for me to hear You when You speak to me.
6. They have ears, but they cannot hear; They have noses, but they cannot smell;	**6.** Idols have ears carved or made but they are useless. I am grateful that when I talk to You, You listen and You answer me. I bless You for all the evidences of answered prayers.
7. They have hands, but they cannot feel; They have feet, but they	**7.** Idols have hands and feet that are useless as they have to be lifted up

cannot walk; They cannot make a sound with their throat.

by their worshippers. I bless and magnify You for You sit in heaven and the earth is Your footstool. My life is in Your hands.

8. Those who make them will become like them, everyone who trusts in them.

8. Those who made these idols and those who worship them are united in foolishness. Let Your wrath fall on them wherever they are.

9. O Israel, trust in the Lord; He is their help and their shield.

10. O house of Aaron, trust in the Lord; He is their help and their shield.

11. You who fear the Lord, trust in the Lord; He is their help and their shield.

9-10. Help me trust in You completely no matter what anyone around me does. Thank You for being my helper and my protection.

11. Give me the Spirit of the fear of the Lord.

12. The Lord has been mindful of us; He will bless us; He will bless the house of Israel; He will bless the house of Aaron.

12. Thank You Father for it is impossible for You to forget about me. Thank You for keeping Your promises and maintaining Your part of Your covenant. Thank You for all the spiritual and material blessings.

13. He will bless those who fear the Lord, the small together with the great.

13. You are a righteous God and Your blessings have nothing to do with man's situation in life. I bless Your holy name.

14. May the Lord give You increase, You and Your

14. Thank You because You have promised to

children.

increase me more and more. You have enabled me to be fruitful and I will continue to be so in Jesus name.

15. May You be blessed of the Lord, Maker of heaven and earth.

15. Thank You Father for heaven and earth answer to You. Therefore all that You have promised must come to pass.

16. The heavens are the heavens of the Lord, but the earth He has given to the sons of men.

16. The heavens declare Your glory for Your residence is in heaven. Father You have given me power to subdue the earth and eat of all You have provided. I praise You the Almighty God.

17. The dead do not praise the Lord, nor do any who go down into silence;

18. But as for us, we will bless the Lord from this time forth and forever. Praise the Lord!

17-18. The physically dead can no longer praise and the spiritually dead who worship idols are too foolish to yield to You. I thank You that I am alive and by Your grace as long as I have breathe in me, I will praise You forever. Amen

Psalm 116 ESV

The Psalm tells of the love of the Psalmist for God. It shows that in all situations when we call upon the name of God, He answers

BIBLE	PRAYER
1. I love the Lord, because He has heard my voice and my pleas for mercy.	**1.** I love You Lord. Thank You for hearing my voice and answering my prayers.
2. Because He inclined His ear to me, therefore I will call on Him as long as I live.	**2.** My Lord You have been good to me. Nothing will stop me from calling upon You as long as I live.
3. The snares of death encompassed me; the pangs of Sheol laid hold on me; I suffered distress and anguish. **4.** Then I called on the name of the Lord: "O Lord, I pray, deliver my soul!"	**3-4.** When the thought of untimely death brings fear and sorrow to me, with Your grace I will call on You to deliver my soul.
5. Gracious is the Lord, and righteous; our God is merciful.	**5.** Thank You for being gracious and merciful unto me. Your righteousness continues to shine through in Your actions.
6. The Lord preserves the simple; when I was brought low, He saved me.	**6.** Thank You for preserving me, right from birth up until this moment. In times of danger thank You for helping me.
7. Return, O my soul, to Your rest; for the Lord	**7.** Help me to stop being anxious. Let me remem-

	Psalm		Prayer
	has dealt bountifully with You.		ber what You have done in the past. Help me return into the safety of Your bosom.
8.	For You have delivered my soul from death, "All mankind are liars."	**8.**	Thank You for delivering me from death, for wiping away my tears and for stopping me from falling and failing.
9.	I will walk before the LORD in the land of the living.	**9.**	As long as I live help me walk before You. Let my daily walk give You pleasure in Jesus name.
10.	I believed, even when I spoke: "I am greatly afflicted"	**10.**	Let my belief in You grow stronger by the day. Help me testify of Your goodness at every opportunity.
11.	I said in my alarm, "All mankind are liars."	**11.**	Help me depend on You rather than on man for man will always disappoint.
12.	What shall I render to the Lord for all His benefits to me?	**12.**	I count my blessings and I thank You but it is impossible to give You more than I have received from You. What can I give the One who owns the heavens and the earth? I ask that You help me show gratitude to You at all times in Jesus name.
13.	I will lift up the cup of salvation and call on the name of the Lord,	**13.**	Help me take the cup of salvation and enjoy every blessing associated with it.
14.	I will pay my vows to the	**14.**	Help me pay every vow I

	Lord and in the presence of all His people.		make and by Your grace let it be in the presence of people as a means of encouragement to them.
15.	Precious in the sight of the Lord is the death of His saints.	**15.**	Thank You Lord for You have made me precious in Your sight. Thank You for I know I will not die before the appointed time.
16.	O Lord, I am Your servant; I am Your servant, the son of Your maidservant. You have loosed my bonds.	**16.**	I declare that all I am and all I have are owned by You. I surrender completely to You. Thank You for the blood of Jesus which has washed away my sins and I am no longer slave to sin.
17.	I will offer to You the sacrifice of thanksgiving and call on the name of the Lord.	**17.**	With Your grace I will thank You with all my heart and I will be appreciative of all You have done for me in the presence of Your people.
18.	I will pay my vows to the Lord in the presence of all His people,	**18.**	Help me pay my vows.
19.	In the courts of the house of the Lord, in Your midst, O Jerusalem. Praise the Lord!	**19.**	I ask that You order my steps to Your house so I can come in to worship You and to pay my vows too.

Psalm 117 ESV

The Psalm is a call to all nations to praise God.

BIBLE

1. Praise the Lord, all nations! Extol Him, all peoples!

2. For great is His steadfast love toward us, and the faithfulness of the Lord endures forever. Praise the Lord!

PRAYER

1. I pray the nations would come to God and praise him. Lord open the eyes of the people; let them see why they should praise You.

2. I pray the nations praise God for his merciful kindness, for the things we can see, and the innumerable things that we take for granted. Lord receive praise because all Your words have come to pass and will continue to come to pass. From the beginning of time till date no word of Yours is unfulfilled. May Your name be praised.

Psalm 118 ESV

The Psalm asks that thanksgiving be given to God for all that He has done for us.

BIBLE

1. Oh give thanks to the Lord, for He is good; for

PRAYER

1. I thank You Lord for You are good and being good

	His steadfast love endures forever!		is Your nature. i thank You because You have continued to have mercy on me despite my failings.
2.	Let Israel say, "His steadfast love endures forever."	**2.**	Help me as I go out to the world and encourage them to appreciate Your mercies that endure forever.
3.	Let the house of Aaron say, "His steadfast love endures forever."	**3.**	I pray that priests and ministers of the gospel will come together and thank You for Your mercies that endure forever.
4.	Let those who fear the Lord say, "His steadfast love endures forever."	**4.**	I pray that You will touch the hearts of those who do not profess You are Lord. Open their eyes to Your mighty works, let them fear You and proclaim that Your mercies endure forever.
5.	Out of my distress I called on the Lord; the Lord answered me and set me free.	**5.**	Give me a praying heart for in my times of pain I called and You answered. Thank You for placing me in a place of peace and protection.
·6.	The Lord is on my side; I will not fear. What can man do to me?	**6.**	Thank You Lord for I am able to say You are on my side. You have caused the hosts of heaven to fight for me. That has taken away my fear and I am no longer afraid of men. I bless and

	magnify Your name.
7. The Lord is on my side as my helper; I shall look in triumph on those who hate me.	**7.** Thank You for You have sent help to me in time of need. With You on my side I am sure I will see the end of all who hate me.
8. It is better to take refuge in the Lord than to trust in man. **9.** It is better to take refuge in the Lord than to trust in princes.	**8-9.** All the kings of this world will disappoint but You O Lord have been faithful from ages past. Help me trust in You and You alone.
10. All nations surrounded me; in the name of the Lord I cut them off!	**10.** Many have ganged up against me but I am sure that because You are for me, they are all destroyed in Jesus mighty name.
11. They surrounded me, surrounded me on every side; in the name of the Lord I cut them off! **12.** They surrounded me like bees; they went out like a fire among thorns; in the name of the Lord I cut them off!	**11-12.** They have gathered together from all sides. I call on fire from heaven to destroy them all in Jesus name.
13. I was pushed hard, so that I was falling, but the Lord helped me.	**13.** They have been waiting for me to fall and give in, but I thank You that out of Your mercy You have helped me stand up to adversity.
14. The Lord is my strength and my song; He has become my salvation.	**14.** Without You I am weak and helpless. Thank You for being my strength and for putting a song of

victory in my mouth.

15. Glad songs of salvation are in the tents of the righteous: "The right hand of the Lord does valiantly,

15. I pray that the joy of victory and salvation will fill my heart. I pray that the voice of singing will be heard continually in my home. I pray that Your righteous right hand will continue to fight for me in Jesus name.

16. The right hand of the Lord exalts, the right hand of the Lord does valiantly!"

16. I exalt Your right hand my Lord. I pray it will continue to lift me up and at the same time destroy my enemies.

17. I shall not die, but I shall live, and recount the deeds of the Lord.

17. I thank You Lord for I am confident in You that I will not die as my enemies wanted, but I shall live to declare Your mighty works in Jesus name.

18. The Lord has disciplined me severely, but He has not given me over to death.

18. Help me respond positively to Your correction my Lord. Thank You for not allowing death to take me away before my time.

19. Open to me the gates of righteousness, that I may enter through them and give thanks to the Lord.

20. This is the gate of the Lord; the righteous shall enter through it.

19-20. Help me live a life of righteousness for only the righteous will enter the kingdom of heaven.

21. I thank You that You have answered me and have

21. Let my heart swell in Your praise. Thank You

become my salvation.

for answered prayers and for saving me from death.

22. The stone that the builders rejected has become the cornerstone.

22. I have been rejected as a nobody but You have made me someone to be reckoned with. Thank You for making me Your child. Help me make a difference. Jesus Christ was rejected and he reigns in heaven and on earth. Thank You Father.

23. This is the Lord's doing; it is marvellous in our eyes.

23. May Jesus Christ continue to be exalted far above all principality and power by You, Lord in Jesus name.

24. This is the day that the Lord has made; let us rejoice and be glad in it.

24. I pray I will continue to rejoice and celebrate both Jesus Christ as my Lord and the Sabbath as the day holy unto the Lord. I pray that every day I wake up, will be celebrated as a day of Your goodness and kindness to me.

25. Save us, we pray, O Lord! O Lord, we pray, give us success!

25. I pray You will continue to save me and deliver me from evil in Jesus name. Let me prosper in every area of my life in Jesus name.

26. Blessed is he who comes in the name of the Lord! we bless You from the house of the Lord.

26. Let all ministers of God and everything they lay their hands on be blessed in the mighty name of Jesus Christ.

27. The Lord is God, and He has made His light to shine upon us. Bind the festal sacrifice with cords, up to the horns of the altar!

27. Let Your light surround me all the days of my life. I pray that every sacrifice I make will be acceptable in Your sight in Jesus name.

28. You are my God, and I will give thanks to You; You are my God; I will extol You.

28. You are my God. I praise You and I magnify Your holy name forever,

29. Oh give thanks to the Lord, for He is good; for His steadfast love endures forever!

29. I give You thanks. I adore You, You are good and Your mercy indeed endures forever.

Psalm 119 ESV

The Psalm is divided into twenty two sections of eight verses each. Each section starts with the English translation of the Hebrew alphabet.

The Psalm teaches how to be impacted by the word of God.

BIBLE

Aleph

1. Blessed are those whose way is blameless, who walk in the law of the Lord!

2. Blessed are those who keep His testimonies, who seek Him with their whole heart,

PRAYER

1. Help me keep away from contamination in my journey of life. Give me a heart that would obey the word of God and as I do so, let me be blessed in Jesus name.

2. Help me keep Your laws, incline my heart to want to know You and as I do so let me be blessed in Jesus name.

3. Who also do no wrong, but walk in His ways!	**3.** I do not want to live a sinful life, help me to resist sin. Teach me to walk in Your ways.
4. You have commanded Your precepts to be kept diligently.	**4.** Help me to take Your commands seriously.
5. Oh that my ways may be steadfast in keeping Your statutes!	**5.** Grant me the grace to keep Your laws. Without Your direction I cannot do it by myself. Help me honour Your commandments by studying them, and making a conscious effort to be led by them, so I will not be ashamed before men and before God. Thank You Father for teaching me Your statutes. Help me praise You with all my heart.
6. Then I shall not be put to shame, having my eyes fixed on all Your commandments.	**6.** Help me keep Your statutes. Let Your grace be available to me. Do not forsake me O God. I ask that the cleansing power of Your word remove every impurity in me now in Jesus name.
7. I will praise You with an upright heart, when I learn Your righteous rules. **8.** I will keep Your statutes; do not utterly forsake me! **Beth** **9.** How can a Young man	**7 - 10.** Incline my heart to yearn for You, put brakes on me so I will not wander away from Your word knowingly or unknowingly.

	keep his way pure? by guarding it according to Your word.		
10.	With my whole heart I seek You; let me not wander from Your commandments!		
11.	I have stored up Your word in my heart that I might not sin against You.	**11.**	Help me store up Your word in my heart, so that when sin comes, it will prevent me from succumbing to it.
12.	Blessed are You, O Lord; teach me Your statutes!	**12.**	I praise my Lord and I thank You for teaching me Your statutes.
13.	With my lips I declare all the rules of Your mouth.	**13.**	Help me, give me boldness, light a fire in me so that all You have taught me, I will be willing to teach people around me.
14.	In the way of Your testimonies I delight as much as in all riches.	**14.**	Let there be rejoicing in my heart as I appreciate that all scripture points to the saving grace of Christ Jesus.
15.	I will meditate on Your precepts and fix my eyes on Your ways	**15.**	Teach me to meditate on Your word, let the word be in my thoughts at all times. Help me obey the word at all times.
16.	I will delight in Your statutes; I will not forget Your word.	**16.**	I pray that my heart will delight in Your word, calling it up and using it at all times.
	Gimel		
17.	Deal bountifully with Your servant, that I may	**17.**	Lord I humble myself in service to You. Let Your

live and keep Your word.

grace and mercy abound towards me. Let me live and as I do so obey Your word.

18. Open my eyes, that I may behold wondrous things out of Your law.

18. Lord open my spiritual eyes so I would see and imbibe all that is in Your law.

19. I am a sojourner on the earth; hide not Your commandments from me!

19. Help me understand and remember at all times that heaven is my home and I am in transition here on earth. I ask that You guide me by Your law always.

20. My soul is consumed with longing for Your rules at all times.

20. Make my heart desire to know Your law earnestly.

21. You rebuke the insolent, accursed ones, who wander from Your commandments.

21. Lord take every element of pride away from me for I do not want to be cursed as I want to keep Your commandments.

22. Take away from me scorn and contempt, for I have kept Your testimonies.

22. I ask that You nullify every reproach upon me arising from the fact that I am Your follower.

23. Even though princes sit plotting against me, Your servant will meditate on Your statutes.

23. Let all opposition against me be nullified in Jesus name.

24. Your testimonies are my delight; they are my counsellors.

24. In spite of all opposition, help me respond with delight to Your testimonies.

Daleth

25. My soul clings to the dust; give me life accord-

25. I ask that You lift me up from distress that is

ing to Your word!	pulling me down. Give me strength.
26. When I told of my ways, You answered me; teach me Your statutes!	**26.** Help me to be open to You as I call on You. I have made a choice to follow Your ways, I want to leave behind my old sins as I desire to learn and obey Your laws.
27. Make me understand the way of Your precepts, and I will meditate on Your wondrous works.	**27.** I ask that You give me a good understanding of Your laws so I will be able to testify of Your great and mighty works.
28. My soul melts away for sorrow; strengthen me according to Your word!	**28.** Lord my heart is heavy because of the challenges I face, and as I encounter Your word let me be strengthened to overcome all my troubles.
29. Put false ways far from me and graciously teach me Your law!	**29.** Take the urge to lie away from me and grant me the grace to overcome this sin.
30. I have chosen the way of faithfulness; I set Your rules before me.	**30.** You are the way and the truth. I have chosen to follow You and no other. Help me live by Your truth.
31. I cling to Your testimonies, O Lord; let me not be put to shame!	**31.** Help me follow Your word in the face of temptation. I ask that You do not allow me to do anything that would put me to shame.
32. I will run in the way of Your commandments	**32.** I ask that You enlarge my heart with the knowled-

when You enlarge my heart!

ge of Your ways and with love for You so I will hasten and joyfully obey Your commandments.

He

33. Teach me, O Lord, the way of Your statutes; and I will keep it to the end.

33. You are the only One who can teach me the theory and practice of Your statutes, do so I ask in Jesus name. By Your grace I will be able to keep them until the very end.

34. Give me understanding, that I may keep Your law and observe it with my whole heart.

34. Pour upon me the spirit of understanding so I know the spirituality behind Your law. This will help me obey the law with my whole heart.

35. Lead me in the path of Your commandments, for I delight in it.

35. Lord I ask that You make me, usher me and guide me in the path so I will be able to walk in thy commandments. I cannot do it by myself.

36. Incline my heart to Your testimonies, and not to selfish gain!

36. Give me a heart that would want to read Your word, a heart that wants to dig deep into all that is in the word. I ask that You move my heart away from covetous-covetousness and all that is associated with the love of money.

37. Turn my eyes from looking at worthless things; and give me life in Your

37. I ask that You turn my eyes and my heart away from the vanities of this

	ways.		world that are there to shift my focus away from You. Rather I ask that You put a fervency in my heart towards Your word.
38.	Confirm to Your servant Your promise, that You may be feared.	**38.**	Let every promise in Your word come to pass in my life. Help me serve You with reverential fear in Jesus name.
39.	Turn away the reproach that I dread, for Your rules are good.	**39.**	I ask that You take away every reproach in my life as You have mercy on me, O righteous judge.
40.	Behold, I long for Your precepts; in Your righteousness give me life!	**40.**	Help me as I continue to learn Your precepts, let Your righteousness be revealed in me quickly.
Waw			
41.	Let Your steadfast love come to me, O Lord, Your salvation according to Your promise;	**41.**	Let me receive Your loving kindness and salvation.
42.	then shall I have an answer for Him who taunts me, for I trust in Your word.	**42.**	Help me silence those who think that there is no help for me. My trust in You cannot be shaken in Jesus name.
43.	And take not the word of truth utterly out of my mouth, for my hope is in Your rules.	**43.**	I pray that in every situation the word of truth will work for me. Help me maintain my trust in Your word.
44.	I will keep Your law continually, forever and ever,	**44.**	Lord enable me to retain Your word in my heart forever.
45.	and I shall walk in a wide	**45.**	Help me walk in the

place, for I have sought Your precepts.

liberty of Your precepts, not enslaved by sin but free in You.

46. I will also speak of Your testimonies before kings and shall not be put to shame,

46. Help me to be proud and bold to speak about my beliefs in the presence of any person, high or low in the society.

47. for I find my delight in Your commandments, which I love.

47. Incline my heart to take delight in Your commandments. Let my love for Your commandments increase more and more in Jesus name.

48. I will lift up my hands toward Your commandments, which I love, and I will meditate on Your statutes.

48. Grant me the strength to put all I am into obeying Your commandments. Teach me to meditate on Your statutes so I will think of how best to obey them.

Zayin

49. Remember Your word to Your servant, in which You have made me hope.

49. I have put all my hope on Your word. I pray all You have promised will come to pass as You are faithful. Let it be so in Jesus name.

50. This is my comfort in my affliction, that Your promise gives me life.

50. Thank You for the word that enabled me survive my affliction. I was dead but Your word gave me life.

51. The insolent utterly deride me, but I do not turn away from Your law.

51. Lord no matter how much ridicule that is poured on me because of my faith, help me stand firm on my beliefs.

52.	When I think of Your rules from of old, I take comfort, O Lord.	**52.**	Help me take comfort from how You dealt with those who reproached the saints of old. Let me be encouraged by Your faithfulness.
53.	Hot indignation seizes me because of the wick-ked, who forsake Your law.	**53.**	Put a dread of sin in my heart so that I would intercede for those who continue in a life of sin.
54.	Your statutes have been my songs in the house of my sojourning.	**54.**	Help me find joy in Your statutes such that I will sing back to You.
55.	I remember Your name in the night, O Lord, and keep Your law.	**55.**	Help me keep Your word in my heart and think about it at all times even as I continue to obey Your word.
56.	This blessing has fallen to me, that I have kept Your precepts.	**56.**	I pray for the grace to know Your word and obey it too.
Heth			
57.	The Lord is my portion; I promise to keep Your words.	**57.**	Help me as I desire to make You all that I would ever need. Help me in my goal to obey Your word.
58.	I entreat Your favour with all my heart; be gracious to me according to Your promise.	**58.**	Be merciful unto me. With my whole heart I ask that You favour me. Envelope me with Your love.
59.	When I think on my ways, I turn my feet to Your testimonies;	**59.**	Help me make the right decision as I consider my ways. Am I living right?
60.	I hasten and do not delay to keep Your command-	**60.**	Help me to be quick in my obedience to Your

ments.

61. Though the cords of the wicked ensnare me, I do not forget Your law.

62. At midnight I rise to praise You, because of Your righteous rules.

63. I am a companion of all who fear You, of those who keep Your precepts.

64. The earth, O Lord, is full of Your steadfast love; teach me Your statutes!

Teth

65. You have dealt well with Your servant, O Lord, according to Your word.

66. Teach me good judgment and knowledge, for I believe in Your commandments.

67. Before I was afflicted I went astray, but now I keep Your word.

68. You are good and do good; teach me Your statutes.

word.

61. As the agents of the wicked one continue to attack, help me keep my focus on Your word.

62. Thank You for Your word. Help me stay awake during the night praying as my heart is inclined to appreciate Your word.

63. Give me good friends who are God fearing and keepers of Your word.

64. Let us continue to enjoy Your mercy O God. I yearn to receive Your word. Teach me Your precepts I pray.

65. Be good to me in every area of my life according to Your promises O God.

66. I ask that You teach me how to discern good from evil. Help me gain knowledge from Your word. Give me a heart that believes the word.

67. Thank You Lord for making me come back into the fold after wandering off. Help me continue obeying Your word.

68. Thank You for You are a good God and You are good to me. Let the Holy Spirit teach me Your word.

69. The insolent smear me with lies, but with my whole heart I keep Your precepts;

69. As I am accused of many things by different people, help me stay focused on Your word, obeying all with my whole heart.

70. their heart is unfeeling like fat, but I delight in Your law.

70. My accusers are comfortable in their skins; I pray that my heart will find joy in Your word.

71. It is good for me that I was afflicted, that I might learn Your statutes.

71. Lord help me learn from every situation that I am confronted with.

72. The law of Your mouth is better to me than thouands of gold and silver pieces.

72. Help me make Your word more important than the transient things of this world.

Yodh

73. Your hands have made and fashioned me; give me understanding that I may learn Your commandments.

73. Thank You Lord for making me what I am today. As I am Your creation, give me understanding that will help me in learning from Your word.

74. Those who fear You shall see me and rejoice, because I have hoped in Your word.

74. I pray I will be able to highlight Your goodness to me to all that are around me.

75. I know, O Lord, that Your rules are righteous, and that in faithfulness You have afflicted me.

75. Thank You for being my Lord. You do not make mistakes for Your faithfulness is forever more.

76. Let Your steadfast love comfort me according to Your promise to Your servant.

76. I pray that Your mercy and kindness will give me comfort as You have promised in Your word.

77. Let Your mercy come to me, that I may live; for Your law is my delight.	**77.** Show me Your compassion so I can live. Do not allow affliction to cause my death. Give me a heart that will continually delight in Your word.
78. Let the insolent be put to shame, because they have wronged me with falsehood; as for me, I will meditate on Your precepts.	**78.** I ask that You pour shame upon all who have acted wickedly towards me without reason. I pray that no matter the situation I am in, You will help me in my desire to meditate on Your word day and night.
79. Let those who fear You turn to me, that they may know Your testimonies.	**79.** I ask that You turn the hearts of those who used to love me back to me. I pray that despite the mistakes I have made in the past, they will find a place in their hearts to forgive me.
80. May my heart be blameless in Your statutes, that I may not be put to shame!	**80.** Give me a pure heart such that I will have no reason to be ashamed before You.
Kaph	
81. My soul longs for Your salvation; I hope in Your word.	**81.** Help me as I wait for You to deliver me for I am dependent on Your promises.
82. My eyes long for Your promise; I ask, "When will You comfort me?	**82.** Help me so that I do not give up as I wait for Your word to come to pass in my life. I need Your

83. For I have become like a wineskin in the smoke, yet I have not forgotten Your statutes.

84. How long must Your servant endure? When will You judge those who persecute me?

85. The insolent have dug pitfalls for me; they do not live according to Your law.

86. All Your commandments are sure; they persecute me with falsehood; help me!

87. They have almost made an end of me on earth, but I have not forsaken Your precepts.

88. In Your steadfast love give me life, that I may keep the testimonies of Your mouth.

Lamedh

89. Forever, O Lord, Your word is firmly fixed in the heavens.

90. Your faithfulness endures to all generations; You have established the earth, and it stands fast.

91. By Your appointment they stand this day, for all

comfort to sustain me.

83. Even though I am exhausted by my situation, help me so I don't forget Your word.

84. Lord I ask that You execute judgement on all who prosecute me now.

85. Open my eyes to see every pit or barrier the enemy has laid for me.

86. I ask that You help me overcome all persecution, for they are all baseless.

87. Deliver me from my enemies as they have almost succeeded in taking me out. Help me continue following Your word.

88. Lord out of Your loving kindness, lift me up for Your name to be glorified.

89. As Your word is settled in heaven, let it be settled in my heart.

90. You have been faithful from ages past. You said let there be and there was. Blessed be Your holy name.

91. Lord, what You said in the beginning is in

things are Your servants.

92. If Your law had not been my delight, I would have perished in my affliction.

93. I will never forget Your precepts, for by them You have given me life.

94. I am Yours; save me, for I have sought Your precepts.

95. The wicked lie in wait to destroy me, but I consider Your testimonies

96. I have seen a limit to all perfection, but Your commandment is exceedingly broad.

Mem

97. Oh how I love Your law! It is my meditation all the day.

98. Your commandment makes me wiser than my enemies, for it is ever with me.

99. I have more understanding than all my teachers, for Your testimonies are my medita-

existence today. Your word answers to You. Glory and honour to You.

92. Help me delight in Your word so that affliction will not get the better of me.

93. Help me remember Your word for it is life unto me.

94. Deliver me from my enemies for I am Your child. Help me to continue seeking to follow Your word.

95. Help me as the enemy looks out to destroy me. I will continue to depend on You.

96. Help me appreciate that You are indeed Almighty and that Your word is complete.

97. Incline my heart to love Your law. Teach me how to meditate every day.

98. Lord give me a better understanding of Your word and of my relationship with You. Let this understanding make me wiser than my enemies as I never depart from Your word.

99. Help me meditate on Your word so that I can have better understanding.

tion.

100. I understand more than the aged, for I keep Your precepts.

101. I hold back my feet from every evil way, in order to keep Your word.

102. I do not turn aside from Your rules, for You have taught me.

103 How sweet are Your words to my taste, sweeter than honey to my mouth!

104. Through Your precepts I get understanding; therefore I hate every false way.

Nun

105. Your word is a lamp to my feet and a light to my path.

106. I have sworn an oath and confirmed it, to keep Your righteous rules.

107. I am severely afflicted; give me life, O Lord, according to Your word!

108. Accept my freewill

100. As I obey Your word give me better understanding than those who have gone ahead of me.

101. Keep my feet away from evil so I don't fall foul of Your word.

102. Thank You for all You have taught me and all You continue to teach me. I pray with Your help I will not depart from Your word.

103. I pray for the heart to enjoy and take delight in the study of Your word.

104. Grant me a good understanding of who You are and what my place is in You. As I do so, I pray that I develop hatred for sin.

105. I pray Your word will show me the way around every obstruction in my path and also provide me direction in life.

106. I want to follow Your word with all my heart. Help me achieve my desire.

107. Lord give me the strength to overcome every affliction.

108. Let my offerings be

offerings of praise, O Lord, and teach me Your rules.

109. I hold my life in my hand continually, but I do not forget Your law.

110. The wicked have laid a snare for me, but I do not stray from Your precepts.

111. Your testimonies are my heritage forever, for they are the joy of my heart

112. I incline my heart to perform Your statutes forever, to the end.

Samekh

113. I hate the double-minded, but I love Your law.

114. You are my hiding place and my shield; I hope in Your word.

115. Depart from me, You evildoers, that I may keep the commandments of my God.

116. Uphold me according to

acceptable unto You O God.

109. As there is always danger lurking around because of the enemy, let me live with confidence that You are always with me.

110. Even though the wicked will always be around, help me so I do not depart from Your word.

111. Let my knowledge of You become the most important thing in my heart. Let this knowledge lead to perfect rejoicing in me forever.

112. Incline my heart to hear and to obey You no matter the circumstances.

113. Help me focus on Your word alone, taking captive every thought to the obedience of Christ.

114. As You shield me from the enemy Lord, protect me from all evil activity.

115. I command every agent from the enemy to depart from me now. Help me so I do not succumb to temptation O God.

116. Help me overcome my

Your promise, that I may live, and let me not be put to shame in my hope!

117. Hold me up, that I may be safe and have regard for Your statutes continually!

118. You spurn all who go astray from Your statue statutes, for their cunning is in vain.

119. All the wicked of the earth You discard like dross, therefore I love Your testimonies.

120 My flesh trembles for fear of You, and I am afraid of Your judgments.

Ayin

121. I have done what is just and right; do not leave me to my oppressors.

122. Give Your servant a pledge of good; let not the insolent oppress me.

123. My eyes long for Your salvation and for the fulfilment of Your righteous promise.

124. Deal with Your servant according to Your stead-

enemies Lord, let Your grace see me through all difficulties that come my way. Let my hope not be in vain.

117. You are the guarantee of my safety. I ask that You keep me from the fiery darts of the enemy.

118. Lord let all who defy Your word be brought down in Jesus name.

119. Let all agents of the devil be destroyed by fire. You are a holy God.

120. I ask for a heart that would fear You, a heart that would stand in awe of You.

121. Help me live a life of righteousness and holiness. Do not allow the enemy to hurt me.

122. I ask that You speak to my heart a word of assurance that I am Yours. Do not allow the wicked to oppress me.

123. Do not allow my heart to fail, I long for freedom from the hands of my enemy. Let Your word work for me.

124. Have mercy on me my Lord. I ask that You take

fast love, and teach me Your statutes.	time to teach me Your law.
125. I am Your servant; give me understanding, that I may know Your testimonies!	**125.** Lord I want to do Your will. I ask that You give me a good understanding of what I need to know.
126. It is time for the Lord to act, for Your law has been broken.	**126.** Come down and show Your power. I ask Lord that You rouse Your children to stand up against the break down in our society.
127. Therefore I love Your commandments above gold, above fine gold.	**127.** Help me love You more so that I will be a good example to my generation. Let my love for You and Your word be more important than everything else in my life.
128. Therefore I consider all Your precepts to be right; I hate every false way.	**128.** Give me a heart that will appreciate that as You are the Almighty, You are and You will always be right. Let me hate evil with passion in Jesus name.
Pe	
129. Your testimonies are wonderful; therefore my soul keeps them.	**129.** Teach me Your word and help me see the beauty in them. I want to be both a hearer and doer of Your word.
130. The unfolding of Your words gives light; it imparts understanding to the simple.	**130.** Let the entrance of Your word bring light into my life. I ask that You give me a good understanding of Your word.

131. I open my mouth and pant, because I long for Your commandments.

132. Turn to me and be gracious to me, as is Your way with those who love Your name.

133. Keep steady my steps according to Your promiise, and let no iniquity get dominion over me.

134. Redeem me from man's oppression, that I may keep Your precepts.

135. Make Your face shine upon Your servant, and teach me Your statutes

136. My eyes shed streams of tears, because people do not keep Your law.

Tsadhe

137. Righteous are You, O Lord, and right are Your rules.

138. You have appointed Your testimonies in righteousness and in all faithfulness.

139. My zeal consumes me, because my foes forget Your words.

131. Let me have a heart that would yearn for Your commandments.

132. Give me a heart that loves You Lord, and as I do so show me mercy. I am desperate.

133. You are my God. Help me as I submit to You. Order my steps. Do not let me be overcome by sin.

134. Deliver me from the hands of my enemies. Incline my heart to obey You at all times.

135. Let Your light shine upon me and all that concerns me. Bless me O God. Teach me Your laws I pray.

136. Give me a heart that hates sin.

137. You deserve to be worshipped and adored for You are righteous and perfect.

138. Lord Your word is righteous and holy just as You are righteous and faithful. Thank You for giving me instruction in righteousness.

139. Give me a heart that will be zealous for You. As the wicked do not pay

	attention to Your word, help me remember Your word at all times.
140. Your promise is well tried, and Your servant loves it.	**140.** Thank You for the purity of Your word.
141. I am small and despised, yet I do not forget Your precepts.	**141.** Lift me up O Lord for I am small and despised by many. Help me so I don't forget Your word.
142. Your righteousness is righteous forever, and Your law is true.	**142.** Thank You Lord that Your righteousness has never changed. Thank You for giving me something to hold on to. Your word is true.
143. Trouble and anguish have found me out, but Your commandments are my delight.	**143.** I am going through many troubles. Help me maintain my dependence on Your word.
144. Your testimonies are righteous forever; give me understanding that I may live.	**144.** I thank You for Your words are based on truth and justice. They have never changed. Give me understanding of Your word so that I can live.
Qoph	
145. With my whole heart I cry; answer me, O Lord! I will keep Your statutes.	**145.** I cry with my whole heart, help me O God. I promise to keep Your word.
146. I call to You; save me, that I may observe Your testimonies.	**146.** Let my cry come unto You. Save me from every situation keeping me down. Help me keep Your word.
147. I rise before dawn and cry for help; I hope in	**147.** Grant me the grace to rise early to pray to You.

Your words.

Answer my cry O God. Let my hope be stayed on You.

148. My eyes are awake before the watches of the night, that I may meditate on Your promise.

148. Teach me the importance of meditating on Your word and also praying to You.

149. Hear my voice according to Your steadfast love; O Lord, according to Your justice give me life.

149. In Your lovingkindness answer my prayers. Your word must work for me.

150. They draw near who persecute me with evil purpose; they are far from Your law.

150. Keep me away from mischief makers.

151. But You are near, O Lord, and all Your commandments are true.

151. Thank You Lord for You are my protection. You are the truth and all Your words are true.

152. Long have I known from Your testimonies that You have founded them forever.

152. Thank You for Your testimonies that have not changed from the beginning of time.

Resh

153. Look on my affliction and deliver me, for I do not forget Your law.

153. Look upon me and deliver me from every affliction that is troubling me. Help me not to forget Your word.

154. Plead my cause and redeem me; give me life according to You promi-r se!

154. Your Son Jesus has paid the supreme price for me. Deliver me from the hold of the evil one.

155. Salvation is far from the wicked, for they do not seek Your statutes.

155. Touch the hearts of the wicked. Turn their hearts back to You. Help them to start seeking You just as I continually want to seek You.

156. Great is Your mercy, O Lord; give me life according to Your rules.

156. Thank You for Your mercies over me. I would not be here without You.

157. Many are my persecutors and my adversaries, but I do not swerve from Your testimonies.

157. I have one enemy who has many agents, help me maintain my integrity.

158. I look at the faithless with disgust, because they do not keep Your commands.

158. As I see the lives of those who perpetually sin against You, my heart is touched. I pray You touch their hearts and cause them to give up the life of sin.

159. Consider how I love Your precepts! Give me life according to Your steadfast love.

159. Help me to love Your word. Let it continue to impact me in every area of my life. Show me Your lovingkindness O God.

160. The sum of Your word is truth, and every one of Your righteous rules endures forever.

160. Thank You Lord for I have tasted Your word and it is true. Thank You for as it was in the beginning so it is now.

Sin and Shin

161. Princes persecute me without cause, but my heart stands in awe of Your words.

161. Help me withstand every form of persecution. Let Your word continually uphold me.

162. I rejoice at Your word like one who finds great spoil.

162. Give me a heart that would rejoice at Your word. Give me insight that will cause rejoicing in my heart.

163. I hate and abhor falsehood, but I love Your law.

163. My heart must hate lying. Let it be so in Jesus name.

164. Seven times a day I praise You for Your righteous rules.	**164.** Give me a heart that will continually praise You for You are worthy to be praised.
165. Great peace have those who love Your law; nothing can make them stumble.	**165.** I pray that out of Your word I will find peace and as I stay in Your word, I will be shielded from offence in Jesus name.
166. I hope for Your salvation, O Lord, and I do Your commandments.	**166.** Thank You for giving up Your son so that I can be
167. My soul keeps Your testimonies; I love them exceedingly.	**167.** Help me keep Your word. I pray for a heart that would love Your word willingly.
168. I keep Your precepts and testimonies, for all my ways are before You.	**168.** There is nothing that can be hidden from You. Help me keep Your word.
Taw	
169. Let my cry come before You, O Lord; give me understanding according to Your word!	**169.** Do not allow anything to hinder my prayers. Hear me O Lord and answer me speedily. Give me understanding, let me live in Your truth.
170. Let my plea come before You; deliver me according to Your word.	**170.** Have mercy upon me, hear my prayers O God. Your promises always come to pass. Deliver me from all that trouble me.
171. My lips will pour forth praise, for You teach me Your statutes.	**171.** Give me a teachable heart, and as You teach me let Your praise fill my heart.
172. My tongue will sing of	**172.** Lord as I learn from You,

Your word, for all Your commandments are right.

173. Let Your hand be ready to help me, for I have chosen Your precepts.

174. I long for Your salvation, O Lord, and Your law is my delight.

175. Let my soul live and praise You, and let Your rules help me.

176. I have gone astray like a lost sheep; seek Your servant, for I do not forget Your commandments.

saved. Help me do Your will at all times.

help me teach people around me the righteousness of Your word.

173. Help me make the right choices, let Your word be my guide.

174. Lord I am desperate for my salvation. Save me O God.

175. Deliver me from physical and spiritual death so that I can live to praise You.

176. Lord I am lost without Your direction. Connect with me again; do not let me forget Your word. Halleluiah

Psalm 120 NKJV

The Psalm is a cry to God for deliverance.

A Song of Ascents.

BIBLE

1. In my distress I cried to the Lord, and He heard me.
2. Deliver my soul, O Lord, from lying lips and from a deceitful tongue.
3. What shall be given to You, or what shall be

PRAYER

1. Lord in my troubles I cry to You, hear my cry speedily O God.
2. They want to ruin me with the words of their mouth, deliver me from their hands Father.
3. I bring them to Your courts; deal with them in

done to You, You false tongue?	Your righteousness.
4. Sharp arrows of the warrior, with coals of the broom tree!	**4.** Release sharp arrows from heaven and let them roast in coals of fire.
5. Woe is me, that I dwell in Meshech, that I dwell among the tents of Kedar!	**5.** Help me Father, I live in the midst of the wicked.
6. My soul has dwelt too long with one who hates peace.	**6.** Protect me Father from their hostility; help me live in peace even where my neighbour behaves as one who hates peace.
7. I am for peace; But when I speak, they are for war.	**7.** Make me a man of peace despite the proclamation of war from those around me.

Psalm 121 NKJV

The Psalm teaches us that wherever we are, our confidence should be in God.

A Song of Ascents.

BIBLE	PRAYER
1. I will lift up my eyes to the hills—From whence comes my help?	**1.** Lord I lift my eyes to You who created the heavens and the earth.
2. My help comes from the Lord, who made heaven and earth.	**2.** I look up to the hills and the mountains; You are above the hills, thank You for being my help. There is nothing You cannot do.
3. He will not allow Your	**3.** Thank You as You help

	foot to be moved; He who keeps You will not slumber		me stand firm. I know I am safe because You are ever watchful, You do not sleep and neither do You slumber.
4.	Behold, He who keeps Israel shall neither slumber nor sleep.	**4.**	You are God, You do not need sleep, and I am assured of my protection.
5.	The Lord is Your keeper; The Lord is Your shade at Your right hand.	**5-6.**	You are the covenant keeping God. Thank You because You will never leave me nor forsake me. You are all around me watching carefully to ensure I am safe. I pray that the heat of the day will not harm me neither will the cold of the night too.
6.	The sun shall not strike You by day, nor the moon by night.		
7.	The Lord shall preserve You from all evil; He shall preserve Your soul.	**7.**	Thank You Lord as You continue to protect me from all evil, seen and unseen. My soul is Yours; preserve me as You preserve all that are dear to You.
8.	The Lord shall preserve Your going out and Your coming in from this time forth, and even forevermore.	**8.**	Lord I ask that You preserve my going out and my coming in, all the days of my life in Jesus name. Amen

Psalm 122 NKJV

The Psalm expresses the joy of entering the presence of God.

A Song of Ascents. Of David.

BIBLE		PRAYER	
1.	I was glad when they said to me, "Let us go into the house of the Lord.	1.	I pray I will be surrounded by people who will encourage me to come to You. Lord help me encourage people to attend church meetings. Let gladness fill my heart whenever it is time to come to church.
2.	Our feet have been standing within Your gates, O Jerusalem!	2.	I pray the feet of Your people shall always stand within Your gates where there is protection, provision, peace and joy.
3.	Jerusalem is built as a city that is compact together,	3-4.	Help churches to be joined together in love for Your name to be glorified. Father I give You thanks.
4.	Where the tribes go up, the tribes of the Lord, to the Testimony of Israel, to give thanks to the name of the Lord.		
5.	For thrones are set there for judgment, the thrones of the house of David.	5.	Let there be justice in Your house all over the world.
6.	Pray for the peace of Jerusalem: "May they prosper who love You.	6.	I pray for the peace of Jerusalem, peace in my country and peace in my

local church. Teach me to love Jerusalem and indeed my own Jerusalem. As You have promised, let me prosper I pray in Jesus name.

7. Peace be within Your walls, prosperity within Your palaces."	7. I pray that leaders and the people being led all over the world will enjoy peace. I pray that I would enjoy peace and prosperity too in Jesus name.
8. For the sake of my brethren and companions, I will now say, "Peace be within You."	8. I pray that my family, neighbours and all that I love find salvation and are blessed.
9. Because of the house of the Lord our God I will seek Your good.	9. I pray that I am continually stirred up to seek the good of the house of God.

Psalm 123 NKJV

This Psalm is a call to God for mercy.
A Song of Ascents.

BIBLE	PRAYER
1. Unto You I lift up my eyes, O You who dwell in the heavens.	1. I lift up my eyes unto You who reign in the heavens.
2. Behold, as the eyes of servants look to the hand of their masters, as the eyes of a maid to the hand of her mistress, so our eyes look to the Lord our God, until He has	2. I want to be able to look up to You at all times, whether I am in trouble or not. Help me come to a complete understanding that You are in charge of all things.

mercy on us.

3. Have mercy on us, O Lord, have mercy on us! For we are exceedingly filled with contempt.

4. Our soul is exceedingly filled with the scorn of those who are at ease, with the contempt of the proud.

Have mercy upon me O God.

3. My need for mercy is urgent and desperate. Take reproach away from me. Do not let the wicked continue to ask me where my God is.

4. Set me free from all who mock me. Let there be a turnaround in the areas of my life that are being used to mock me in Jesus name.

Psalm 124 NKJV

This Psalm teaches us that with the Lord on our side, victory is certain.

A Song of Ascents. Of David.

BIBLE

1. "If it had not been the Lord who was on our side," Let Israel now say—

2. "If it had not been the Lord who was on our side, when men rose up against us,

3. Then they would have swallowed us alive, when their wrath was kindled against us;

PRAYER

1. Thank You Father for being with me and all Your children, in our times of trial and tribulation. Once again I say thank You for being on my side.

2. My enemies rose up against me, they have tried to destroy me completely.

3-5. They certainly went overboard and it was as if I was under water and I was almost swept away.

4. Then the waters would have overwhelmed us, the stream would have gone over our soul;	
5. Then the swollen waters would have gone over our soul."	
6. Blessed be the Lord, who has not given us as prey to their teeth.	**6.** I praise You Lord for setting me free from all these troubles.
7. Our soul has escaped as a bird from the snare of the fowlers; The snare is broken, and we have escaped.	**7.** You have not allowed the attacks of my enemies to succeed. You have enabled me escape all the traps laid for me. The traps will never be strong enough to hold me down in Jesus name.
8. Our help is in the name of the Lord, who made heaven and earth.	**8.** Thank You Lord for helping me. No man could have delivered me but You, the creator of the heavens and the earth.

Psalm 125 NKJV

The Psalms teaches that trust in God leads to peace.
A Song of Ascents.

BIBLE	PRAYER
1. Those who trust in the Lord are like Mount Zion, which cannot be moved, but abides forever.	**1.** I thank You Lord because You have given me a heart that trusts You. You are my protection and I

depend on You for all my care. Thank You because I cannot be moved. I am secure in You, the devil cannot touch me.

2. As the mountains surround Jerusalem, so the Lord surrounds His people from this time forth and forever.

2. Thank You Father because You surround me and there are no loopholes for the enemy to come through; You are with me forever more.

3. For the sceptre of wickedness shall not rest on the land allotted to the righteous, lest the righteous reach out their hands to iniquity.

3. I pray that nothing the devil and his agents do to me will cause me to doubt You and sin against You. I know You will always intervene and make a way out for me. I am desperate that You keep me away from indulging in sin.

4. Do good, O Lord, to those who are good, and to those who are upright in their hearts.

4. Help me do good at all times and keep me upright I pray. As You have promised, be good to me O God.

5. As for such as turn aside to their crooked ways, the Lord shall lead them away with the workers of iniquity. Peace be upon Israel!

5. Punish all who continue in wickedness. Thank You Father for granting me peace.

Psalm 126 NKJV

The Psalm shows when we turn to God for deliverance, the outcome will be joy.

A Song of Ascents.

BIBLE	**PRAYER**
1. When the Lord brought back the captivity of Zion, we were like those who dream.	**1.** Thank You Father for changing my story. The restoration of my past losses is like a dream to me.
2. Then our mouth was filled with laughter, and our tongue with singing. Then they said among the nations, "The Lord has done great things for them."	**2.** As I am filled with joy, I will sing songs of praise to You.
3. The Lord has done great things for us, and we are glad.	**3.** As I testify of Your goodness, I give You all the glory; let the unbeliever see the mighty things You have done for me.
4. Bring back our captivity, O Lord, as the streams in the South.	**4.** Lord there are some areas that I am waiting for Your touch, answer me speedily.
5. Those who sow in tears shall reap in joy.	**5.** Grant me the grace to sow my time and resources with the expectation that I will reap in joy.
6. He who continually goes forth weeping, bearing seed for sowing, shall doubtless come again with rejoicing, bringing his sheaves with him.	**6.** In Your mercy as I serve You let me enjoy the harvest in every area I have sowed into.

Psalm 127 NIV

This Psalm teaches complete dependence on God in every area of our lives.
A song of ascents. Of Solomon.
A Song of Ascents.

BIBLE	PRAYER
1. Unless the Lord builds the house, the builders labour in vain. Unless the Lord watches over the city, the guards stand watch in vain.	**1.** I need You to be involved in all I have to do. I surrender my family, my home and work and every other thing to You. I surrender my heart to You, I want to live a holy life and I cannot do it by myself. You are essential to my success in life. I ask that You protect my home, and as You do so, I know I will be at peace.
2. In vain You rise early and stay up late, toiling for food to eat—for He grants sleep to those He loves.	**2.** I ask that You bless every effort that I put into my activities, be it rising early or working late. Lord take away every anxiety or sorrow from my life. Help me to be truly dependent on You. I ask that You grant me true rest after I have laboured knowing that Your blessings on my labours are assured.
3. Children are a heritage from the Lord, offspring a reward from Him.	**3.** I thank You for the children that You have given me and those that

You will give me. Thank You because You have made me fruitful.

4. Like arrows in the hands of a warrior are children born in one's Youth.	4. I pray that my children will be useful to me, supporting me at all times in Jesus name.
5. Blessed is the man whose quiver is full of them. They will not be put to shame when they contend with their opponents in court.	5. I pray my children will walk the way of God and they will be terrors to the enemy in Jesus name. I pray You will give me faith to succeed in a hostile world.

Psalm 128 NKJV

This Psalm is about what it takes to be blessed by God.
A Song of Ascents.

BIBLE	PRAYER
1. Blessed is everyone who fears the Lord, Who walks in His ways.	1. I want to be blessed. Help me Lord; give me a heart that fears You. Let me know what fearing You entails. Help me walk in Your ways, help me obey You.
2. When You eat the labour of Your hands, You shall be happy, and it shall be well with You.	2. Lord let my labour be fruitful, give me good health to enjoy my labour. I pray that other people will not snatch the fruit of my labour from me. Thank You Father because it is well with me.

3. Your wife shall be like a fruitful vine in the very heart of Your house, Your children like olive plants all around Your table.

3. I pray that my wife shall be fruitful in every area and my children shall grow gracefully.

4. Behold, thus shall the man be blessed who fears the Lord.

4. I pray there will be peace and fellowship in our home between the whole family.

5. The Lord bless You out of Zion, and may You see the good of jerusalem all the days of Your life.

5. Lord I ask that You bless me beyond my wildest dreams.

6. Yes, may You see Your children's children. Peace be upon Israel!

6. I pray that I will see my grandchildren and I will enjoy my relationship with them. I pray for peace in Israel.

Psalm 129 NKJV

The Psalm shows the righteousness of God in delivering His children. Despite the many afflictions from the enemy, we know God would in justice destroy the enemy.

Song of Ascents

BIBLE

1. "Many a time they have afflicted me from my Youth," Let Israel now say—
2. "Many a time they have afflicted me from my Youth; Yet they have not prevailed against me.

PRAYER

1. Lord I have been afflicted from the days of my Youth.
2. I thank You because You have kept me and preserved me, You have not allowed my enemies

3. The plowers plowed on my back; They made their furrows long.
4. The Lord is righteous; He has cut in pieces the cords of the wicked.
5. Let all those who hate Zion be put to shame and turned back.
6. Let them be as the grass on the housetops, which withers before it grows up,
7. With which the reaper does not fill his hand, nor he who binds sheaves, his arms.
8. Neither let those who pass by them say, "The blessing of the Lord be upon You; We bless You in the name of the Lord!"

to prevail over me. I am alive today by Your grace and Your grace alone.

3. The enemy did their best to put difficulties in my path, yes they sowed wickedness all over me.
4. In Your righteousness You rolled back all the difficulties, You cut off all cords used to slow me down. Thank You for delivering me.
5. Let all who hate me be shocked that they have failed despite all efforts.
6. I ask that You be a wall between them and myself such that they would give up and turn away from their evil deeds.
7. Let all my enemies wither under Your fire in Jesus name.
8. Let prosperity be far from my enemies in Jesus name. Let them not receive any blessings from You.

Psalm 130 NKJV

This Psalm shows our hope is in God for forgiveness of our sins. It also shows sometimes there is a waiting period before we get a response from God.

A Song of Ascents.

BIBLE	PRAYER
1. Out of the depths I have cried to You, O Lord;	**1.** I cry to You from being deep down in trouble. I am alone but I know You are close by to me. Lord be merciful to me and come to my aid.
2. Lord, hear my voice! Let Your ears be attentive to the voice of my supplications.	**2.** Hear my prayer and answer me speedily.
3. If You, Lor, should mark iniquities, O Lord, who could stand?	**3.** You have not closed the door to me despite my sin, You still allow me to enter into Your presence, Most Holy God. I thank You Father.
4. But there is forgiveness with You, that You may be feared.	**4.** I come to You asking for forgiveness of my sins. I pray that Your kindness will produce reverence for You in my heart.
5. I wait for the Lord, my soul waits, and in His word I do hope.	**5.** I wait in hope believing You will answer my prayer.
6. My soul waits for the Lord more than those who watch for the morning—Yes, more than those who watch for the morning.	**6.** Grant me the grace to wait in the place of prayer. Let the end of my waiting bring comfort to my soul.

7. O Israel, hope in the Lord; For with the Lord there is mercy, and with Him is abundant redemption.

7. All my trust is in You and in Your mercy towards me. Thank You for teaching me the benefit of waiting on You. I thank You that redemption by You is never ending.

8. And He shall redeem Israel from all his iniquities.

8. Thank You Father for redeeming me from every iniquity.

Psalm 131 NKJV

This Psalm is a profession of humility in man borne out of relationship and hope in God.
A Song of Ascents. Of David.

BIBLE

1. Lord, my heart is not haughty, nor my eyes lofty. Neither do I concern myself with great matters, nor with things too profound for me.

2. Surely I have calmed and quieted my soul, like a weaned child with his mother; Like a weaned child is my soul within

PRAYER

1. I ask that You take away pride from my heart such that I will not look down on anyone no matter their situation in life. Whenever I lift up my eyes let it be in prayer to You alone. Help me not to meddle in things that are of no concern to me. Yes help me to mind my own business. Help me to be focussed on You and You alone.

2. As I wait on Your promises to come to pass in my life, help me behave like a child that is well brought up. Grant me

me.	the strength to look at areas of my life that I need to improve upon and change, see me through this process in Jesus name. Lord a child weaned of his mother is no longer dependent on the mother; help me to be totally dependent on You.
3. O Israel, hope in the Lord from this time forth and forever.	**3.** I pray my hope will be on You forever and ever.

Psalm 132 NKJV

The Psalm shows David's great desire to build a house for the Lord and also gives us the covenant promises of God.

A Song of Ascents.

BIBLE	**PRAYER**
1. Lord, remember David and all his afflictions;	**1.** Lord I ask that You remember that You gave up Your only Son, Jesus Christ to die for my sins on the cross. Let me rerap the benefits of the covenant He entered into on my behalf.
2. How he swore to the Lord, and vowed to the Mighty One of Jacob: **3.** "Surely I will not go into the chamber of my house, or go up to the	**2-4.** Help me remember the vows that I made and I have forgotten in the past. Lord help me keep every vow that I make to You. I ask for com-

fort of my bed;

4. I will not give sleep to my eyes or slumber to my eyelids,
5. Until I find a place for the Lord, a dwelling place for the Mighty One of Jacob."
6. Behold, we heard of it in Ephrathah; We found it in the fields of the woods.
7. Let us go into His tabernacle; Let us wor- ship at His footstool.
8. Arise, O Lord, to Your resting place, You and the ark of Your strength.
9. Let Your priests be clothed with righteousness, and let Your saints shout for joy.
10. For Your servant David's sake, do not turn away the face of Your Anointed.
11. The Lord has sworn in truth to David; He will not turn from it: "I will set

forgiveness because of the vows that I have made and I did not keep.

5. I desire to be a builder of Your kingdom here on earth for Your name to be glorified. Help me day by day to fulfil this promise in Jesus name.
6 Help me seek You with all my heart and as I do so Lord, let me find You.
7. Help me find my way into Your presence at all times. Give me a heart of worship. Let me understand that You made me to worship You.
8. Let Your presence dwell mightily in every church that Your name is called. Bless the meetings with Your mighty power.
9. Help me lead a life of righteousness and I pray that my heart will be filled with joy at all times.
10. I pray with every fibre of my being that You do not turn Your face away from me. Hear me and answer me speedily at all times in Jesus name.
11. Thank You Lord for every promise to me that has come to pass. As You do

	upon Your throne the fruit of Your body.		not change, every promise concerning me will surely come to pass in Jesus name.
12.	If Your sons will keep My covenant and My testimony which I shall teach them, their sons also shall sit upon Your throne forevermore."	**12.**	Help me play my part by obeying You so that Your promises will come to pass. Give me a teachable heart that will want to learn from You.
13.	For the Lord has chosen Zion; He has desired it for His dwelling place:	**13-14**	I pray that the Holy Spirit will dwell within me forever.
14.	"This is My resting place forever; Here I will dwell, for I have desired it.		
15.	I will abundantly bless her provision; I will satisfy her poor with bread	**15.**	Thank You Father for divine provision; Thank You for meeting all my needs. Thank You for catering for the poor out of Your riches in Jesus name. I pray that I will be an instrument in Your hands for providing the needs of the poor in Jesus name.
16.	I will also clothe her priests with salvation, and her saints shall shout aloud for joy.	**16.**	Let Your power rest upon me such that when I share the good news of the gospel, people will respond and receive the free gift of salvation. I pray that across the world You will use men as instruments to draw souls into Your kingdom.
17.	There I will make the	**17.**	Help me grow from

horn of David grow; I will prepare a lamp for My Anointed.

18. His enemies I will clothe with shame, but upon Himself His crown shall flourish."

grace to grace with Your light around me never fading in Jesus name.

18. Let my enemies end up ashamed and disgraced in Jesus name

Psalm 133 NKJV

This Psalm shows that men in unity receive blessing from God.

A Song of Ascents. Of David.

BIBLE

1. Behold, how good and how pleasant it is for brethren to dwell together in unity!

2. It is like the precious oil upon the head, running down on the beard, the beard of Aaron, running down on the edge of his garments.

PRAYER

1. Help me to see that all Your children are my brothers and sisters of the same family. Grant me the grace to live with fellow men in unity. Let me enjoy the benefits of making the decision to live as You want me to do.

2. I pray that the love I share with my family will be precious, pure, holy and beautiful. I pray the love I show will be abundant and will envelope my whole being. I pray my love will bring blessings and remove hatred and malice. I also pray it will

soften the hearts of all I interact with in Jesus name.

3. It is like the dew of Hermon, descending upon the mountains of Zion; For there the Lord commanded the blessing —Life forevermore.	3. Thank You Father for everlasting life. I pray all blessings commanded by God will be received in Jesus name.

Psalm 134 NASB

The Psalm is a prayer for ministers of God.

A Song of Ascents.

BIBLE	PRAYER
1. Behold, bless the Lord, all servants of the Lord, who serve by night in the house of the Lord!	1. Help me; I want to serve in Your house. Grant me the grace to stand by night faithfully without fail in Your presence. Let all those who serve in the house of God all over the world be blessed in Jesus name.
2. Lift up Your hands to the sanctuary and bless the Lord.	2. Let Your servants lift up holy hands to bless You. Let them teach the people to bless You. Give them hearts that will not want to depart from Your presence. You are worthy to be praised.
3. May the Lord bless You from Zion, He who made heaven and earth	3. I ask that You bless your servants out of Zion. I thank You for the

uncountable blessings You have given Your servants and for the blessings that are on the way.

Psalm 135 NASB

The Psalm is a call to praise God because He loves us and He is a great God too. The Almighty God is contrasted with the gods of the heathen.

BIBLE	PRAYER
1. Praise the Lord! Praise the name of the Lord; Praise Him, O servants of the Lord,	**1.** Lord I give You praise. I call on all believers to praise Your holy name.
2. You who stand in the house of the Lord, in the courts of the house of our God!	**2.** Grant me the grace to stand in Your house and as I stand let Your praise never depart from my lips.
3. Praise the Lord, for the Lord is good; Sing praises to His name, for it is lovely.	**3.** Yes I will praise You with all my heart for You are good. I want to enjoy praising You. Let it be so in Jesus name.
4. For the Lord has chosen Jacob for Himself, Israel for His own possession.	**4.** Out of the abundance of Your grace I am a part of Your family through Your Son, Jesus Christ. I have no choice but to praise You forever.
5. For I know that the Lord is great and that our Lord is above all gods.	**5.** Thank You for allowing me to experience Your greatness. No god can

be compared with You.

6. Whatever the Lord pleases, He does, in heaven and in earth, in the seas and in all deeps.

6. No one can question Your authority my Lord. You do as You please in the heavens, on earth and in the seas, unlike the lesser gods of the heathen.

7. He causes the vapours to ascend from the ends of the earth; Who makes lightnings for the rain, who brings forth the wind from His treasuries.

7. I praise You for the wisdom You exhibited during creation. Rain, thunder and wind are all crafted in heaven. Blessed be Your holy name.

8. He smote the firstborn of Egypt, both of man and beast.

9. He sent signs and wonders into Your midst, O Egypt, upon Pharaoh and all his servants.

8-9. You smote the first born of Egypt. You sent plagues, tokens of Your mighty power into the land of Egypt. I ask that You send disappointment, frustration and destruction into the land of every enemy of Your children in Jesus name.

10. He smote many nations and slew mighty kings,

11. Sihon, king of the Amorites, and Og, king of Bashan, and all the kingdoms of Canaan;

12. And He gave their land as a heritage, A heritage to Israel His people.

10-11. I ask that You come down on all who gang up against me. Let all who keep me away from my blessing suffer for it in Jesus name.

12. I thank You for every spiritual and physical blessing You have promised me in Jesus name. Every inheritance including those taken away from the enemies of Your people will not pass us by in Jesus name.

13. Your name, O Lord, is everlasting, Your remembrance, O Lord, throughout all generations.

13. Lord help me remember all Your deeds. Your greatness will cause Your name to endure forever. Men even generations yet unborn will continue to call on You in Jesus name.

14. For the Lord will judge His people and will have compassion on His servants.

14. You are a caring Father. I ask that You take care of me and protect me from my enemies. Let the world know that I am Your child. Answer my prayers my Lord I pray.

15. The idols of the nations are but silver and gold, the work of man's hands.
16. They have mouths, but they do not speak;
17. They have ears, but they do not hear, nor is there any breath at all in their mouths.

15-17. Lord You cannot be compared to gods made by the hands of men. These idols have mouths, ears and noses carved into them but they are all useless.

18. Those who make them will be like them, Yes, everyone who trusts in them.

18. Help me trust in You and You alone. I pray the foolishness of those who trust in idols will never be found in me in Jesus name.

19. O house of Israel, bless the Lord; O house of Aaron, bless the Lord;
20. O house of Levi, bless the Lord; You who revere

19-21. I ask that You endow me with the heart of praise. As for me and my household we will bless You all the days of our

the Lord, bless the Lord.

21. Blessed be the Lord from Zion, who dwells in Jerusalem. Praise the Lord!

lives. I call on all who serve You to sing praises unto You. I call on all who fear You and all who believe in Your name to humble themselves before You and bless Your holy name.

Psalm 136 NASB

The Psalm is a song of praise to God the creator, the deliverer, and the merciful.

BIBLE		PRAYER	
1.	Give thanks to the Lord, for He is good, for His lovingkindness I everlas everlasting.	**1.**	I thank You because You have continuously been good to me. I bless Your name for the unchanging love You have bestowed upon me.
2.	Give thanks to the God of gods, for His loving-kindness is everlasting.	**2.**	I thank You for You are the God of all gods. You are the God who is worthy to be praised. All other gods are the works of men and are therefore irrelevant.
3.	Give thanks to the Lord of Lords, for His loving-kindness I everlasting.	**3.**	I give You thanks for You are the Lord of lords. You correct every injustice perpetrated by the Lords of the land.
4.	To Him who alone does great wonders, for His lovingkindness is ever-lasting;	**4.**	I give You thanks for You have performed won-ders from the beginning of time and by Your

5. To Him who made the heavens with skill, for His lovingkindness is everlasting;

6. To Him who spread out the earth above the waters, for His loving-kindness is everlasting;

7. To Him who made the great lights, for His lovin-gkindness is everlasting:

8. The sun to rule by day, for His lovingkindness is everlasting,

9. The moon and stars to rule by night, for His lovingkindness is ever-lasting.

10. To Him who smote the Egyptians in their first-born, or His lovingkind-ness is everlasting,

11. And brought Israel out from their midst, for His lovingkindness is everla-sting,

12. With a strong hand and an outstretched arm, for

grace I experience new wonders day by day.

5. We see the exhibition of Your wisdom in creation. All You created at the beginning are still in existence today.
We give You thanks.

6. The waters have a boundary and the earth has stayed where You created it a long time ago. We give You thanks.

7-9. Thank You for making the lights that enables us live in comfort. The sun, moon and stars have different roles to play in the existence and com-fort of man. Your stead-fast love indeed endures forever.

10. Just as You struck at the heart of the oppressors of the people of Israel, I ask that You strike at the heart of every agent of satan being used to oppress every one of Your children.

11. Have mercy on me, I ask that You bring me out of every cage that the devil has put me into.

12. I know that none can escape Your outstretch-

His lovingkindness is everlasting.

13. To Him who divided the Red Sea asunder, for His lovingkindness is everlasting,

14. And made Israel pass through the midst of it, for His lovingkindness is everlasting;

15. But He overthrew Pharaoh and his army in the Red Sea, for His lovingkindness is everlasting.

16. To Him who led His people through the wilderness, for His lovingkindness is everlasting:

17. To Him who smote great kings, for His lovingkindness is everlasting,

18. And slew mighty kings, for His lovingkindness is everlasting:

19. Sihon, king of the Amorites, for His lovingkindness is everlasting,

20. And Og, king of Bashan,

outstretched arm, therefore let Your strong hand completely destroy every agent of the devil and all their works in Jesus name.

13. Let every obstruction before me part like the Red sea now in Jesus name.

14. As every obstruction parts, let me see the miracle before my eyes and courageously move forward in Jesus name.

15. As Your power makes a way for me through every obstruction, let Your power destroy all my pursuers in Jesus mighty name.

16. Out of Your steadfast love, I ask that You lead me through every wilderness before You. Grant me staying power so I do not give up in these times.

17-20. I am praying that You will strike down all who stand between me and my promised land. No matter how mighty, powerful, important or great, let them give up what belongs to me in Jesus name.

for His lovingkindness is everlasting	
21. And gave their land as a heritage, for His lovingkindness is everlasting,	**21-22.** You have promised that the wealth of the sinner will be passed to the just. Let me be a partaker of this blessing in Jesus name.
22. Even a heritage to Israel His servant, for His lovingkindness is everlasting.	
23. Who remembered us in our low estate, for His lovingkindness is everlasting,	**23.** Thank You Father for I know You will never forget me because Your love endures forever.
24. And has rescued us from our adversaries, for His lovingkindness is everlasting;	**24.** Thank You Father for You have rescued me from my enemies. Importantly the power of sin over me has been broken. Glory be to You.
25. Who gives food to all flesh, for His lovingkindness is everlasting.	**25.** You care for all flesh. You provide all my needs out of the abundance of Your riches. I honour and reverence You.
26. Give thanks to the God of heaven, for His lovingkindness is everlasting.	**26.** I give thanks to You the God of the heavens and the earth. Thank You for Your unending love.

Psalm 137 NASB

The Psalm was written in captivity and we learn we should weep when we are far away from God.

BIBLE

1. By the rivers of Babylon, there we sat down and wept, when we remembered Zion.

2. Upon the willows in the midst of it we hung our harps.

3. For there our captors demanded of us songs, and our tormentors mirth, saying, "Sing us one of the songs of Zion."

4. How can we sing the Lord's song in a foreign land?

5. If I forget You, O Jerusalem, may my right hand forget her skill.

6. May my tongue cling to the roof of my mouth If I do not remember You, if I

PRAYER

1. Give me a heart that will long for Your presence. When I am separated from You for any reason, let me weep and find my way back to You.

2. Give me a heart that will sing at all times no matter the circumstances, good or bad. I pray I will never have to hide or hang my instruments of praise to You. Lord put me in a position where no man can mock me.

3-4. Make it impossible for any enemy to ask me to bring dishonour to Your holy name.

5. Help me never to forget the aroma of Your presence. Let my heart be filled with Your presence.

6. Help me never to forget the songs of praise. You will always be my source

do not exalt Jerusalem above my chief joy.

7. Remember, O Lord, against the sons of Edom the day of Jerusalem, who said, "Raze it, raze it to its very foundation."
8. O daughter of Babylon, You devastated one, how blessed will be the one who repays You with the recompense with which You have repaid us.
9. How blessed will be the one who seizes and dashes Your little ones against the rock.

of joy. I pray Your glory will be totally restored in my life and in the world at large.

7-9. Remember O Lord all who perpetuated evil, deal with them justly in Jesus name.

Psalm 138 NASB

The Psalm calls for the praise of God for His word and for answered prayers. A Psalm of David.

BIBLE

1. I will give You thanks with all my heart; I will sing praises to You before the gods
2. I will bow down toward Your holy temple and give thanks to Your name for Your loving-kindness and Your truth;

PRAYER

1. Help me praise You with my whole heart, not leaving anything behind

.

2. I bow down before You and I honour You. I praise You for Your loving-kindness towards me and all that concerns

	Scripture		Prayer
	For You have magnified Your word according to all Your name.		me. You are forever faithful to me. Everything You have said is sure. You have made Your word greater than Your name.
3.	On the day I called, You answered me; You made me bold with strength in my soul.	**3.**	Thank You for answering me when I cry unto You. Thank You for the strength You have graciously given unto me to bear all that has come my way. The testimony of Your children shall continually draw people to You and they will join hands in praising You.
4.	All the kings of the earth will give thanks to You, O Lord, when they have heard the words of Your mouth.	**4.**	I pray earthly kings will be drawn to You and they will submit to You the king of all the earth and join hands to praise You.
5.	And they will sing of the ways of the Lord, for great is the glory of the Lord.	**5.**	Your glory covers the whole earth. You are greatly to be praised.
6.	For though the Lord is exalted, yet He regards the lowly, but the haughty He knows from afar.	**6.**	Thank You for caring for the lowly. Give me a heart like Yours too. I pray that pride will not be found in me.
7.	Though I walk in the midst of trouble, You will revive me; You will stretch forth Your hand against the wrath of my	**7.**	I ask that You keep and protect me in times of trouble. I pray You will stretch forth Your hand and stop every action of

enemies, and Your right hand will save me.

8. The Lord will accomplish what concerns me; Your lovingkindness, O Lord, is everlasting; Do not forsake the works of Your hands.

the enemy against me in Jesus name.

8. Whatever You start You have always completed. Remember me O Lord. I ask that You perfect all that concerns me. Halleluiah

Psalm 139 NASB

This Psalm shows to us that God is everywhere, knows everything and is all powerful. (Omnipresent, Omniscient and Omnipotent)

For the choir director. A Psalm of David.

BIBLE

1. O Lord, You have searched me and known me.

2. You know when I sit down and when I rise up; You understand my thought from afar.

3. You scrutinize my path and my lying down, and are intimately acquainted with all my ways.

PRAYER

1. Thank You Lord for the confidence You have enabled me to have in You. You have searched me and You know everything about me. There is nothing to hide from You.

2. Lord every movement I make, You are aware of. It is amazing that my innermost thoughts are not hidden from You. You are a very great God.

3. I need You Lord to help me get my mind around the fact that everywhere I go, You are there; when I lie down thinking about what has happened You

	are there with me and everybody else. My prayer today is that my praise of You should do You enough justice.
4. Even before there is a word on my tongue, behold, O Lord, You know it all	**4.** Every word I speak and the words left unspoken are known by You. Lord there is nothing I can hide from You.
5. You have enclosed me behind and before, and laid Your hand upon me.	**5.** Thank You for laying Your hand upon me for my benefit.
6. Such knowledge is too wonderful for me; It is too high, I cannot attain to it.	**6.** The knowledge You have is incomprehensible to a human being. You are the Almighty God, All glory and honour to Your name.
7. Where can I go from Your Spirit? Or where can I flee from Your presence?	**7.** There is no hiding place from You because You are everywhere. Jehovah Shammah.
8. If I ascend to heaven, You are there; if I make my bed in Sheol, behold, You are there.	**8.** No man except Jesus Christ has been to heaven, but if I could ascend to heaven, You are there. I know that from Your abode in heaven You control what happens in hell, so hiding in there is futile. You are all powerful and ever present.
9. If I take the wings of the dawn, if I dwell in the remotest part of the sea, **10.** Even there Your hand	**9-10.** Thank You Lord for no matter how far away I run, even the uttermost parts of the sea I am safe

will lead me, and Your right hand will lay hold of me.

11. If I say, "Surely the darkness will overwhelm me, and the light around me will be night,"

12. Even the darkness is not dark to You, and the night is as bright as the day. Darkness and light are alike to You.

13. For You formed my inward parts; You wove me in my mother's womb.

14. I will give thanks to You, for I am fearfully and wonderfully made; Wonderful are Your works, and my soul knows it very well.

15. My frame was not hidden from You, when I was made in secret, and skilfully wrought in the depths of the earth;

16. Your eyes have seen my unformed substance; And in Your book were all written the days that were ordained for me, when as yet there was

because Your right hand will uphold me.

11-12. I realise that darkness can't cover my actions because it makes no difference because You are everywhere. Thank You Father for I am safe in Your hands.

13. You knew my beginning before I was conceived. You have known my innermost thoughts right from my beginning. I thank You because You have always been in charge of my life.

14. You put in special efforts when I was conceived in my mother's womb. Your completed work is marvellous in my sight. I praise You from the bottom of my heart.

15-16. I praise You for nothing was left to chance. You were attentive to every detail even though my parents conceived me in secret.

Scripture	Prayer
not one of them.	
17. How precious also are Your thoughts to me, O God! How vast is the sum of them! **18.** If I should count them, they would outnumber the sand. When I awake, I am still with You.	**17-18.** I thank You Lord for Your thoughts towards me are beautiful, good and not of evil. Your word tells me that I am in Your thoughts all the time for I am inscribed on the palm of Your hands.
19. O that You would slay the wicked, O God; Depart from me, therefore, men of bloodshed.	**19.** As You have seen everything the wicked people have done, I pray they do not go unpunished. Let destruction come upon them now. Henceforth let me be separated from every form of wickedness in Jesus name.
20. For they speak against You wickedly, and Your enemies take Your name in vain.	**20.** I ask that You steer me away from those who will speak wickedly against You.
21. Do I not hate those who hate You, O Lord? And do I not loathe those who rise up against You? **22.** I hate them with the utmost hatred; They have become my enemies.	**21-22.** Let my love for You grow continuously such that Your enemies become my enemies.
23. Search me, O God, and know my heart; Try me and know my anxious thoughts;	**23.** Look into my heart Lord and if there is anything in me that is not right, impress it upon me so that I can change for the better.
24. And see if there be any	**24.** Lead me to a place

hurtful way in me, and lead me in the everlasting way.	where there will be no traces of wickedness in my life. Lead me to a place where my life will be pleasing to You, in the everlasting way in Jesus name.

Psalm 140 ESV

The Psalm is a call for rescue from the arms of the wicked and for God to fight on behalf of His children.

To the choirmaster. A Psalm of David.

BIBLE	PRAYER
1. Deliver me, O Lord, from evil men; preserve me from violent men,	1. Lord deliver from all who want to harm me.
2. Who plan evil things in their heart and stir up wars continually.	2. Every gathering against me will come to nothing in Jesus name.
3. They make their tongue sharp as a serpent's, and under their lips is the venom of asps. Selah	3. I cancel every word spoken and every curse uttered against me with the blood of Jesus Christ.
4. Guard me, O Lord, from the hands of the wicked; preserve me from violent men, who have planned to trip up my feet.	4. Do not let me fall into the trap of the wicked that are out to steal, kill and destroy me.
5. The arrogant have hidden a trap for me, and with cords they have spread a net; beside the way they have set snares for me. Selah	5. Let the proud and the wicked fall into the snares they have laid out for me.
6. I say to the Lord, You are	6. My Lord and my God,

my God; give ear to the voice of my pleas for mercy, O Lord!

7. O Lord, my Lord, the strength of my salvation, You have covered my head in the day of battle.

8. Grant not, O Lord, the desires of the wicked; do not further their evil plot, or they will be exalted! Selah

9. As for the head of those who surround me, let the mischief of their lips overwhelm them!

10. Let burning coals fall upon them! Let them be cast into fire, into miry pits, no more to rise!

11. Let not the slanderer be established in the land; let evil hunt down the violent man speedily!

12. I know that the Lord will maintain the cause of the afflicted, and will execute justice for the needy.

13. Surely the righteous shall give thanks to Your

hear my voice as I call on You. There is none looking out for me except You.

7. My God, I thank You for my safety, my protection depends on You. I pray You will continue to be my shield and my buckler in Jesus name.

8. Do not let the plans of the wicked come to pass, lest they gloat and ask me where my God is.

9. My Lord You have done it before; let every mischief organised against me come upon the heads of the organisers in Jesus name.

10. Let Your fire come down on them destroying them and their works in Jesus name.

11. Let all who do and speak evil fail in Jesus name. Let the evil that they do come back to haunt and destroy them in Jesus name.

12. Thank You Father for You will always be our defence, protecting all who are under the siege of the enemy.

13. I thank You for You are deserving of praise and

name; the upright shall dwell in Your presence.	adoration. Help me never to depart from Your presence, dwelling with You and in You always.

Psalm 141 ESV

The Psalm starts with a desperate call to God for help and ends with a request for vindication.

A Psalm of David.

BIBLE	PRAYER
1. O Lord, I call upon You; hasten to me! Give ear to my voice when I call to You!	**1.** Lord as I call on You, please recognise that I am crying to You, answer me quickly.
2. Let my prayer be counted as incense before You, and the lifting up of my hands as the evening sacrifice!	**2.** My hands are lifted up to You, so is my heart, let the sincerity of my heart and the words of my mouth be as a sacrifice unto You.
3. Set a guard, O Lord, over my mouth; keep watch over the door of my lips!	**3.** Help me keep my mouth from saying things that are sinful. I ask that You ensure that I do not partake in evil talk.
4. Do not let my heart incline to any evil, to busy myself with wicked deeds in company with men who work iniquity, and let me not eat of their delicacies!	**4.** Turn my heart away from evil, help me keep away from evil people not joining them in their undesirable pleasures.
5. Let a righteous man strike me—it is a kind-	**5.** Lord lead good and truthful people to correct

	ness; let him rebuke me—it is oil for my head; let my head not refuse it. Yet my prayer is continually against their evil deeds.		me when I make mistakes, give me a heart that accepts when I am wrong. Give me a compassionate heart that prays for all people including those who are a blessing to me.
6.	When their judges are thrown over the cliff, then they shall hear my words, for they are pleasant.	**6.**	Let my enemies lose every battle with me, let them have no choice but to listen to me and accept whatever I say.
7.	As when one plows and breaks up the earth, so shall our bones be scattered at the mouth of Sheol.	**7-8.**	Lord I am under severe attack, I look up to You to deliver me, for my trust is in You. Do not let me suffer.
8.	But my eyes are toward You, O God, my Lord; in You I seek refuge; leave me not defenceless!		
9.	Keep me from the trap that they have laid for me and from the snares of evildoers!	**9.**	Protect me from every obstacle and trap that has been laid for me.
10.	Let the wicked fall into their own nets, while I pass by safely.	**10.**	Help me escape, let the wicked fall into every trap that they have set for me.

Psalm 142 ESV

This is a Psalm written in distress, a call to God for deliverance with the expectation that He will hear and do as He has always done.

A Maskil of David, when he was in the cave. A Prayer.

BIBLE

1. With my voice I cry out to the Lord; with my voice I plead for mercy to the Lord.

2. I pour out my complaint before Him; I tell my trouble before Him.

3. When my spirit faints within me, You know my way! In the path where I walk they have hidden a trap for me.

4. Look to the right and see: there is none who takes notice of me; no refuge remains to me; no one cares for my soul.

5. I cry to You, O Lord; I say, "You are my refuge, my portion in the land of the living."

6. Attend to my cry, for I am brought very low! Deliver

PRAYER

1. I cry out loud to You, for I am in distress.

2. I bring all my troubles, fears, worries, anxieties and feelings to You, not keeping anything away. I can run no further; there is no strength in me any longer, help me O Lord.

3. You know all things; the wicked have laid a trap for me. I come to You for there is no help any-where. In times of trouble friends are no-where to be seen.

4. You are the only one who never changes. You are all that I truly need to be safe, all that I need to succeed; all that I need to excel in life.

5. Hear me and deal with my situation here and now O Lord.

6. Deliver me from the hands of those per-

me from my persecutors, for they are too strong for me!	secuting me, cut their hands off me and turn their hearts away from me. Make a way for me; let Your blood which was shed on the cross of Calvary work for me.
7. Bring me out of prison, that I may give thanks to Your name! The righteous will surround me, for You will deal bountifully with me.	**7.** Let praise come out of my lips. Let the righteous surround me and join in thanking You for You have done me well.

Psalm 143 ESV

This is a Psalm for God's attention by David asking for deliverance

A Psalm of David

BIBLE	**PRAYER**
1. Hear my prayer, O Lord; give ear to my pleas for mercy! In Your faithfulness answer me, in Your righteousness!	**1.** Let nothing stand between me and You. Hear my prayers out of Your faithfulness and rightousness.
2. Enter not into judgment with Your servant, for no one living is righteous before You.	**2.** I have no righteousness in my own right, for all have sinned and come short of Your glory.
3. For the enemy has pursued my soul; he has crushed my life to the ground; he has made me sit in darkness like those long dead.	**3.** I need Your help Lord for the enemy wants to destroy me completely.
4. Therefore my spirit faints	**4.** I am troubled within my

within me; my heart within me is appalled.

soul for the battles are becoming overwhelming.

5. I remember the days of old; I meditate on all that You have done; I ponder the work of Your hands.

5. Help me remember the victories and the blessings You have given me in the past. Let the reality of creation be ever present before me.

6. I stretch out my hands to You; my soul thirsts for You like a parched land. Selah

6. Let there be a hunger and a thirst for You. Lord let me feel Your presence. Let Your presence bring light into the darkness that surrounds me.

7. Answer me quickly, O Lord! my spirit fails! Hide not Your face from me, lest I be like those who go down to the pit.

7. Answer me speedily for without You I face destruction.

8. Let me hear in the morning of Your stead- fast love, for in You I trust. Make me know the way I should go, for to You I lift up my soul.

8. Let me perceive in my spirit Your loving kindness for I know the battles cannot last forever. Help me develop my trust in You. Therefore I ask that You show me the path to my destiny. Help me lift up my soul to You in prayer continuously so that I can be lifted up.

9. Deliver me from my enemies, O Lord! I have fled to You for refuge.

9. I have no power of my own. I run to You for my deliverance. You are my shield and buckler.

10. Teach me to do Your will, for You are my God! Let Your good Spirit lead me on level ground!

10. Help me to know Your will and to do it. Put Your will in my heart, direct me through Your word. You are my God and there is none like You. You are a good God; help me to be good just as You are good. I ask that You hold me by my hand and help me to be upright.

11. For Your name's sake, O Lord, preserve my life! In Your righteousness bring my soul out of trouble!

11. Move fast O Lord; let Your name be glorified. Deliver me from all afflictions.

12. And in Your steadfast love You will cut off my enemies, and You will destroy all the adversaries of my soul, for I am Your servant.

12. Cut all my enemies off from me. Let destruction come upon them and all that is theirs.

Psalm 144 ESV

The Psalm shows that the all-powerful God is our strength. We should ask God to rescue us from our enemies

Of David

BIBLE

1. Blessed be the Lord, my rock, who trains my hands for war, and my fingers for battle;

2. He is my steadfast love and my fortress, my

PRAYER

1. I praise You for teaching me to fight.

2. Thank You for Your mercies towards me. I

	stronghold and my deliverer, my shield and He in whom I take refuge, who subdues peoples under me.		bless You for being my shield and protection. Thank You for peace all around me.
3.	O Lord, what is man that You regard him, or the son of man that You think of him?	**3-4.**	I am like nothing before You. Lord I am forever grateful that You are interested in me and I matter to You.
4.	Man is like a breath; his days are like a passing shadow.		
5.	Bow Your heavens, O Lord, and come down! Touch the mountains so that they smoke!	**5.**	Come down from heaven to my rescue; let Your fire consume my enemy for You are a consuming fire.
6.	Flash forth the lightning and scatter them; send out Your arrows and rout them!	**6.**	Show Your power on my behalf; send lightning and scatter them, let arrows be unleashed from heaven to take them all down.
7.	Stretch out Your hand from on high; rescue me and deliver me from the many waters, from the hand of foreigners,	**7.**	Deliver me from the hands of agents of the devil. They are strangers who want to overwhelm me. Let Your outstretched hand reach out and free me.
8.	Whose mouths speak lies and whose right hand is a right hand of false-hood.	**8.**	Lord everything about them is falsehood. Shut them up permanently I pray.
9.	I will sing a new song to You, O God; upon a ten-stringed harp I will play to You,	**9.**	Put new songs in my mouth O God; Let me sing praises unto You.

10. who gives victory to kings, who rescues David His servant from the cruel sword.

11. Rescue me and deliver me from the hand of foreigners, whose mou-mouths speak lies and whose right hand is a right hand of falsehood.

12. May our sons in their Youth be like plants full grown, our daughters like corner pillars cut for the structure of a palace;

13. May our granaries be full, providing all kinds of produce; may our sheep bring forth thousands and ten thousands in our fields;

14. May our cattle be heavy with Young, suffering no mishap or failure in bearing; may there be no cry of distress in our streets!

15. Blessed are the people to whom such blessings fall! Blessed are the people whose God is the Lord!

10. Thank You Lord for my deliverance comes from You.

11. Deliver me from the hands of the wicked. Let my family and I be safe, let us live in peace I pray.

12. I pray my children will grow up in righteousness and holiness.

13. Help me use my resources judiciously, providing adequately for my family in Jesus name.

14 I ask that You protect all my sources of income from the devourer. Every bit of Your creation will be beneficial to me in Jesus name.

15. Thank You for a heart that will worship You; thank You for every blessing in Jesus name.

Psalm 145 ESV

- **The Psalm is a Psalm of praise. The Psalmist praises God from the depths of his heart.**

A Song of Praise. Of David.

BIBLE	PRAYER
1. I will extol You, my God and King, and bless Your name forever and ever.	**1.** Help me praise You all the days of my life. Let my praise be a blessing unto You.
2. Every day I will bless You and praise Your name forever and ever.	**2.** Let me always have a reason to praise You every day.
3. Great is the Lord, and greatly to be praised, and his greatness is unsearchable.	**3.** As no man can know the full extent of Your greatness, I ask that You open my heart to how much You want to show me.
4. One generation shall commend Your works to another, and shall declare Your mighty acts	**4.** Help me teach my children why they should praise You, so that when I am gone they will continue praising You.
5. On the glorious splen-our of Your majesty, and on Your wondrous wor-ks, I will meditate.	**5.** I pray nothing will stop me from speaking about Your majesty and the greatness of the works of Your hands.
6. They shall speak of the might of Your awesome deeds, and I will declare Your greatness.	**6.** I pray men will be bold to give credence to Your mighty works. Help me shout about Your great-ness on the rooftops.
7. They shall pour forth the fame of Your abundant	**7.** As I think of Your good-ness day by day let my

goodness and shall sing aloud of Your righteousness.

8. The Lord is gracious and merciful, slow to anger and abounding in steadfast love.

9. The Lord is good to all, and his mercy is over all that he has made.

10. All Your works shall give thanks to You, O Lord, and all our saints shall bless You!

11. They shall speak of the glory of Your kingdom and tell of Your power,

12. To make known to the children of man Your mighty deeds, and the glorious splendour of Your kingdom.

13. Your kingdom is an everlasting kingdom, and Your dominion endures throughout all generations. The Lord is faithful in all His words and kind in all His works.

14. The Lord upholds all who are falling and raises up all who are bowed down.

15. The eyes of all look to You, and You give them

heart bust forth into singing at all times.

8. Thank You for the abundance of grace towards me, thank You for despite my unfaithfulness at times, You have been slow to anger.

9. Lord, You are good and Your mercies endure forever; I thank You.

10-11. Let my heart have words that will be enough to give You all the praise that You deserve O Lord.

12. Help me teach my children and all I contact, Your great and mighty works so that they will never be forgotten.

13. Lord, You have reigned from the beginning in Your power and majesty; I pray that all men will come to worship You.

14. I ask that You do not let me stay down when I fall, in Your grace and mercy lift me up and let Your name be glorified.

15. All that wait on You are never disappointed. I

their food in due season.

ask that You provide for me as You have promised in Jesus name.

16. You open Your hand; You satisfy the desire of every living thing.

16. Thank You Lord for I know my waiting cannot be in vain; You will supply all I need for life and godliness JEHOVAH JIREH

17. The Lord is righteous in all His ways and kind in all His works.

17. Everything You do is always right; I give You praise.

18. The Lord is near to all who call on Him, to all who call on Him in truth.

18. Help me call on You with all my heart for I have nowhere else to turn to.

19. He fulfils the desire of those who fear Him; He also hears their cry and saves them.

19. Help me to continue living in reverential fear of You. Hear the cry of my heart and save me from the evil one.

20. The Lord preserves all who love Him, but all the wicked He will destroy.

20. Preserve my life O Lord for I love You. I ask that You destroy every agent of the devil.

21. My mouth will speak the praise of the Lord, and let all flesh bless his holy name forever and ever.

21. By Your grace I will not keep silent. I will praise You forever.

Psalm 146 ESV

The Psalm praises the trust worthiness and power of God

BIBLE

1. Praise the Lord! Praise the Lord, O my soul!

PRAYER

1. Lord I praise You with all that I am and all that is within me.

2. I will praise the Lord as long as I live; I will sing praises to my God while I have my being.

3. Put not Your trust in princes, in a son of man, in whom there is no salvation.

4. When his breath departs, he returns to the earth; on that very day his plans perish.

5. Blessed is he whose help is the God of Jacob, whose hope is in the Lord his God,

6. who made heaven and earth, the sea, and all that is in them, who keeps faith forever;

7. who executes justice for the oppressed, who gives food to the hungry. The Lord sets the prisoners free;

8. The Lord opens the eyes of the blind. The Lord lifts up those who are bowed down; the Lord loves the righteous.

2. By Your grace I will praise You as long as I live.

3-4. Help me to be completely determined and also to remain committed to trusting You at all times. Help me so I do not put my trust in any human being who one day will die unlike You who is eternal.

5. I prayerfully ask for Your help in every area of my life for I cannot achieve anything without You.

6. You who made the heavens and the earth and everything that are in it. Everything You have said is true, and will all be accomplished in Jesus name.

7. I thank You Lord because You are on the side of the oppressed, You provide food for the hungry and yes You came to set the captives free.

8. Thank You Father for opening the eyes of the blind and You also lift up all who are down in different circumstances. You are righteous and You also love all who are righteous.

9. The Lord watches over the sojourners; He upholds the widow and the fatherless, but the way of the wicked He brings to ruin.

9. I pray that You will continue to show mercy on the Fatherless, the widow and all who need You to comfort them and provide for them. I pray that the way of the wicked be cut short, every activity of the wicked You will nuullify and make of no effect in Jesus name.

10. The Lord will reign forever, Your God, O Zion, to all generations. Praise the Lord!

10. My God and my King, You will reign forever, You are the self-existing God. JEHOVAH EL OLAM. All praise and honour to You.

Psalm 147 NASB

The Psalm praises God for creation, healing for the afflicted, provision for the weak and for sending His word.

BIBLE

1. Praise the Lord! For it is good to sing praises to our God; For it is pleasant and praise is becoming.

PRAYER

1. With all my heart I praise You. Let my praise be pleasant to You and give You all the glory that You deserve. Let me enjoy singing praises to You too.

BIBLE

2. The Lord builds up Jerusalem; He gathers the outcasts of Israel.

PRAYER

2. Build Your church all over the world. Let there be hunger in the hearts of Your ministers for all who are outcasts in the

			society.
3.	He heals the broken-earted and binds up their wounds.	**3.**	Thank You for healing the broken in heart, for forgiveness of sin and reconciling them back to You.
4.	He counts the number of the stars; He gives names to all of them.	**4.**	You are the creator of the heavens and the earth. You created the stars, You know how many they are and they have no choice but to respond to You. Blessed be Your holy name.
5.	Great is our Lord and abundant in strength; His understanding is infinite.	**5.**	You are great and greatly to be praised. I bless You for You are my Lord and Master. None can be compared to You for Your power, wisdom and understanding is infinite.
6.	The Lord supports the afflicted; He brings down the wicked to the ground.	**6.**	I desire humility. Give me a humble heart and I ask that You lift me up. I also pray that every trace of wickedness in me be destroyed in Jesus name for I do not want to be cast down by You my Father.
7.	Sing to the Lord with thanksgiving; Sing praises to our God on the lyre,	**7.**	I am thankful to You for who You are and for all You have done and for all You will do. Help me use all I can lay my hands on to praise You.
8.	Who covers the heavens with clouds, who provi-	**8-9.**	Thank You for giving us clouds who give birth to

des rain for the earth, who makes grass to grow on the moun-tains.

9. He gives to the beast its food, and to the Young ravens which cry.

10. He does not delight in the strength of the horse; He does not take plea-sure in the legs of a man.

11. The Lord favours those who fear Him, those who wait for His lovingkind-ness.

12. Praise the Lord, O Jerusalem! Praise Your God, O Zion!

13. For He has strengthened the bars of Your gates; He has blessed Your sons within You.

14. He makes peace in Your borders; He satisfies You with the finest of the wheat.

15. He sends forth His command to the earth; His word runs very swiftly.

rain. You provide rain so that the earth can be fruitful both for man and animals. What a great God You are.

10. I accept that I do not have any strength on my own. Help me work in Your strength.

11. Help me live with the fear of God in me. Have mer-cy on me. I ask that You take pleasure in my de-pendence on You. Let Your perfect will be done in my life.

12 I will praise You where-ver I am, in my home and in the church I will bless Your holy name.

13. Thank You for being my security. Thank You for making me fruitful and for blessing my children and I. You are worthy to be praised.

14. Thank You for divine favour, for in this situa-tion even my enemies will be at peace with me.

15. Thank You for sending Your angels to carry out Your instructions. Help me receive Your word so I can reap the benefits of obedience.

16. He gives snow like wool; He scatters the frost like ashes. **17.** He casts forth His ice as fragments; Who can stand before His cold?	**16-17.** You are the God who created the seasons. Thank You for the heat and the cold both fulfilling their purposes.
18. He sends forth His word and melts them; He causes His wind to blow and the waters to flow.	**18.** Let Your word melt the hardness in the heart of men, such that there will be repentance and they will surrender to Your Sovereignty.
19. He declares His words to Jacob, His statutes and His ordinances to Israel.	**19.** Show me Your word. Give me understanding so I can obey all You bring before me.
20. He has not dealt thus with any nation; And as for His ordinances, they have not known them. Praise the Lord!	**20.** Thank You for You will deal with me with mercy and with favour in Jesus name. Halleluiah

Psalm 148 NKJV

The Psalm is a call for creation both in the heavens and on earth to rise and praise God

BIBLE	PRAYER
1. Praise the Lord! Praise the Lord from the heavens; Praise Him in the heights!	**1.** Lord I ask that You open my spiritual eyes to see how praise is done in heaven. This will help me in praising You the way that You deserve.
2. Praise Him, all His angels; Praise Him, all	**2.** Let all the hosts of heaven praise God the

	His hosts!		way they only can praise the Lord.
3.	Praise Him, sun and moon; Praise Him, all You stars of light!	**3.**	Let the moon and all the stars join the party and praise their Maker.
4.	Praise Him, You heavens of heavens, And You waters above the heavens!	**4.**	Let all who reside in the heaven of heavens praise the Most High God. Let the waters that are above the heavens respond to the One who placed them there by praising Him.
5.	Let them praise the name of the Lord, For He commanded and they were created.	**5.**	Let all creation show their appreciation of God by praising Him.
6.	He also established them forever and ever; He made a decree which shall not pass away.	**6.**	Your word established all creation for ever and ever. All creation operaates according to Your decree. May You be praised forever and ever.
7.	Praise the Lord from the earth, You great sea creatures and all the depths;	**7.**	Only God knows why sea dragons were created. Let them all join in the praise of their Maker.
8.	Fire and hail, snow and clouds; Stormy wind, fulfilling His word;	**8.**	Fire and hail show the power of God. Wind and vapour respond to Him too. Let them all join in the praise of God.
9.	Mountains and all hills; Fruitful trees and all cedars;	**9.**	Let the mountains and all the hills praise God. Let the fruitful trees and the cedars praise God.

. Beasts and all cattle; Creeping things and flying fowl;

10. Let the beasts and all the cattle join in the praise, let the birds sing their praises to the Lord too.

11. Kings of the earth and all peoples; Princes and all judges of the earth;

11. Let kings and all the people, let those in authority and those that are being led come together to declare the goodness of God. God desires that we praise Him and He deserves to be worshipped and adored.

12. Both Young men and maidens; Old men and children.

12. Let families come together, old and young joining hands to sing to the Almighty God.

13. Let them praise the name of the Lord, for His name alone is exalted; His glory is above the earth and heaven.

13. Lord I praise Your name alone for Your name is excellent above all and worthy to be praised. Your glory exceeds what the human mind can imagine.

14 And He has exalted the horn of His people, the praise of all His saints —Of the children of Israel, a people near to Him. Praise the Lord!

14. Thank You for exalting my horn, for giving me victory in every area. I thank You for adopting me into Your family through Jesus Christ. As You have lifted me up, I will lift You up forever.

Psalm 149 NKJV

The Psalm praises God and also shows the victory of the righteous over the wicked.

	BIBLE		PRAYER
1.	Praise the Lord! Sing to the Lord a new song, and His praise in the assembly of saints.	**1.**	I praise You Almighty God. I sing a new song unto You for the uncountable things You have done in my life. I praise You because You have given me an opportunity and privilege to join hands in a holy assembly to give praise unto You.
2.	Let Israel rejoice in their Maker; Let the children of Zion be joyful in their King.	**2.**	I pray the church worldwide will praise as we all realise that You have made all things possible and You are the very essence of our being.
3.	Let them praise His name with the dance; Let them sing praises to Him with the timbrel and harp.	**3.**	Teach me to praise You in dance and with instruments. Let my praise be acceptable unto You. Thank You for taking pleasure in me. Thank You for loving me, favouring me and finding me acceptable to You.
4.	For the Lord takes pleasure in His people; He will beautify the humble with salvation.	**4.**	Thank You for cleaning me up with salvation.
5.	Let the saints be joyful in	**5.**	I pray I would find joy in

glory; Let them sing aloud on their beds.

Your glory. I pray my focus would be on my relationship with You. I pray I would not tire of singing Your praises.

6. Let the high praises of God be in their mouth, and a two-edged sword in their hand,

6. I pray the praise of God would continue to be in my mouth.

7. To execute vengeance on the nations, and punishments on the peoples;

7. As I use the word of God as a sword, every enemy of the Kingdom shall be destroyed and punishment meted out to the wicked in Jesus name.

8. To bind their kings with chains, and their nobles with fetters of iron;

8. I bind all kings and their nobles with chains and fetters of iron in Jesus name.

9. To execute on them the written judgment—This honour have all His saints. Praise the Lord!

9. I receive the victory over enemies and the wicked wherever they are in Jesus name. Thank You Father; it is an honour to have You on my side. Halleluiah

Psalm 150 NKJV

The Psalm teaches why we should praise God and how to praise Him.

BIBLE

1. Praise the Lord! Praise God in His sanctuary; Praise Him in His mighty firmament!

PRAYER

1. I want a heart that would want to praise You. Give me a heart that would always find its way to the

location wherever there is a call to praise. As You are being praised on earth let the hosts of heaven praise You too.

2. Praise Him for His mighty acts; Praise Him according to His excellent greatness!

3. Praise Him with the sound of the trumpet; Praise Him with the lute and harp!

4. Praise Him with the timbrel and dance; Praise Him with stringed instruments and flutes!

5. Praise Him with loud cymbals; Praise Him with clashing cymbals!

6. Let everything that has breath praise the Lord. Praise the Lord!

2. I thank You for all the great and mighty things You have done and the things that are perceived as small too.

3-5. Thank You for the different instruments that are used in praising You. Thank You for the talents that are exhibited in playing these instruments.

6. I pray that my praise is acceptable to You. I pray that praise will continually be in my mouth till the end of my days.